Hector + Petra →
2006♀

RAW MEATY BONES

RAW MEATY BONES

Promote Health

TOM LONSDALE

RIVETCO P/L

First published in 2001 by:
Rivetco P/L
PO Box 6096
Windsor Delivery Centre
NSW 2756
Australia

Telephone: +61 2 4574 0537
Facsimile: +61 2 4574 0538
E-mail: rivetco@rawmeatybones.com
Web: www.rawmeatybones.com

National Library of Australia Cataloguing-in-Publication entry:

Lonsdale, Tom, 1949-
Raw meaty bones: promote health.

Bibliography.
Includes index.

ISBN 0 646 39624 2

1. Pets - Feeding and feeds. 2. Pets - Nutrition.
3. Pets - Health. 4. Pet food industry - Australia. I. Title.

636.089

This book has been written and published in good faith. However, when dealing with biological systems, for instance the health of animals, problems can occur. The publisher is therefore unable to guarantee that, in every circumstance, the information presented here will be of benefit and neither does the information constitute professional advice upon which you should rely.

If you find errors of fact or interpretation contained within these pages please contact the publisher.

FOREWORD

—————⇒❯●❮⇐—————

Tom Lonsdale has written this book with his hand on his academic heart. He is refreshingly straight forward in his condemnation of convenience foods for pet dogs and cats.

He was a rumbustious, active-minded student. I have cause to recall one occasion while delivering a final summary lecture on the renal system prior to Membership of the Royal College of Veterinary Surgeons finals, due in eight weeks. I had taken enormous trouble to give not only my own views but included many references for student study. The heavily silent worried students listened, but halfway through there was a bang as someone — yes it was T L — slammed down the desk top and said in a shattering bold voice of scepticism: 'I don't believe a word of this.' In the ensuing shocked silence of the other 65 students I asked him: 'Why?' He then parried by declaring that I had no proof of the veracity of what I was saying, nor of the references.

We have remained friends ever since tho' my career took me through the army in the war, private practice and appointments as Senior Veterinary Officer at London Zoo and senior lecturer Royal Veterinary College, London, where memorably Tom and I first met. It was entirely Australia's gain to acquire such an outstanding practitioner who has never taken anything for granted. Indeed it was this very quality that helped him write these informative common sense observations about pet diets, disputing prepared foods and commending the raw meaty bones philosophy. You will learn much from this book and enjoy so doing.

Oliver Graham-Jones FRCVS
CHICHESTER

January 2001

Contents

PREFACE

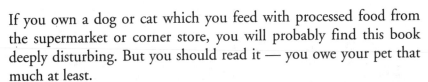

If you own a dog or cat which you feed with processed food from the supermarket or corner store, you will probably find this book deeply disturbing. But you should read it — you owe your pet that much at least.

The book is about what happens to dogs and cats if their diet is inadequate. These days most pet owners give their animals processed pet food. It may seem a convenient way of feeding but such a diet, on its own, is likely over time to cause the pets considerable ill health and suffering. And the signs of the ill health may not be obvious to many owners.

But ask yourself the question: Is it likely that a carnivore — a meat eater — whose species evolved on a diet of the whole carcasses of other animals, will benefit from bland processed food with never a bone in sight?

The book is also about the fight that some veterinarians — who see the problem every day in their surgeries — are engaged in to get the issues out in the open. These vets face powerful forces, not just in the pet food industry, and some have put their professional future on the line by taking part in the campaign.

As well, we take a look at some of the scientific issues, the politics and the marketing practices surrounding the pet food industry. These are matters, regrettably, that make the process of reform a long and arduous one.

Finally, we take a short journey into a realm of ideas that may seem strange or unfamiliar, but which help us to see the whole question of diet and health of our pets in a wider context.

1

Disturbing the peace

The greatness of a nation and its moral progress can be judged by the way its animals are treated.

Mahatma Gandhi[1]

Natural diets based on raw meaty bones promote the health of pets, the human economy and the natural environment but, I admit, I used to believe the opposite. As a 1972 graduate of the Royal Veterinary College at the University of London I was trained to believe that pet dogs and cats are best fed on processed food hygienically sealed in cans and packets. Oral disease and 'dog breath' were scarcely considered, being accepted as a commonplace condition of the domestic carnivore. As a student, sitting at the back of the class, it suited me to subscribe to the prevailing orthodoxy.

Fortunately, discussion with colleagues and the hard lessons of practical experience later overturned my faith in the commercial offerings — but it took time. There was no 'Road to Damascus' style of conversion but rather a series of events over a number of years. Meanwhile I fought against the creeping realisation — after all the majority of my profession still believed in processed foods and the regulatory authorities were known to deal harshly with those who took an independent line. When my inner turmoil finally subsided and the contradictions dissolved I was convinced that I should actively help my clients towards the new understanding.

Where previously diet hadn't featured in my consultations — whether for serious disease or routine health checks — it was now elevated to a central position. The usual starting point for the discussions involved a consideration of the dental health of the animal patient. Bad breath, unsightly staining of teeth, and sore and bleeding gums were, once pointed out, things that concerned my clients. And for those clients who embarked on the new way of feeding their dog or cat the benefits soon flowed. Gone were the bad breath and bleeding gums and in their stead the pets developed a new vitality.

Of course, we were on the lookout for problems of any kind. Raw bones were said to be responsible for broken teeth, constipation and nasty bacterial diseases. Happily, in the short term, none of those things came to pass. As for the long term no one could be sure because that was in the future. But clients, seeing the short-term benefits, were prepared to trust in the future. My staff and I gained in confidence too. We began to streamline our service and illustrate our message with charts and diagrams.

But if this information on more natural feeding was of benefit to our clients the same could be said for the clients of veterinarians everywhere. However the TV was an ever constant source of artificial pet food ads and the pet food propaganda mill continued to churn within the veterinary profession. Students were actively encouraged to recommend processed food — university nutrition lectures frequently being conducted by guest lecturers from the pet food companies. Magazine advertisements and 'scientific' articles extolled the benefits of commercial diets and company-sponsored 'educational' meetings kept veterinarians informed.

In August 1991 the Uncle Ben's pet food company, a division of the Mars Corporation, sponsored a series of symposia in Australia. Two speakers hailed from the Royal Veterinary College, London, and two from the Mars research and development institute, Waltham Centre for Pet Nutrition — 'Waltham, the World's Leading Authority on Pet Care and Nutrition' proclaims their logo.[2] Dr Alan Bennet, my associate in the veterinary practice, and I decided to attend the Sydney meeting. Our objectives were twofold: discover what was on the menu and then ask some public, hard to answer questions.

Living and working in the outer western suburbs of Sydney meant that we had a one hour drive to the meeting — an easy run against the ebbing rush hour traffic. By the time we had reversed the car into the parking bay at the Australian Veterinary Association headquarters, the venue for the meeting, we had already enjoyed a lively conversation on the failings of the pet food industry/veterinary profession alliance.

The meeting was full to overflowing, with a video link to an upstairs room. As latecomers we took seats in front of the video screen, where we were obliged to watch and listen — asking questions of the video screen was pointless. In the event the speakers were protected from us and more importantly we were protected from ourselves — our line in questions would not have been welcome. Time soon passed and as the evening drew to a close the chairman called for a round of applause for the speakers. Alan and I continued to stare at the video screen which flickered and went blank and signalled the time to leave.

As we descended the stairs and crossed the car park our voices returned. Infuriated by the sessions, at least we could laugh and rage together on the journey home. For many of the other 200 veterinarians the evening probably reinforced their own (opposite) prejudices. Whether the extra reinforcement of the company message justified the expense is not something that can easily be judged. It suits my sense of justice to know that the evening acted as a turning point — henceforth I would seek to alert the veterinary profession to the dangers of artificial pet foods.

First show of dissent

In winter the work in a small-animal veterinary practice slows down. There are not so many fleas, the snakes and ticks are hibernating, and folks stay at home with the dog. With the extra free time available I fretted over what I hoped would be a decisive article in repudiation of the artificial pet food industry/veterinary profession alliance. Of course I was handicapped by lack of detailed research knowledge but set against this were my experience as a clinician and what that had convinced me of. Within days the initial draft was ready and within three weeks the typewritten version was dispatched to Dr Douglas Bryden, Director of The Post Graduate Foundation in Veterinary Science of the University of Sydney. I hoped to gain publication in the bimonthly newsletter *Control and Therapy*.

It is true that I was aiming for maximum impact without alienating the audience and, like any self-protective scientist, was anxious not to say anything that could be found to be embarrassingly inaccurate. Favouring the direct approach, I spoke as if the problems and their solution were self-evident.

ORAL DISEASE IN CATS AND DOGS

The stench of stale blood, dung and pus emanating from the mouths of so many of my patients has finally provoked this eruption of dissent. The sheer numbers passing through the practice, when extrapolated to the world situation, tells me that oral disease is the source of the greatest intractable pain and discomfort experienced by our companion animals. This is a great and mindless cruelty we visit upon our animals from the whelping box to the grave. Just imagine having a toothache for a lifetime.

> oral disease is the source of the greatest intractable pain and discomfort experienced by our companion animals. This is a great and mindless cruelty we visit upon our animals from the whelping box to the grave.

THE INTERNAL FACTORS ARE THESE:

Puppies and kittens cut their deciduous teeth between 2 and 6 weeks of age. An inevitable consequence of this is gingivitis. A diet of processed food ensures lack of gum massage and the gingivitis persists. The growing animal develops grooming behaviour and adds hair and faecal material to the accumulated food scraps clogging the interdental spaces.

Between 4 and 6 months of age the permanent teeth erupt into a soup of blood, pus and saliva. The gingivitis is now well established and not infrequently one finds a young kitten or puppy with a complete set of deciduous teeth hanging from inflamed gingival shreds.

Even on a diet of processed food the deciduous teeth must eventually fall out. The permanent teeth come to occupy a diseased mouth and by this time the animal has learned not to chew on anything because of the pain involved.

The exquisite mechanism of teeth and gums designed by nature to be cleaned, massaged and stressed in use is left to rot. Compare mining machinery properly maintained which can excavate a mountain but by disuse can be rendered useless.

A lifetime of inescapable pain is bad enough. The sequelae of endocarditis, iliac thrombosis, nephritis, and all those other entities attributable to a permanent septic focus finally condemn this situation as being intolerable.

THE EXTERNAL FACTORS ARE THESE:

Foremost are the pet food manufacturers who have effectively promoted their 'complete diet ... only water needed'. Along with petroleum and coffee, pet food is one of the biggest industries world wide.

Reacting to the now universal dental needs of our animals, the dental instrument, the dental machine and even the imitation bone industries have flourished.

I believe many veterinary practitioners have reacted passively, perhaps providing some dental care as an afterthought and virtually no advice. Since cats and dogs don't complain, owners don't realise and don't seek advice. Many vets just don't seem to be proactive in this vital area.

As vets we need to provide more than palliative care. Brushing teeth and regular prophys [dental treatment under general anaesthetic] are not enough when advice on diet and food to massage the gums is so vitally important.

WHAT'S TO BE DONE?

a. The internal system
Simple, give our cats and dogs their basic rights of a healthy functioning mouth. Supply raw chicken wings, chicken necks or ox tail to young/small kittens and puppies when they most want to chew and explore. Help them to control their two bouts of physiological gingivitis before it becomes pathological.

Older larger dogs need raw bones and cats need raw meat on the bone.

b. The external system

The external commerce-driven system may take a while to dismantle. It did not exist before the 50s [it originated in England in the 1860s and flourished after World War II[3]] and now it seems such an inescapable part of life. It may take a while to alter course.

The veterinary profession can do much to re-educate itself and in turn the public. A few practice surveys and university-based research projects would set the course.

The pet food manufacturers will need advice on the problems caused by processed food. One pet food company gives biannual 'prophys' to its research animals…

However, they may be persuaded to voluntarily print cautionary advice on their packaging.

WHAT BENEFITS CAN WE EXPECT?

Innumerable. Pets will be fed on cheap unprocessed byproducts some of the time. The environment will benefit, clients will be an average $1000 per animal/per lifetime better off. Certainly the pets can be expected to live longer as they enjoy their lives seeking to 'steal the bones out of the freezer'. As vets we will be happy to see more pain-free, healthier pets and grateful owners.[4]

Would Douglas Bryden, the editor, publish such a straightforward set of pronouncements? Outright rejection seemed possible. As it turned out, I didn't have to wait long for his answer. Two changes were deemed necessary, otherwise the article would be published as submitted. This was good news for I knew that the *Control and Therapy* series is widely read and has an influence beyond Australian shores. Accordingly I accepted the editorial changes and awaited the anticipated publication in October.

Meanwhile life in veterinary practice, which is never dull, gained an unusual richness. Everywhere Alan and I looked, tripped and stumbled we found more connections and implications of our central hypothesis — that artificial pet foods underpin most pet diseases. We eagerly gobbled up the new revelations. For us it was like stepping onto a new and previously undiscovered continent. At times we came close to pinching ourselves to ensure that we were not in a trance or completely self-deluded.

One day in October the mail bundle arrived, with a familiar envelope from the Post Graduate Foundation in Veterinary Science. I opened the envelope and scanned the documents. Nowhere could I find the article. Thomas by name and doubting by nature, I first checked the documents again. When the evidence was undeniable I wondered if Dr Bryden had thought better of publishing the article. Just as in science, where the simplest answer is usually the best, so it is in life. The article had missed the October deadline and would appear in the December edition.

Coincidences and chance encounters have helped fuel the challenge to orthodox views on diet and disease in pets. Serendipity, some might say. But in any case a chance meeting with my old mate Breck Muir was certainly to make a difference. The occasion was a veterinary meeting where general practitioner vets gathered to hear a mixture of scientific and commercial presentations and enjoy a chat and the hospitality of pharmaceutical suppliers.

Back in the early 1980s Breck used to complain of the stench associated with canned-food-fed dogs. At our reunion the conversation soon turned to our common dislike of the commercial offerings. Glad to be in the company of like-minded vets, Breck, Alan Bennet and I joined forces and sought to impress our ideas on a few bystanders. Progress was slow, which led me to mention the coming publication. Breck straightaway said that he would join in the effort and would submit a letter to the monthly *Australian Veterinary Association News*.[5] The timing was uncanny as, with the shorter publication schedule of *AVA News*, both of our pieces appeared in December 1991.

The debate gets under way

Breck came straight to the point in his published letter. Under a headline proclaiming 'Canned pet food not the healthiest' he condemned the modern way of feeding pets.

The pet food situation has concerned me for some years, my feelings brought to this by the current competitive marketing of various dental work stations for veterinary use… Here we have the perfectly engineered commercial circle — a problem doesn't exist, so we create one, and then come up with all the remedial treatments…

We as a profession have been led by the nose by vested interests into a current situation where most younger vets actually recommend commercial pet foods as the best available way of feeding domestic pets — because they have never known of any other way. Before they had their first pet they were bombarded with constant mass media advertising instilling into them that various commercial foods are the only way to go, and when they graduated and went to postgraduate nutrition courses again they had this idea reinforced by visiting lecturers who actually mentioned brand names in their notes.

My experience with commercial canned and dry pet foods is that they:

- are a prime cause of periodontal disease in all breeds of dogs and cats
- are associated with an increased incidence of gastric dilatation and/or torsion [gas accumulation and twisting of the stomach with generally fatal consequences]
- are a cause of diarrhoea in a substantial number of dogs
- cause intestinal 'allergies' with associated dermal pruritus [skin itch] and behavioural changes in a significant number of cases
- are a prime cause of flatulence and offensive odour in dogs — some brands [of pet food] more than others.

For readers of the *AVA News* this was their first notification of dissent in the ranks. Of Australia's 6800 vets about 4800 are paid-up members of the professional association. Membership is not cheap. For $430 annually members obtain a range of social and professional services including publication of a journal of refereed articles. Most vets lend their moral support and pay their dues without taking a close interest in the internal workings which, as with most organisations, is left to the few.

For Breck and me this was our first experience of dealing with the few in control of the AVA. We were delighted that Breck's letter had been published but concerned that pet food manufacturers had been given the opportunity to respond in the same edition of *AVA News*. In due course we were to discover the significance of the special relationship between the parties, but for now the response was published under the title 'Far Fetched Claims'.

The President of the Pet Food Manufacturers Association of Australia Inc signed the Association's statement, which sought to nullify dissent and shepherd the wayward sheep back into the fold. 'We are surprised by the content of Dr Muir's letter, which is an attack on the integrity of the pet food manufacturers of this country' was the opening line. One and half columns later the President concluded: 'With the economic strife Australia now faces, we would have thought it more appropriate to encourage ever increasing standards of excellence in a successful export industry such as the prepared pet food industry. Instead this letter attempts to cut the "tall poppy" down.'

Breck and I discussed tactics on the telephone. We were pleased to see debate getting under way and both submitted letters for the next edition of *AVA News*. Breck ridiculed the Pet Food Manufacturers' letter and condemned modern marketing methods which promoted the idea of dogs slurping their food in 30 seconds. This, he remarked, was good for the manufacturers but not for 'Fido'. My letter referred to income that American veterinarians derive from dental and related diseases. 'Why is it that 40 percent [estimated] of US veterinary time is devoted to this cascade of misery?' I asked. 'Simply because the pet food manufacturers hold such sway and have effectively persuaded almost everyone (but not Breck Muir) that their pulverised, packaged processed pap is all that pets need.'

In the March 1992 edition two more correspondents joined in — both from the state of Victoria. John Sandford spoke out against the artificial pet food culture and concluded: 'The challenge then, is up to the veterinary profession to be more honest, realistic and [to] actively promote preventive dental care and a balanced diet — in a practical way bones, bones and more bones.' Dr Duncan Hall, a pet food company vet, sought to deflect criticism away from the industry and on to dental plaque. 'Plaque is not a food residue', he declared. His final paragraph revealed that the industry is aware of and seeks to ameliorate the plaque problem.

> The pet food industry currently commits considerable financial resources towards researching pet nutrition and product development. An example of this is the work at the Waltham Centre for Pet Nutrition where a technique for staining and objectively grading plaque development in dogs is now being used to examine the effect of different food textures on canine dental health. The ultimate aim of such research is to develop products which can assist in preventing the development of this complex and distressing disease.

Breck fired back in the April edition: 'Duncan K Hall's letter is a good example of how the English language can be used to cast shadows of varying intensity on the original meaning of the written word! Neither Dr Lonsdale nor myself stated that "plaque is food residue".'

Those who specialise in veterinary dentistry could be expected to lead the way on plaque prevention strategies, but Stephen Coles, President of the Australian Veterinary Dental Society, sought to justify the prevailing orthodoxy.

> Veterinary dentistry has not been invented as a new source of income for vets... Dental disease is not a pet food industry conspiracy... The increasing prevalence of periodontal disease has resulted from several factors... Periodontal disease is a bacterial disease... Many breeds have been altered genetically and cannot chew bones... Some pets with moderate to severe periodontal disease should have multiple extractions.[6]

While Dr Coles acknowledged the benefits of bones — 'most dogs fed a good bone once weekly have better teeth' — he advised pet owners that: 'These should be fed in conjunction with a nutritionally sound diet.' A message acceptable to artificial pet food manufacturers, pet toothbrush makers and a majority of veterinarians.

There could be no mistaking the position adopted by Dr Ian Billinghurst writing in the June 1992 edition of the *AVA News*. Ian is credited with being the first Australian veterinarian to raise the issue of natural diets for dogs. His clients, tutored on the dietary needs of pet carnivores, reaped the benefits and in 1986 Ian wrote down his philosophy for the benefit of the veterinary profession.[7] The ability of the profession to ignore essential truths meant that Ian's article went largely unnoticed. In 1989 he handed me his writings. When, in 1992, I tracked him down and encouraged him to participate in the debate Ian explained that he had cancelled his AVA membership, no longer read the *AVA News* and was unaware of the controversy. Gladly he took up the pen in defence of his essential truths:

> As a profession we will shortly be hanging our heads in shame as we realise that we have acted as unpaid sales staff for an industry that has not promoted the health of our clients' pets. An industry that has pushed products that are clearly and demonstrably responsible for much of the misery suffered by pet dogs and cats in the western world while generating huge profits.

Publication of the *AVA News* became a focal point each month. Prior to publication it was necessary to have letters prepared, proofread by colleagues and sometimes checked by my legal adviser. On the day when the *News* arrived there was a general flurry and downing of tools until the latest exchanges were read out loud. Interpreting the shades of meaning was never easy but always enjoyable. Alan and Jason Pollard, the new vet in our practice, would provide opinions and then there was the need to consult by telephone with Breck Muir. Occasionally a month would go by without any mention of raw bones. Did this mean, we wondered, that the AVA authorities had summarily terminated the correspondence? We expected some form of gag or retaliation, and sure enough our premonitions proved correct.

An unfortunate setback

'Periodontal campaign — wearisome', said the headline above Dr Hugh Southwood's letter in the March 1993 *AVA News*. Despite his suggestion that 'most small animal clinicians agree with Tom that raw bones or some other form of oral hygiene measure should form part of a pet's life', he followed with: 'Finally, I congratulate the pet food industry on their patience and tolerance in the face of this attack. I have no vested interest in this matter yet my patience is exhausted.' More important than Hugh Southwood's fatigue was the seemingly bland statement at the foot of the column. '*AVA News* believes that this issue has been aired fully over the last year and does not intend to run further correspondence. — Ed.'

We felt insulted as much by their method as by their message; this was the first and only official AVA response. Without prior warning they had imposed the guillotine. 'Aired fully' — how could anyone believe that? Nevertheless, sixteen letters had been published, ten for the campaign and six against. Of those against, two came from pet food industry sources, three from veterinary dentists and one from Hugh Southwood. Notably there were no letters appearing from veterinary academics on either side of the debate, despite the implied criticisms of veterinary teaching. We shall examine the motives of those living in the 'ivory tower' later, but by remaining silent they managed a temporary postponement of their embarrassment. However these are peripheral issues when one considers that veterinarians were now severely limited in discussing both diet affecting all their patients, and periodontal disease affecting most of them. Paid pet food advertisements and other pieces favourable to the industry continued to appear.

Something had to be done and done fast, but the question was What? Followed by How? Resignation from the Australian Veterinary Association was one option but we rejected it, partly on principle and partly as an act of defiance against the AVA.

In the end Jason and I prepared a notice of motion for the forthcoming AVA annual general meeting.

Notice of motion — AVA AGM, Jupiters Casino, Gold Coast, Friday May 21 1993

A resourceful AVA must provide forums for the membership in order that they may better serve animals, people and the wider environment.

The current *AVA News* letters page ban on open discussion of diet and disease in companion animals hinders this process.

A committee, without present or past affiliations to the processed pet food industry, must be formed to report on all aspects of diet and disease in companion animals.

The ban on member contributions on this vital subject must be lifted.

Tom Lonsdale and Jason Pollard

With the conference just three weeks away, preparations were made at a gallop. Compiling a 'Fact File' for the conference was fun. Susan Rutter had been helping with secretarial duties and now we worked closely on the project. The File contained a mixture of scientific truth, common sense observations, and various comments from the artificial pet food advocates. Here is a selection:

- Public relations manager from Uncle Ben's Australia (makers of PAL), Doug Hyslop said Mr Lonsdale's claims were "ridiculous", however he did recommend a couple of bones each week. *Hills Mercury*, 30 June 1992
- Dr Coles, President of the Australian Veterinary Dentists Society said dogs should chew bones twice a week and cats should chew chicken necks once a week to help prevent dental disease. Dr Stephen Coles, reported in *Sunday Telegraph*, 17 May 1992
- Most dogs are now on more convenience foods and we have to accept that. The best thing to do would be to go and give your dog probably an ox tail with the hide still on it once a week but that's just not socially acceptable. Dr S Coles, *The Investigators*, ABC 27 April 1993
- A single letter in *The Lancet* initiated the medical profession response to suggestions that thalidomide had toxic

consequences. It would appear to us that a similar obligation
rests with the veterinary profession if the consumption of
dietary products by animals leads to an unnecessary buildup of toxins. Rather than closed forums of debate, we
believe they should be opened and accordingly place this
motion on the agenda.

Half of the last page was given over to a cartoon depicting a faceless
giant — with puppets in his pocket and one suspended from the ends
of his dirty fingers.

Striking it lucky on the Gold Coast

Sydney to the Queensland Gold Coast is best travelled over two days
but can be achieved in one long day's drive. As a Queenslander Jason
knew the route well. His pleasure at the prospect of a few days at
home was balanced by apprehension. Few other young veterinarians
would be at the conference, none of whom would have an item on
the AGM agenda.

It was late, raining and cold as we cruised into that artificial
pleasure and retirement strip known as the Gold Coast. A few turns off
the highway we drew up at Jason's house and he disembarked. Tired
from the journey I was reluctant to search for a cheap motel and
instead headed for the opulent Jupiters Casino and Conference Centre.
Discount rates applied for delegates and yes, a room was available on
the executive floor alongside the AVA officers. In retrospect, setting up
camp in the midst of the enemy was quite a coup. Our proximity and
apparent constant activity, I now believe, gave the impression of a well-
planned operation.

Jason may have been nervous but, apart from when he was warned
that the Veterinary Board were taking a keen interest, showed great
courage. Word soon spread that we had arrived and we were often to
be seen at the lobby desk collecting and sending faxes. The next day,
during the coffee interval, we raced around the various lecture rooms
dropping our Fact File onto chairs. We felt like daredevil terrorists
hurling grenades, but in reality it was more like we were planting land
mines. By the end of the day many of the delegates had read the File,

leading us to believe that our 'explosive device' was having an effect.

Judging whether this effect was assisting our cause was not easy. We had checked and crosschecked the Fact File for discrepancies and a solicitor had approved the final draft. The initiative was ours, with the AVA attempting to manoeuvre and respond as best they could. By Thursday afternoon word came to us that Jakob Malmo, the Acting President, would like to meet with Jason and me. At six we gathered in the twilight on the terrace of his suite. Bill Scanlan, AVA Treasurer, was also there, as was Michael Banyard, the President elect.

They sought to appear composed but instead their resentment took control. Our disruptive tactics, we ought to know, were unnecessary and counterproductive. Didn't we realise that the Executive always acted in the best interests of the AVA? Their plan was for the Australian Small Animal Veterinary Association (ASAVA) to carry out an investigation into the connection between diet and disease. This, Jakob assured us, was the competent authority to investigate and report on our claims. We should withdraw our motion.

In time I came to understand that Michael Banyard exerted influence as a small animal practitioner with a doctorate in immunology. Michael, like the others, doubted that there was much in our claims, even if they were based on the work of scientists. After all, he reasoned, if there was so much of consequence, and scientists being scientists, why were they not rushing to claim the kudos of being the first to make the discoveries? At the time I felt this to be a rather difficult paradox to explain in a few seconds. However, keen not to show any sign of uncertainty I looked him in the eye and spoke about this being a political and philosophical matter to do with a 'paradigm shift' in the affairs not only of the AVA but of veterinary science generally. I suggested that the average scientist might be interested in playing safe rather than risking ridicule over unconfirmed theories.

It made no difference what we said — the AVA officers were unwilling to budge. Should we compromise?, was my nagging thought. Could the ASAVA be trusted to adopt suitable terms of reference and then complete a thorough investigation? Should we persist with our democratic appeal to the membership despite the knowledge that many members still lacked a full grasp of the issues? A loss was likely on the floor of the meeting but perhaps, by demonstrating a degree of AVA intransigence, we could pave the way for a later victory.

In the end, perhaps the main motive for persisting with our motion was less noble. Having got the AVA Executive to a showdown we were keen to see the matter through.

The AGM proceedings were under way as Jason and I sat down at the back of the auditorium. Douglas Bryden, I noticed, was positioned in the middle of the room. As part of my address to the meeting I intended tabling a chapter from the Post Graduate Committee book *Veterinary Dentistry*. Although I had written the chapter, because it was as yet unpublished I needed Douglas's consent to making it public. I moved alongside him and whispered my request, to which he warmly assented.

Jakob Malmo, the Acting President, introduced my talk in a flat voice, seeking to establish calm. I approached the lectern from where I could see a full meeting of the AVA establishment and a heavy contingent of pet food company vets. A shouting match had been predicted, but as I began to speak I knew that I had to steady myself and avoid provoking anger. Ten minutes, the allotted time, soon passed and Jakob opened the motion for debate. Three prominent veterinarians spoke against the motion, but nobody spoke in support. Prospects looked poor, at which moment Douglas Bryden rose to his feet. 'I wish to move an amendment to the motion which may not be seen as speaking for the motion or against it.' His measured tones had delegates leaning forward as he spoke. (His remarks are set out in Appendix A.)

The amendment Douglas moved was:

> That in keeping with the AVA policy of providing forums for the membership, the AVA establish an independent committee to prepare a report on the interaction between diet and disease in companion animals.

The debate meandered along on procedural matters without the anticipated fury. Pet food company veterinarians sat quietly watching. Professor Mike Rex, from the University of Queensland, sitting immediately behind Jason and me, moved 'That the motion be now put'. To Jason's relief this motion obtained a large majority, meaning debate was curtailed, and consequently he was not required to speak.

Now for the fateful moment. Jakob put our motion and asked for all those in favour to raise their hands. Jason and I stretched our hands to the rafters and scanned the room for supporters. Not one was to be seen. (One veterinarian later told us that he voted with us but was hidden from view.) So this was the end, or so we thought. But fate was playing strange tricks. Dr Bryden's amendment was deemed to be sufficiently different from the original motion that it should be treated as a separate entity.

This time Jakob's request for a show of hands evoked a different response — the Bryden amendment was supported 46 votes for and 38 against.

As icing on the cake another motion, effectively giving a nod to the final point of our original one, was put to the vote:

> That the *AVA News* Editor continue to exercise judgment in publishing letters in the *AVA News*.

This motion also gained majority support — reaffirming editorial discretion but implying that it should be exercised with care.

Professor Rex was first to congratulate us in a public and uninhibited way. Such a gesture from an elder statesman of the profession was not to be underestimated. Douglas Bryden's speech had been the decisive factor. Douglas's first words to us after the vote were that the hard work was just beginning.

AVA members appeared to have asserted themselves — against the wishes of the Executive — for the community. No one was admitting defeat; in fact quite a number were claiming victory. Pet food industry vets were seen heading for the telephone and soon the wire was alive with their media release.

VETERINARIANS FOCUS ON GOOD NUTRITION AND PET HEALTH

The Annual General Meeting of the Australian Veterinary Association focussed on the importance of nutrition to the overall health and well-being of companion animals by setting up a committee to review scientific data on the role of nutrition and disease.

The Petfood Manufacturers Association of Australia, representing all major manufacturers, endorsed the establishment of a committee composed of informed veterinarians and nutritional experts and believes this will benefit the welfare of our pets through a greater scientific understanding of their nutritional requirements.

The PFMA particularly welcomes an investigation into the therapeutic benefits of so-called 'natural diets', which it believes are being promoted without any semblance of scientific support.

The PFMA endorses the Australian Veterinary Association as the appropriate body to conduct the review and looks forward to the findings of such a committee and the greater understanding of the importance of a balanced diet, as part of responsible pet ownership.

No respite

Buoyed by the resolutions of the AGM — I must confess misreading the results as being a sign that the membership were beginning to see things our way — I returned to the letters column of the *AVA News*:

PROBITY IN FINANCIAL AFFAIRS

Open discussion and democratic principles proved their worth once again. Only good can come of the establishment of an independent committee to report on the interaction of diet and disease in companion animals. Independence is the key and 'perception is everything'. The committee must not only be independent but be seen to be independent...

But the AVA Executive reverted to their earlier intentions. They asked Dr Jill Maddison, president of the ASAVA, to nominate a researcher. She nominated Associate Professor David Watson, veterinary physician at Sydney University, as the principal researcher. Dr Peter Groves, an epidemiologist, and Douglas Bryden were to be the other members of the Committee. Rather than covering diet and *all* diseases the Committee brief was limited: 'To explore the relationship between diet and oral health in dogs and cats and the possibility that poor oral health may contribute to other disease conditions in these species.' No original research was to be performed, just a review of the existing literature. Although the AGM motion called for an independent committee, Dr Watson acknowledged the assistance provided by veterinary dentist Stephen Coles and Uncle Ben's pet nutrition adviser Dr Barbara Fougere.

Despite the fact that the Committee raked over (what I believe was) old misapplied science the results were worth waiting for. The *AVA News* of February 1994 carried a front page article:

DIET AND DISEASE LINK — FINAL REPORT

In summary the committee found, 'there is sufficient evidence to incriminate an association between diets of predominantly soft consistency and periodontal disease' and that veterinarians 'need to be concerned about the relationship between diet and health'.

The reasons for restricting the terms of reference as compared to the very broad specification in the motion were as follows:

- The committee believed the concerns raised required urgent attention and comment. It was considered that within the time frame set by the AVA it was not possible to explore every aspect of dietary interaction with disease.
- Information which could be gathered on the broader issues would be unlikely to add more than is already well known.
- Concentration should be placed on periodontal disease and diet because this was the principal area of current concern to the Australian veterinary profession.

- It was felt that if periodontal disease could be prevented then any secondary complications from this problem would be reduced.

There is *prima facie* evidence to justify concern by veterinarians. Pet owners should consider the need to provide some 'chewy' material as well as the basic nutrient intake of their dog or cat.

Periodontal disease may be associated with the occurrence of other diseases but the available evidence is inconclusive. Periodontal disease is arguably the most common disease condition seen in small animal practice and its effects on the gums and teeth can significantly affect the health and well being of affected animals. This is sufficient in itself to give reason for concern. Proof of additional systemic effects is not necessary to justify further action.

Further research is required to better define the relationship between particular diet types and oral health in dogs and cats. Those investigating small animal health problems should also take diet and diet consistency into account when researching systemic diseases — possible confounding effects of diet and poor oral health must be considered in such studies.

RECOMMENDATIONS

- A suitable ration for dogs and cats should be nutritionally adequate and have physical qualities (texture, abrasiveness, chewiness) that will help control plaque and maintain oral health.
- Diets consisting largely of soft foods, even if nutritionally complete, may be physically inadequate and favour development of periodontal disease.
- Soft foods of home-prepared or commercial origin may not differ in this regard.
- When soft foods form the basis of a pet's ration, additional methods are advisable to remove plaque.
- Dry foods made by pet food companies are, on balance, likely to be more effective than soft foods in removing plaque. However they are far from ideal in this regard at

present and are likely to perform variably depending on size, shape and consistency of individual pieces. Until data becomes available on these products, veterinarians should make their own assessments from the animals they see.

- Raw meaty bones have good physical characteristics to promote oral health, but they do not provide complete and balanced nutrition by themselves. Other food items are needed to provide essential nutrients.

In our battles with the AVA their constant cry was that there was an absence of evidence and as such our claims were without foundation. Now at a cost of $7000 they had destroyed their own argument and elevated our claims by providing official endorsement. Previously the information was known, but scattered throughout the literature. Gathered together in one place with the added advantage of being a 'current' piece of work, the findings, so we thought, would demand attention. If an AVA committee found so heavily in our favour what were the real implications?

> In our battles with the AVA their constant cry was that there was an absence of evidence and as such our claims were without foundation. Now at a cost of $7000 they had destroyed their own argument and elevated our claims by providing official endorsement.

In February 1994 Breck Muir and I were engaged in other strategies, and now the preliminary report gave us a welcome boost. As candidates in the AVA elections we assumed, quite wrongly, that our vindication by the Committee would provide us with extra votes and the possibility of gaining election. In the event I received 18 percent of the vote for president of the association and Breck received 38 percent for the position of board member. (My vote of around 8 to 10 percent at subsequent elections reflected the true level of support for the radical anti pet food stance.) Official announcement of the election results was scheduled for the AGM on the last day of the annual conference. The full report of the Committee was to be made public at the same event.

Pressure rise, pressure drop: the 1994 Canberra Annual Conference

Breck and I anticipated that the full Diet and Disease Report would build on the preliminary report. This we reasoned would place considerable obligations upon the AVA, whose Code of Conduct states:

> Veterinarians occupy a trusted, privileged position in society because of unique knowledge and training... members agree to act in a manner consistent with the following principles:
>
> - The primary concern of the profession is for the welfare of animals...
>
> - That veterinarians, individually, act to promote cohesion within the profession and the trust of the profession by the general public.

we believed that veterinarians should neither recommend nor sell artificial pet foods.

According to the Code and in light of the Report we believed that veterinarians should neither recommend nor sell artificial pet foods. Furthermore, we believed that the AVA ought to terminate sponsorship arrangements with the companies, correct past mistakes and seek to promote healthy diets. These ideas we enshrined in two motions for debate at the annual general meeting.

With the election behind us all strands of our campaign converged on Canberra, the nation's capital and venue of the AVA annual conference. Our plan was for Breck to fly down for the AGM on the final day of the conference. Michael Scasny, a young associate veterinarian, and I would travel down by car a few days earlier. Canberra, being the seat of government, is also home to a large press contingent. We hoped to contact members of the press and persuade them of the importance of the issues confronting the veterinary profession. In support of our submissions we carried various documents, videos and 500 copies of a four page press release. The release said:

Pet Diet and Widespread Disease

Since December 1991 indignant private practitioner veterinarians have slammed the hypocrisy of a 'healing profession' being in collusion with the multinational pet food monopolists. It was alleged that widespread disease of pet animals was accompanied by serious national economic and environmental consequences. Parallels were drawn with the exploitation of Third World communities by baby milk formula companies in league with local health care professionals.

Despite the depths of concern the leaders of the profession failed to act until March 1993 when the first and only public response was to ban member discussions in the Australian Veterinary Association Newsletter. '*AVA News* believes that this issue has been aired fully over the last year and does not intend to run further correspondence. — Ed.' The same issue carried extensive coverage of pet food company matters.

Lacking action and denied a voice some members took the matter to the floor of the Association AGM. Despite the AVA Executive and pet food industry opposition the ban was lifted and a committee established to investigate the links between diet and disease. Now it is official, the committee says: 'Periodontal disease is arguably the most common disease condition seen in small animal practice and its effects on the gums and teeth can significantly affect the health and well being of affected animals. This is sufficient in itself to give reason for concern. Proof of additional systemic effects is not necessary to justify further action.'

This begs the question when, and in what form, will action be taken.

The press release detailed various activities of the AVA and concluded:

The outline report of the Diet and Disease Subcommittee has regained sight of the need to protect domestic pets and consumers from the unwarranted side effects of feeding processed food. In anticipation of this fact two motions allowing for beneficial change are to be debated at the 11 March, 1994 AGM. It is to be hoped that the AVA Executive will recognise the national interest and steer away from their commercial affiliations. The funny thing is that the outline report contains nothing that cannot be readily gleaned from any university or pet food company library. It is ironical that those with best access to libraries have, since the debate commenced in December, 1991, either put up great resistance or been slow to act.

Accompanying the text was a cartoon, the preliminary Diet and Disease Report and a letter from Dr Jill Maddison rebutting suggestions of conflict of interest over her consultancy to Friskies Pet Foods.

Four hours after leaving Riverstone Veterinary Hospital, Michael Scasny and I reached the leafy streets of Canberra. Luckily we found a convenient hotel in which to set up headquarters. Once established we hailed a cab and set off in search of Pekka Paavonpera, *AVA News* editor and the press liaison officer. In the job for the last twelve months or so, he was a man I'd learnt to admire for his sense of humour and firm grasp on reality. We hoped he would provide us with introductions to journalists.

As we neared the press office in the conference building Pekka came striding down the corridor towards us. His look of recognition faded to dismay — he was happy to see us but not happy to be seen with us. In an instant he reached for the nearest door, the entrance to a storage closet, pulled on the handle and pushed us inside. Squeezed in the dark space we informed Pekka of our plans and asked for any 'hot news'. Pekka protested that, while there had been plenty of talk, as an AVA employee he could not divulge information — if we wished to speak with the press we should go to the Parliament House complex where newspaper and TV reporters had offices.

A short cab ride later we rolled up to Parliament House with the clear impression that the adventure was under way and going our way. Peter Harvey, a well-known TV reporter, appeared at the press lobby entrance. Without hesitation he provided directions on how to deliver our message. Soon Michael Scasny and I were tape-recording interviews with journalists keen to learn of our story. Before leaving

the Parliament building we dropped copies of our media release in
letter boxes belonging to the various radio and TV stations. Our luck
appeared to be riding high such that by the time we arrived back at
the conference centre there was already a clutch of telephone
messages — radio stations wanted interviews and television stations
wished to arrange film sessions. In the ensuing broadcasts the AVA
became unwilling participants, their representatives trying to remain
calm under pressure.

Surely the AVA would waver and turn under the barrage of
unfavourable publicity, or so I thought. With the AGM scheduled
for Friday morning we did not have long to wait for the verdict.
Breck arrived on the early flight from Sydney and after quick consultation we made our way into the auditorium. As we walked to our
seats I surveyed the 200 or so assembled veterinarians for signs of a
friendly gesture. Instinctively I knew that our run of good luck had
come to an end. The three and half hour marathon was described by
AVA News as 'vigorous debates on a series of controversial issues'.
Fully one year later one veterinarian complained: 'I was stunned by
the level of animosity palpable in the room, and appalled by what
Tim Winton refers to as the "bed rock of incuriosity" exposed in the
comments of several members.'[8]

For the record our motion to establish a Diet and Disease Action
Committee was overwhelmingly defeated, receiving just five votes.
The motion seeking cessation of AVA financial arrangements with
pet food companies gained nine votes. For the AVA and the pet food
companies it was back to business as usual. In a media release
intended for communication to the general public, the AVA 'refuted
media reports condemning pet foods'. Seven months later, when the
Diet and Disease issue was safely out of the public spotlight, an article in *AVA News* stated:

DIET VITAL, SAYS REVIEW

There is 'reasonable evidence' that soft diets are associated
with increased frequency and severity of periodontal disease
in dogs and cats, according to a new report published in the
October issue of the *Australian Veterinary Journal.*[9]

PART I

PET HEALTH

2

⎯⎯⎯⎯⎯⎯⎯⎯◈⎯⎯⎯⎯⎯⎯⎯⎯

Mouth rot and dog breath

Nowadays periodontal disease fascinates me but I must admit that until I was twenty years of age I remained oblivious to the existence of the condition. My first introduction occurred during a lecture at the Royal Veterinary College, London. Robert Churchill-Frost, the lecturer, had an easy manner, a sense of irony and an ability to make things seem simple. And in the case of this student he certainly did impart a simple understanding. I don't believe that the words 'periodontal disease' were employed. As I recall, Churchill-Frost set the scene and described the origin, diagnosis and treatment in a single sentence. 'Once poodles reach about six years of age it is necessary to perform dental treatments, and thereafter every six months.' Even to me with my minimalist approach this seemed a brief description, but there was no pressure to enquire further.

The next learning experience that I recall took place five years later. By that time I had been a qualified vet for three years and had recently joined a London small animal practice. I have to admit that I was barely coping with the work — my previous jobs had been teaching in Kenya and treating cows in Wales — and I needed instruction. Malcolm Corner, the senior assistant in the practice, patiently coached me in the art and science of the small animal practitioner. 'That's periodontal disease,' he said as he pointed to the swollen gums overlaying the canine teeth of an old cat undergoing dental extraction. Subliminally I had become aware of the term 'periodontal disease' and I was pleased, as I thought, to learn how to label the condition.

On that occasion Malcolm was only partially right. The swollen gums of old cats are a rather dramatic aspect of periodontal disease

— but only an aspect of what is the most prevalent and multifaceted disease affecting domestic cats and dogs. And in a limited sense our ignorance was blissful as we went about our busy lives attending to the endless stream of sick animals presented by their owners. Some clients presented their animals to have their teeth cleaned and, if the teeth were loose, then to have extractions. All of these animals were suffering severe periodontal disease, but we did not stop to consider. Dental work was disparaged and, as dirty work, always done last and in a hurry.

> The swollen gums of old cats are a rather dramatic aspect of periodontal disease — but only an aspect of what is the most prevalent and multifaceted disease affecting domestic cats and dogs.

How I wince now at the clues missed and the suffering compounded. So often the nurses were in better touch with reality and, without trying too hard, could prick a young vet's ego. Desexing cats was a major part of our work which, given the time constraints, was done at great speed. According to the nurses my predecessor had not only completed the task in quick time but had shown the necessary empathy to check the ears and clean the teeth as add-on extras for the comfort of the animals. Meeting the nurses' expectations, I could see, was going to be a difficult task. Little did I realise that my exemplary predecessor had been almost as guilty of the same neglect as myself. He had cleaned away the evidence of foul accretions coating the teeth of young cats, but had not then instituted any form of preventative maintenance. Within days the cat's periodontal problems would be as before with no one the wiser.

Occasionally a client commented upon what he or she believed was halitosis. Whereas others presented animals with obvious lameness or a torn ear, here was someone complaining about smelly breath, which by the majority was considered normal. Circular discussion ensued. I attempted to show interest but at the same time downplay the issue — for I had no useful explanation or treatment. Simultaneously the pet owner would try to communicate his or her concerns without appearing unnecessarily fussy. Invariably neither party succeeded. By way of closing those awkward consultations I prescribed antibiotics for presumed 'tonsillitis' or 'gastritis' — periodontal disease, the true source of the breath odour, was never mentioned. At subsequent consultations the pet owner and I would steer clear of breath odour, and of course the patient never complained. And so like thousands of other vets, I entered into an unconscious acceptance of serious disease affecting the majority of animals under my care.

Over the next few years I gained confidence in my abilities as a vet, to the point where I felt able to open my own practice. Ancient mariners went to sea using charts of a flat earth and for all practical purposes were successful — similarly guided by misconceptions, I embarked on my new venture. The year was 1981 and the place Riverstone, an outer suburb of Sydney — I had emigrated to Australia the year before. Happily the practice grew and soon I had to employ other veterinarians in order to meet the demand for our services. Riverstone is semi-rural and some of our patients were horses and farm animals but by far the majority were family pets. That the majority of our patients had a smelly breath and bad teeth did not seem to intrude on our daily cares.

Gradually things began to change. There was no single wake-up call but a series of events which alerted me to the pandemic of periodontal disease affecting my patients. In the mid-1980s veterinary dentistry, imported from the US, began to be reported in the veterinary literature. Dental equipment manufacturers spearheaded the new information and extolled the profit opportunities. Dental 'carts' costing vets $12,000 each, toothbrushes and toothpaste for pets appeared on the market. Contrary to the intentions of the merchants, I at first became suspicious and then resentful of their sales pitch. I started to think independent thoughts and take an active interest.

> There was no single wake-up call but a series of events which alerted me to the pandemic of periodontal disease affecting my patients.

Taking an active interest

For my colleagues Alan Bennet and Jason Pollard and me, 1991 and 1992 were peak years of periodontal disease learning and discovery. Almost on a daily basis new and perplexing details came to light. We were amazed that with little prior knowledge or training we at

Riverstone Veterinary Hospital could seemingly be so successful. This cut across the grain of established thought which suggests that the framework of useful information has been established by past researchers and that new information emerges only as a result of large scale efforts in universities and commercial settings.

As keenly as we enjoyed the challenge and our numerous discoveries we felt that in some ways we had exceeded our station — almost that we had disobeyed the unwritten code requiring conformity and obedience. And since our credentials were not of the highest then perhaps our newfound information was not of the highest worth either. The best solution appeared to be to relay our findings to the veterinary authorities. In this way our duty would be done. The authorities would, we reasoned, take note and commit resources to fleshing out the details and discovering the big picture.

Getting the message of our concerns across to the veterinary authorities proved to be a difficult task. Luck changed slightly when I spoke with Dr Rick LeCouteur, a renowned veterinary neurosurgeon and at the time President of the Sydney Branch of the Australian Veterinary Association (AVA). Although somewhat skeptical, Dr LeCouteur agreed to allow me to speak at a meeting of the Association. A date was set for six months hence.

During the intervening time I attempted to drum up interest in the subject of periodontal disease. Dr Marilyn McKenzie, AVA Branch Secretary, assisted with the circulation of a 'tick the box' style questionnaire on diet and oral health. Two hundred veterinarians were asked to sniff the breath — 'Please assess the breath odour of open mouth 5 cms from incisors' — and examine the mouths of cats and dogs attending their clinics. I hoped that this self-help style of epidemiological survey would serve to alert practitioners to the widespread disease affecting pets and provide quantification of the Sydney situation. Of the four veterinarians who responded, two were of the opinion that periodontal disease was not a matter for concern.

Absence of survey results was no bar to the lecture proceeding since there was plenty of other important information. In fact I worried as to how I could deliver the message in the 30 minutes allocated. The obvious solution was to provide lecture notes and these I prepared under the title 'Pandemic of periodontal disease: a malodorous condition'. Some of the material had already been published by Dr Douglas Bryden and as a precaution I obtained his consent for reproduction of the material. As a further safeguard against possible misunderstandings, and at risk of discomfiting the audience, I arranged for the proceedings to be recorded on video-tape.

On the appointed night the auditorium was packed — in hindsight I suspect the other speakers on the program provided the main attraction. Among the audience were influential veterinarians including three specialists and six lecturers from the University of Sydney. Catching sight of the Nestlé and Mars veterinary advisers I blessed the decision to film the meeting. Under the watchful eye of the camera the audience watched each other. In a show of bravado some swilled beer while the majority found mirth helped release their tensions. Many Sydney veterinarians, it seemed, were determined to 'laugh off' the threats and contradictions posed by the pandemic of periodontal disease.

During question time Dr Barbara Fougere, pet nutrition adviser to the Mars Company Uncle Ben's of Australia, addressed the audience. She used the word 'bravery' to describe my willingness to share my opinion. If 'bravery' was a precondition for the research and communication of periodontal disease issues then my hopes for university participation were doomed. Who among them would risk unpopularity? Who would be prepared to confront Mars Inc.? As I made my final plea for a concerted research effort I knew it was hopeless — my words were falling on deaf ears and for them the subject was closed.

> 'More than 85 percent of dogs and cats over the age of three years are suffering from periodontal disease to a degree that would benefit from treatment.'
>
> *Drs Peter Emily and Susanna Penman*

The disease

According to Peter Emily and the founding president of the British Veterinary Dental Association, Susanna Penman: 'More than 85 percent of dogs and cats over the age of three years are suffering from periodontal disease to a degree

that would benefit from treatment.'[1] Of the other 15 percent we can
fairly assume most have the condition, but not yet severely enough to
warrant treatment. As it is the most prevalent disease affecting
domestic pets we need to concern ourselves with the underlying science.

Derived from the Greek words *peri*, around, and *odontos*, tooth,
the name periodontal describes the area affected which includes the
gums and jawbones. The old term 'mouth rot' evokes a clearer impression of the process where bacteria rot gums and dissolve living bone.
Until recent times bacteria inhabiting the mouth were blamed for the
disease. Now the body's immune defences are seen as an equal con-
tributor to the rot. The immune system employs cells and chemical
antibodies against the bacteria but in the process the gums and bone
become further damaged. The tissues are then said to be 'inflamed'.

Inflammation and repair

In order to better understand periodontal inflammation it is best to
give some thought to the 'normal' processes of injury, healing and
repair. As an example think about the processes affecting a cut finger.
After the bleeding subsides the wound is likely to swell with fluid
which also leaks from the cut surface. Some blood congeals into a
clot in the wound which looks red, feels hot and is painful. Cells
move into and around the injury site, some of which can be seen with
the naked eye. Pus — dead white blood cells and other debris —
might ooze from the wound. Over a few days bruising might appear
through the translucent skin. The change in colour goes from red
through dark blue to yellow, being the stages through which trapped
blood is changed and finally removed from the tissues.

The toughness and normal 'architecture' of all organs and tissues
are maintained by a protein known as collagen arranged in a
'connective tissue network'. Pot scourers and loofahs have a similar
structure. In the early stages of inflammation the wound is weakened
as the collagen fibres are dissolved by enzymes called collagenases.
Scavenger cells remove the debris — much as builders first remove old
timbers from a house undergoing renovation. As the repair process
progresses new blood-carrying capillaries penetrate the healing tissue.
Simultaneously cells called 'fibroblasts' migrate into the site and

recreate the fibrous connective tissue framework. In large wounds a large amount of connective tissue may leave a visible scar. Providing the wound is kept clean and protected during the healing phase then healing can be expected in a week and full use in two weeks.

Now imagine a situation where wood splinters are forced into the nail bed. Instead of the wound being kept clean and dry the finger, in constant use, is often wet and dirty. The rapid two week healing cycle does not occur. Physical aggravation and infection leads to a chronic condition where the body makes constant attempts to repair the injury. Large numbers of dead cells accumulating at the site release toxic chemicals which in a controlled situation assist with healing, but in this contaminated wound create more damage. More tissue damage provides more food for bacteria and a vicious cycle is well under way.

Of course this scenario tends to remain hypothetical in humans, and even in pets superficial chronic wounds get noticed and treated. Inflamed gums are hidden from view, and like the contaminated finger wound, remain wet and aggravated by bacterial chemicals. Absence of the usual healing with collagen connective tissue is an important feature. By dissolving collagen which anchor teeth, and preventing its reformation, the bacteria are able to penetrate alongside teeth deep into the sockets. Unless the body can fight back, the situation becomes progressively worse with teeth being lost from sockets. When teeth fall out the gums can finally heal. This fact confirms another important point. Periodontal bacteria need to attach to a hard surface. Without teeth there can be no periodontal disease.

Factors affecting periodontal disease

A complex array of factors encourage the growth of plaque micro-organisms and thus assist in the development of periodontal disease. On the other side of the equation many factors affect the immune system in its battle with plaque. The paradox here is that whether the immune system be depressed or boosted the periodontal destruction continues apace. What is the likely explanation? First a depressed immune system permits the growth of bacteria deep into the tissues. Second a robust immune system, which attacks the plaque vigorously, also damages the periodontium. Increased damage provides plaque with greater access to the tissues and increased nutrients for growth. In the presence of plaque it seems that the body cannot win. But do not be depressed. By keeping teeth clean and gums massaged the disease can be prevented. (I find brushing necessary and flossing essential for keeping my own gums healthy. Your dentist can advise on correct technique.)

Genetics

Genetics plays a major part in the periodontal disease equation. At a simple level it makes a big difference if you are a human, horse or dog. While humans and horses do develop the disease, dogs appear to be more susceptible. Reasons for this are numerous and probably relate to the number of teeth in the jaw, acidity and composition of the saliva. This natural selection probably serves important and subtle functions as we shall see in Chapter 14. In the case of dogs, artificial selection has changed their size and shape and thus the susceptibility to periodontal disease. The worst affected are the toy breeds, such as Poodles, Pomeranians and Maltese, which have large teeth relative to small jaw bones. It seems that the bacterial toxin to bone ratio is greater and hence the rate of destruction more rapid.

Physiology and health status

General health, nutrition and age influence the body's ability to mount a defence and repair damage. All diseases can be said to 'stress' the body and set up complex interrelationships between the different body systems. 'Trench mouth' refers to an acute mouth infection common among troops in the First World War. Presumably they felt many stresses including extremes of temperature, nutrition, fatigue and fear. Outbreaks of the disease are now seen in groups of students fearful of approaching exams. With the recent discoveries of neuro-immunology we can conceive how neurological and psychological processes activate the immune system.

Any factor which changes the microenvironment of the mouth and gums influences periodontal disease. The increased levels of glucose and ketones in the blood of diabetics and the toxins in the blood of kidney patients facilitate the development of gum disease. In humans the hormones during pregnancy increase the incidence of periodontal disease, as does smoking tobacco. Changes in the flow of saliva have an impact. We commonly experience a dry mouth, and sometimes 'stale' breath, when we wake after a night's sleep.

Injury

Any injury to the teeth and gums gives rise to varying degrees of periodontal disease. Wild carnivores lead a hazardous life fighting between themselves, chasing and killing prey. The mouth takes the brunt of the injuries. Domestic dogs suffer additional hazards. Bored pets frequently chew on wood and are fed cooked bones which either break teeth or get stuck between teeth and damage the gums. Broken teeth are painful so animals avoid chewing on

Teeth which are not used are not cleaned and consequently plaque accumulates.

that tooth or that side of the mouth. Teeth which are not used are not cleaned and consequently plaque accumulates.

The diet

For domestic pets the single most important factor which helps increase plaque accumulation on teeth is an artificial diet. People ask me what chemicals in artificial pet foods create the problem. I explain that while the sticky sugars and other chemicals may provide nutrients for the bacteria the main problem concerns the failure of the food to clean away the bacteria. Wolves hungrily tearing at a carcass gain a vigorous wash, scrub and polish of the teeth and oral cavity. Providing the time interval between feeds is not too great the plaque can be kept at bay and the gums maintained in good health.

Professor Colin Harvey, one of only two veterinary periodontologists in the world, says: 'In a healthy dog or cat fed a "natural" diet that requires tearing and separation of swallowable pieces, the teeth and gingival tissues are largely self-cleaning; that is, plaque is wiped off before it has time to mature to a pathogenic thickness and bacterial mix. When circumstances change so that plaque accumulates, the disease process starts.'[2] In 1947 Sir Frank Colyer wrote that 'cats and dogs which lead a freer life and obtain a diet more nearly approaching their natural food, are practically free from the disease'.[3] In the foremost reference work on the subject, *Periodontitis in Man and Other*

Animals, the authors state that Colyer's observations 'were extremely far sighted and, in fact, have generally been corroborated by later detailed studies of periodontal disease in mice, rats, hamsters, minks, dogs, sheep and several non-human primates'.[4]

In 1947 Sir Frank Colyer wrote that 'cats and dogs which lead a freer life and obtain a diet more nearly approaching their natural food, are practically free from the disease'.

Plaque, teeming alive

Early in the history of the earth's atmosphere water vapour and carbon dioxide were plentiful but oxygen gas was scarce. The first inhabitants, more than 3.5 billion years ago, were anaerobes — meaning that they lived without oxygen. Slowly, over the next two billion years, microbes evolved and spread throughout the waters, air and land. In order to accomplish this remarkable colonisation they developed most of the biochemical processes still in use by complex plants and animals. Photosynthesis was a critical step which enabled some bacteria to derive energy from the abundant carbon dioxide and water. Proliferation of photosynthesising organisms meant that the waste product, oxygen, also proliferated with toxic effect on the anaerobes. In order to survive the challenge anaerobes faced two choices: either hide away from the oxygen gas or turn the threat into an opportunity and evolve as aerobes.

Aerobes, at first sight, appear to have been the most successful. Gradually the single-celled organisms combined into larger accretions of cells dependent on the oxygen gas. This symbiosis achieves its ultimate in warm-blooded mammals such as cats, dogs and humans where billions of cells unite together for the mutual benefit of all. Getting oxygen from the outside air to the innermost cells dependent on the gas is achieved by an elaborate transport system involving the lungs and circulatory system. We breathe air by action of the respiratory muscles. The inspired oxygen gas diffuses across the lungs to circulating red blood cells (which are made in the bone marrow). These are then pumped around the body by the heart. Once in the tissues of the body the red cells give up their oxygen to the surrounding aerobic cells. When we stop to admire this aerobic miracle we should pause and consider what became of the anaerobes.

Anaerobes are not the unfortunate losers we might suppose. They live prolific lives in mud, soil, the bowels of animals and the plaque on teeth. While we may not be able to see them we can often smell their foul vapours. In plaque the anaerobic bacteria live under layers of aerobes. The surface aerobes consume the oxygen and thus protect the anaerobes. As plaque-induced periodontal disease develops and the pockets alongside the teeth increase in depth it is the anaerobes which prosper. It's as if these calculating creatures are determined to hang on to their 3.5 billion-year-old lifestyle regardless of the changing fashions of contemporary life.

Biofilms — what's that?

How living systems fit together is, I suspect, about to change with the rediscovery that bacteria do not live in random groupings. Some scientists now believe that 99 percent of bacteria live in carefully ordered ecosystems called biofilms. Bacterial plaque is a biofilm. I discovered this fact quite by accident as I wandered through the bacteriology laboratory during a University of Western Sydney open day. A display showed dental plaque to be akin to the slime lining oil pipelines, sewage treatment works and rocks on the sea shore.

Until recently bacteriologists depended on methods pioneered by Pasteur and Koch. They studied bacteria in artificial colonies or dead and preserved on a microscope slide. Now with the development of powerful microscopy natural biofilms can be observed directly. Biofilm inhabitants live in different 'neighbourhoods' and different-shaped 'skyscrapers' according to their species requirements. 'Sparkling with reflections from the microscope light, the skyscrapers resemble Manhattan at night.'[5] The whole complex metropolis is enveloped in protective slime, 'permeated at all levels by a network of channels through which water, bacterial garbage, nutrients, enzymes, metabolites and oxygen travel to and fro'.[6] Biofilms, such as dental plaque, living in direct contact with the air have aerobe colonies on the surface with anaerobes hiding beneath.

Once established in the protected environment of the biofilm, bacteria switch to using different genes to those employed by their free-floating counterparts. At a fundamental level their biochemistry changes with the biochemical waste of one species forming the raw materials for another. The symbiotic benefits of the communal lifestyle are considerable. An oft quoted example is that biofilm bacteria can be 1500 times more resistant to antibiotics than a single colony living in a laboratory culture. From the time the first bacteria attach to a surface, the enamel of a tooth for instance, through to the organisation of the mature biofilm there seems to be a remarkable coordination which cannot be explained by chance events alone.

Gradually, we can expect, scientists will unravel the mysteries of bacterial communal life. But first of all they will need an introduction to biofilm biology. As previously remarked it was by chance that I discovered the significance of biofilms and the conceptual framework that provides. Dentists are often unaware of the term. Our family dentist exclaimed, 'Biofilms — what's that?', when I raised the subject. In my 1999 veterinary dictionary, containing over 65,000 entries, the word biofilm does not appear.[7] Microbiologist J W Costerton complained about errors of understanding by members of his own profession. Deficient teaching methods, he suggested, were the reasons for microbiologists' failure to grasp the significance of biofilms.[8]

Calculus — when bugs build stone houses

Your tartar is your calcified hate. Not only the microflora in your oral cavity, but also your muddled thoughts, your obstinate squinting backwards, the way you regress when you mean to progress, in other words, the tendency of your diseased gums to form germ catching pockets, all that, the sum of dental picture and psyche, betrays you; it is stored up violence, full of murderous designs.

Gunter Grass[9]

A regular feature of biofilms, if left undisturbed, is that they begin to calcify (develop hard calcium deposits). The University of Western Sydney display made special mention of this in regard to the blockage of oil pipelines and sewage treatment works. Calculus or tartar is the name given to the hard brown calcium deposits which accumulate on teeth. I wanted to discover more, but found that the veterinary dentistry textbooks contain little information. When I rang the local human dental teaching hospital for some electron microscope pictures of calculus they could not help since they had none. The chief periodontist kindly offered me the use of the dental school electron microscope for obtaining the pictures on page 52 and 53.

The coral-like formations are beautiful and suggest that perhaps the soft-bodied community of bacteria may have special workers which lay foundations and mould and shape a stone house for the security of their community. Their use of a honeycomb structure, imparting strength with capacity, suggests an 'understanding' of engineering principles. The chemical composition of calculus appears to have further significance. Calculus, teeth and bone are predominantly made from calcium/ phosphorus compounds. Teeth and bone have cells (odontoblasts and osteoblasts) which manufacture the chemicals and other cells (odontoclasts and osteoclasts) which dissolve the chemicals in order to create channels and holes. Could bacteria have mastered the same feat long ago? Could soft dental plaque and hard calculus be considered as parts of a single organism living in balance with the host mammal?

ELECTRON PHOTOMICROGRAPHS OF CALCULUS FROM TWELVE-YEAR-OLD GOLDEN RETRIEVER

SURFACE ORGANISMS X 1,300 MAGNIFICATION

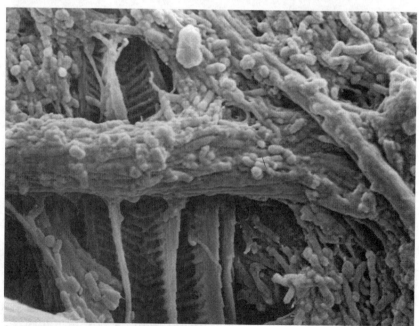

SURFACE ORGANISMS X 1,900 MAGNIFICATION
(The frond-like structures may be trapped material)

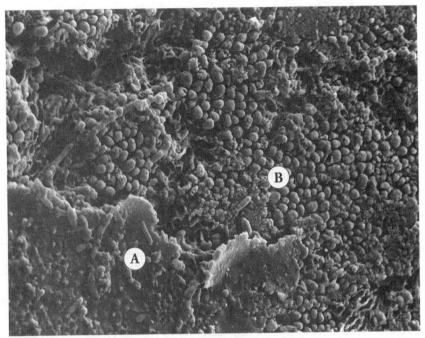

TOOTH ATTACHMENT SURFACE X 1,700 MAGNIFICATION
A. Attachment surface
B. Attachment surface peeled away revealing internal arrangement

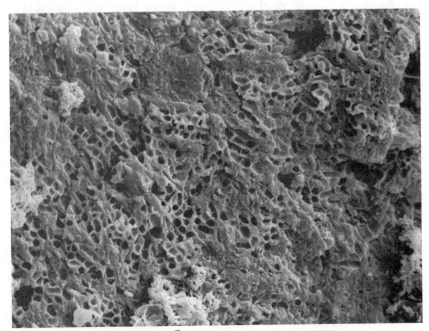

HONEYCOMB STRUCTURE WITHIN CALCULUS X 4,500 MAGNIFICATION

Periodontal disease, more questions than answers

This brief review attempts to draw attention to some factors influencing the biological struggle between the body and the plaque biofilm which consequently gives rise to periodontal disease. Much needs to be done by clinicians and scientists using new methods if we are to fully understand and combat this disease.

Community attitudes will also need to change. The stench of mouth rot affecting so many of our pets is usually dismissed as 'dog's breath'. Children learn forbearance of the problem. In a picture book entitled *Dog Breath, The Horrible Trouble with Hally Tosis*, Hally the 'cute little fuzzy puppy' hero of the story was plagued by a horrible breath.[10] The Tosis children tried various cures for the problem. They took Hally to the top of a mountain with a breathtaking view, they hoped an exciting movie might leave Hally breathless and a roller coaster ride might take her breath away. But all to no avail, until one morning they awoke to find unconscious burglars, laid out by Hally's breath. Hally became an instant 'hero hound' with headlines proclaiming 'Rancid respirations restrain robbers'. The proud Tosis family erected a sign: 'This home protected by DOG BREATH.' In the group picture on the final page of the book the Tosis family are wearing clothes pegs on their noses and Hally is fast asleep. In the next chapter we consider why falling asleep or reaching for the clothes pegs cannot in fact help our situation.

3

Ugly facts

Now that periodontal disease is known to play a significant role in the lives of modern pets, questions need to be asked. What are the consequences of this disease? What impact does periodontal disease have on the overall health, vitality and longevity of the sufferers? Given the magnitude of the problem you might expect to find plenty of information in the veterinary literature. At this stage the small amount of information tends to be hidden and requires interpretation.

This chapter will seek to reveal the hidden and clarify the inconclusive. Each aspect will be discussed separately; however, please keep in mind that nothing happens in isolation. In the living body a multiplicity of interactions bear on the final outcome.

Primary consequences

Asking pets affected by periodontal disease 'How are you feeling today?' cannot help us to understand their pain. Veterinary textbooks are not much help either. While they discuss development and treatment of periodontal disease, how the patient might feel is left unspoken. In attributing feelings to animals we should exercise care. But, in the absence of information to the contrary, feelings should be considered. As an added complication, human periodontal disease patients often feel no pain. Just as lepers may experience slow, painless erosion of nose and fingers, periodontal disease can erode the gums without the patient noticing.

But pain, severe pain, is a feature of periodontal disease for some human sufferers and I believe the same can be said for animals. We empathise with babies cutting their teeth one at a time and help them cope by using teething aids. Imagine the plight of a young kitten or puppy, without teething aids, whose deciduous teeth all cut through the gums in a three week period (between three and six weeks of age, though variations occur).[1] The animal's immature immune system, coupled with a reduced pain tolerance, would likely contribute to its misery. Individual teeth might ache or merge into pain engulfing a row of teeth and reverberating throughout the jaw. With sleep may come relief but upon waking another round of torment begins.

> Asking pets affected by periodontal disease 'How are you feeling today?' cannot help us to understand their pain. Veterinary textbooks are not much help either.

When kittens and puppies attain four months of age teething starts again. A full set of permanent teeth — 28 teeth for cats and 42 for dogs — erupts in a two month period (variations occur). Simultaneously the temporary teeth are shed, or are supposed to be shed. Chewing on natural food serves to dislodge the deciduous teeth and heal the gums of wild carnivores. For domestic pets on artificial diets, the teeth hang by shreds from bleeding gums. Young animals try chewing on wicker baskets and metal feeding bowls — but gain frustration rather than relief.

Eventually the deciduous teeth must fall out and the gums gain some respite. Young adult animals appear to suffer the least oral discomfort. But low-grade persistent periodontal disease takes its toll, such that by late middle age many, perhaps the majority, of domestic pets suffer from severe gum disease. In an attempt to be rid of plaque, sometimes the gums eject whole teeth. Veterinarians speak of teeth 'exfoliating' — a word reminiscent of falling leaves. (Surely a better word is needed to describe the ejection of the 'tools of trade'?) Exfoliating teeth tend to ride up, thus preventing the jaws from closing. With jaws askew the lips cannot seal, swallowing becomes difficult and saliva drools. (Have you ever tried swallowing with your mouth open?)

Loss of teeth, either by exfoliation or by surgical extraction, permits sockets to close over and gums to heal. Unfortunately, opposing teeth, lacking the rudiments of the scissor cleaning action, become encrusted with calculus. Calculus-encrusted teeth suffer from accelerating gum disease. Eventually a lifetime of oral pain and difficulty eating leads to malnutrition, weakness and death. Periodontal disease is the prime culprit but old age gets the blame.

By contrast with domestic pets, animals in the wild are virtually free of periodontal disease. D A Crossley, a UK veterinary dentist, states:

> The body's natural control methods basically revolve around physical removal of plaque bacteria during eating, the antibacterial chemical and flushing actions of saliva and a cellular response involving 'neutrophil' white blood cells. When animals feed in the wild they rarely develop a serious level of periodontal disease unless they are debilitated in some other way. By feeding animals unnatural foods we encourage plaque buildup and the development of periodontal disease.[2]

Secondary diseases

Secondary diseases arising from periodontal disease are many, but there are problems of interpretation. Pets tend to obscure the presence of disease, owners tend not to notice. Even when owners detect problems they do not always seek veterinary advice. Advice when sought seldom connects with the underlying periodontal disease. Partly this failure to connect relates to veterinary training and partly to how evidence is assessed. Because most animals have a diseased mouth and yet not all show outward signs of systemic disease people tend to reject the possible connection.

How can these problems of interpretation be overcome? If periodontal disease is ever present we can ask if it confers benefits on the patient, is neutral in effect or harmful. If we conclude that periodontal disease imposes harmful effects this suggests further questions. Are the effects mild or severe, acute or chronic? Which other organs are affected and how do those effects occur? The Australian Veterinary Association's Diet and Disease Committee had an opportunity to investigate when in 1993 they set out:

> To explore the relationship between diet and oral health in dogs and cats and *the possibility that poor oral health may contribute to other disease conditions in these species* [emphasis added].[3]

The Committee made a connection between diet and periodontal disease but, in considering the second half of their brief, shied away from the issue, suggesting that: 'Periodontal disease may be associated with the occurrence of other diseases but the available evidence is inconclusive.'[4] On this point I believe they were mistaken. There is conclusive evidence and more can be found by looking in the right places in the right way. The Committee, I believe, were correct in saying:

> Periodontal disease is arguably the most common disease condition seen in small animal practice and its effects on the gums and teeth can significantly affect the health and well-being of affected animals. This is sufficient reason in itself to give reason for concern. Proof of additional systemic effects is not necessary to justify further action.[5]

Evidence from the veterinary literature

By assembling 'proof of additional systemic effects' action may be brought forward. Some of the evidence can be found in the veterinary literature. Back in 1950 the author of *Dollar's Veterinary Surgery* stated:

> If dogs are injudiciously fed, receiving mostly soft food instead of that requiring tearing and chewing, the teeth become practically functionless, the gums become soft, and micro-organisms remain in contact therewith without disturbance, and eventually set up a gingivitis. The infection extends from

the gum to the periodontal membrane, and thence to the surrounding bone, giving rise to a varying degree of toxaemia, manifested by different forms of constitutional disturbance. Many of the cases of obscure affections in dogs, characterised by inappetence and general loss of vigour, are believed to be due to pyorrhoea [purulent infection of the gums].[6]

In 1991 Dr Gary Beard, a veterinary dentist based at Auburn University, Alabama, wrote in the proceedings of a dental seminar:

Veterinarians have long suspected and research supports the fact that periodontal disease can become systemic and can predispose the animal to problems such as right sided heart failure, hepatic compromise, renal failure and bone marrow depression. This anachoretic effect [effect in other parts of the body seeded from the original site] can have drastic repercussions on the overall health of the pet and presents one of the greatest health challenges facing small animal practitioners today.[7]

Susanna Penman and Peter Emily, writing in the 1991 edition of *Waltham International Focus*, a Mars Corporation publication, state:

As the disease worsens, the symptoms usually become more evident, including halitosis, dysphagia [difficulty in eating], excessive salivation, haemorrhage, oral discomfort and general malaise. Bacteria from this reservoir of infection in the mouth readily enter the blood through the inflamed gingivae and may spread to other organs, commonly the heart and kidneys. Symptoms of disease of these organs often add to the clinical signs of dental disease.[8]

Also in 1991 Dr Robert Hamlin of Ohio State University hypothesised that: 'Periodontal disease is principal in the pathogenesis of multisystem disease, including diseases of the heart, lungs, and kidneys.'[9]

In 1994 Dr Linda DeBowes, a veterinarian working at Kansas State University, reported the potential consequences of dental bacteremia in dogs and cats. Dr DeBowes included bacterial endocarditis, pulmonary disorders, renal disease, hepatic disease, polyarthritis, polyvasculitis, auto-immune disorders, discospondylitis, and endotoxaemia.[10]

In February 1998 as part of the annual US Pet Dental Health Month several articles, intended for use by the general public, were posted at the promoters' web site.[11] Visitors to the site were advised:

> WITHOUT GOOD DENTAL CARE, most dogs and cats will show signs of oral disease by age three, which puts them at risk for other diseases. That's why the American Veterinary Medical Association, the American Veterinary Dental Society and Hill's Pet Nutrition, Inc. work together to educate pet owners about the importance of pet dental care during National Pet Dental Health Month in February.

Clicking through the links at the site I found a paper from the *Journal of Veterinary Dentistry* which indicated:

> Periodontal disease is a common problem in dogs that may affect their health and quality of life. A greater than 75% incidence of periodontal disease has been reported in dogs. The presence of systemic disease in dogs with chronic periodontal disease has been attributed to bacteremia and absorption of bacterial toxins from the oral cavity. Problems suggested to be associated with chronic periodontal disease in dogs include chronic bronchitis, pulmonary fibrosis, endocardiosis, endocarditis, interstitial nephritis, glomerulonephritis, and hepatitis.[12]

Another link led me to Dr John J Hefferren's research findings. First published in 1996 and sponsored by an Educational Grant from Hill's Pet Nutrition, Dr Hefferren stated:

> The mouth is an integral component of the head. The head is connected to the body. This visual linkage stresses the multi-dimensional dependency of oral to systemic health and disease...

Health vs. wellness

The World Health Organization has defined health as the state of physical, mental, and social well-being and not merely the absence of disease or infirmity. Absence of disease is thus no longer equated with health. For this reason, the quality of life, comfort, and ability to be productive are important considerations that become more important as life is longer. This is true for human beings and animals. Each needs to contribute to be fulfilled.

The definition of dental care has broadened. Infections of the oral cavity require as much attention as do conditions in other parts of the body that may have been treated more aggressively in the human medical and veterinary medical communities. Interdisciplinary teams formed to treat cancer and heart disease or perform transplants are becoming the rule in human medicine, and should be used in veterinary dentistry and medicine where appropriate and possible. Although most oral conditions other than certain carcinomas may not be fatal in themselves, dental disease can contribute to a fatal disease complex. It may be even more important to behavioral and social issues with people and companion animals.[13]

These published statements warrant comment on several levels. It appears that pets are at serious risk of severe systemic disease arising from an infected mouth yet the AVA Diet and Disease Committee make the pallid disclaimer: 'Periodontal disease may be associated with the occurrence of other diseases but the available evidence is inconclusive.' In contrast to the AVA reticence two companies quoted above, Mars and Hill's (a division of Colgate-Palmolive), publish material indicating the devastating effects of their own products on the health of pets. Perhaps they have little choice? If the facts cannot be denied then publishing the information themselves enables the companies to employ timing and emphasis which harms them least.

The Hill's company capitalise on the prevalence of periodontal disease by marketing a dietary product which they claim reduces plaque and tartar. By drawing attention to periodontal disease they draw attention to their range of periodontal disease promoting products. But by having the American Veterinary Medical Association and the American Veterinary Dental Society closely involved they seem to gain innocence by association. In the United Kingdom the Mars Corporation, through its Pedigree Petfoods division, markets a milk and rice based 'artificial bone'. The British Veterinary Dental Association provides endorsement.

Evidence from the human medical literature

While pet food companies may control research and publication of veterinary information, they may not be able to block human medical research. For humans: 'Adult periodontitis, one of the major causes of tooth loss in adults, is a chronic, non-painful, inflammatory disease of the supporting tissues of the teeth. Its prevalence rivals that of the common cold, affecting [about] 75% of the population in the USA.'[14] Some patients, including those with AIDS and 'trench mouth', may suffer a severe and painful form of the disease. But tooth loss, bad breath and pain are not the only matters of concern. The nexus between periodontal and general health of humans increasingly becomes a focus of attention as the British *Sunday Times* reported in July 1997:

> The blood clots that result in heart attacks could be triggered by the activity of bacteria in the mouth. Infection by *Porphyromonas gingivalis* is a cause of gum disease, and a study showed adults with gum disease are nearly three times as likely to suffer a heart attack as those with healthy gums. Now American scientists have found that this bacterium also produces factors that trigger blood clots.[15]

In the 13 March 1993 edition of the *British Medical Journal* Frank DeStefano and his team published results of a survey conducted on 'Dental disease and risk of coronary heart disease and mortality' in 20,749 people.[16] They found a weak correlation between severe periodontal disease and heart disease, although in young men this correlation was much stronger.

In 1994 Dr Linda DeBowes informed the American College of Veterinary Internal Medicine:

> Bacterial endocarditis is a known consequence of dental bacteremia in susceptible humans. Human patients with oral infections may also be at risk for developing acute bacterial myocarditis, brain abscess, ocular and neurological problems, neutrophil dysfunction, and fever of 'unknown' origin.[17]

Doctors have long noticed that women with bad teeth seem more likely to give birth prematurely. Dr Steven Offenbacher, a periodontist at the University of North Carolina, studied 124 women and found those with gum disease were about seven times more likely than usual to deliver dangerously small premature babies.[18] A wider study currently underway involving 5000 poor rural women in Alabama should help clarify the connection.

Dr John Hefferren, in his paper published at the Pet Dental Health web site, notes that medical centres establish guidelines for the treatment of dental disease before treating heart disease and that medical staff and institutions are becoming increasingly aware that oral disease has a bearing on the success of major surgical treatments. Organ transplant patients, a high risk category of patient, routinely undergo dental treatment prior to surgery. While it is possible to overlook or contest some of the evidence for the connection between oral and systemic health, Hefferren recommends:

> One, however, would think twice before debating with the chief counsel of the American Dental Association who is trying to help member dentists when she says you, a member of the American Dental Association, should premedicate a patient with a cardiac condition before doing routine dentistry including a dental prophylaxis. This is a clear re-affirmation that the oral cavity and its treatment is indeed important to the heart especially when the health of the heart is compromised by past or present disease.[19]

Dr Rod Marshall, Lecturer in Periodontology at the University of Queensland, in speaking at a conference on the association of periodontal and systemic health reviewed the evidence linking periodontal and cardiovascular disease. Dr Marshall cautioned dentists in the audience that: 'Failure to screen for periodontal disease may have greater consequences for litigation.'[20] But first things first, Hefferren advises prevention:

> Controlling periodontal disease will minimize the concern for oral disease and its components that contribute to systemic disease. The mouth is the major and primary portal of entry. Pederson suggested [in a 1992 paper] that the best place to stop disease is the portal of entry, the mouth. This is a prudent first step.[21]

Evidence from general veterinary practice

The periodontal disease connection with major disease has begun to gain acceptance among some medical authorities. However, the subtleties of life and the manifestations of disease are inherently more interesting and often do not fit neatly into the textbook classifications of major disease. Experts tend to place an over-reliance on specific diagnosis which misrepresents what happens both in the wider population of animals and that sub-population whose owners take their pets to the vet. Utilising a mixture of subjective and objective observations, a generalisation can be made that the majority of animals are more or less affected by their diseased gums some or all of the time.

In general veterinary practice, treatment is often begun without a specific diagnosis. Case records from a number of clinics reveal that owner observations, such as 'off food', 'seems listless', or 'has a rash', are the main bases for many veterinary treatments. Sometimes the client information is translated into a broad catch-all category such as 'dermatitis', 'skin allergy', 'upper respiratory tract infection', 'gastroenteritis' or 'arthritis'. In consummation of the contract between the clinician and the client, treatment needs to be given and in almost every instance this involves antibiotics and frequently corticosteroids too.

Regardless of the catch-all diagnosis the pre-existing periodontal disease is seldom noticed or diagnosed. Unwittingly, however, the condition does receive treatment as the antibiotics and corticosteroids circulate in the blood and have pronounced effects in the gums. It does not matter which antibiotics are prescribed for most have an effect on periodontal disease. The broad spectrum antibiotics, as their name implies, act against a wide range of bacteria. But narrow spectrum antibiotics frequently appear to be as effective since they inhibit or kill bacterial components of the plaque biofilm upon which the other bacterial species depend.

Antibiotics

Metronidazole is used to treat protozoal infections and also acts against anaerobic bacteria which live in the deepest recesses of inflamed gums. A paradox of Metronidazole treatment is that after only seven days of treatment the clinical improvement seen in the inflamed gums may continue for up to nine months. Vets treating inflammatory bowel disease of cats and dogs have remarked on the benefits of Metronidazole treatment and pondered whether anaerobic bacteria in the inflamed bowel may be at the crux of the problem. While not discounting the significance of anaerobes in the inflamed bowel I speculate that the inflamed gums are a likely source of the systemic immune response. That is to say that the drug would be acting against bacteria in both the gums and bowel simultaneously.

Commonly prescribed Tetracyclines have a double mode of action. Scientists at the New York College of Dentistry reported that these drugs, besides inhibiting bacterial growth, also reduce the effects of collagenases — the enzymes which predominate in the destruction of the gums.[22] Destruction of collagen by collagenases may be a common factor in a range of conditions such as rheumatoid and osteoarthritis, diabetes mellitus, skin and eye diseases. So when clinicians prescribe Tetracyclines for a skin infection they may unwittingly be having a fourfold effect — inhibiting bacteria and collagenase enzymes in the skin and the same two effects in the gums.

Corticosteroids

Veterinarians frequently adopt a grave countenance when prescribing corticosteroids. They advise the owner of the potency of the drug and the welter of unwelcome side effects but they conclude that, in the best interests of the patient, they have no choice. Since 1855, when Sir Thomas Addison found the adrenal cortex to be essential for life, a long list of adrenal hormones has been discovered. In modern medicine synthetic corticosteroids are extensively used for their potent anti-inflammatory and anti-allergic effects. Vets try to use the drugs in small quantity and for a short time. While the condition under treatment may appear to improve the risk of unwanted side effects increases with dose and duration. Animals on corticosteroid medication are at greater risk of developing infections, muscle wasting, thinning of skin, and weakening of connective tissue and bone.

> **Animals on corticosteroid medication are at greater risk of developing infections, muscle wasting, thinning of skin, and weakening of connective tissue and bone.**

But with the millions of animals suffering from allergies, inflammatory skin disease, arthritis and signs of premature aging the use of corticosteroids continues at increasing levels. If, as seems likely, these diseases are at least in part the result of chronic dental disease then the popularity of corticosteroids can be understood. (Periodontal disease and other diseases share immune aspects in common. Each may trigger or exacerbate the others as will be explained later in this chapter.)

Corticosteroid effects in the inflamed gums are the same as in the inflamed skin and other organs. They reduce fluid accumulation, number and activity of immune cells. Thus a twofold effect — reduction of the periodontal and secondary inflammatory disease — is achieved. The immediate benefits may seem considerable but, in the longterm the patient may be much worse off. Millions of pets suffer the primary unresolved periodontal disease, secondary systemic disease and tertiary effects of long-term corticosteroid therapy.

Mechanisms of disease

Periodontal disease exerts its influence on other parts of the body by various mechanisms. Some mechanisms are understood by reference to first principles of biological systems, others require experimental investigation. It would be fair to say that the majority of biochemical mechanisms are not yet discovered and importantly that most disease processes are multifactorial — meaning several factors working together. In broad terms we can consider that three factors arise from periodontal disease. These are the dissemination of bacteria, the dissemination of biochemicals and immune consequences. The various organs and body systems will only then become diseased dependent upon the interaction of various other factors. Such factors include genetic predisposition, age, nutrient status and other environmental considerations.

Bacterial entry

The entry of bacteria into the body via diseased gums was first proposed at the beginning of the twentieth century. Either suspended in the lymph and plasma or encapsulated within defence cells, bacteria are transported to remote sites of the body. This more or less constant process peaks at times of gum disturbance, for instance eating or tooth brushing. At times of extractions considerable numbers of bacteria can gain access to the blood stream. Dentists and vets recognise this fact and especially in vulnerable patients, such as those with heart disease, pretreat with antibiotics. Perhaps of equal concern, the background cumulative source of bacteria entering from the gums is thought to be one thousand times that occurring at a single tooth extraction.[23] So while antibiotic treatment has a place, oral health maintenance is believed to be more important.

Plainly not all bacteria set up infection in remote sites in the body. Most are destroyed without harm occurring. But, in certain instances the destruction of the bacteria creates inflammation and release of chemicals which affect sensitive tissues, for instance the heart or kidneys. Abscesses and infections frequently occur in areas which have a poor blood supply. Bacteria get into cul-de-sacs where the oxygen levels are low and antibodies and scavenger cells cannot reach, in high enough quantity, to destroy the invaders. Infection in bone and joints are common examples. If and when a patient's immune system is depleted for whatever reason, then the risk of oral bacteria gaining entrance to the body increases dramatically.

Immune system

The well-functioning immune system is a wonder of creation. Some cells circulate in the blood, others reside in the tissues. Antibodies (defence proteins) circulate in the blood and body fluids such as saliva, milk and sweat. By some miraculous auto-regulatory process the bone marrow produces the correct numbers of basic cells. From there the cells migrate to key areas of the body. Concentrations of cells occur in the lining of the bowel and airways where intimate contact with the outside world occurs.

The lymphatic system filters body fluids travelling back from the tissues to reunite with the blood stream. Stationed along the path are lymph nodes in which heavy concentrations of immune cells neutralise and remove harmful material. Your doctor is interested in these things and for this reason feels for the lymph nodes in your neck and examines your tonsils when you have a sore throat. Similarly if you cut your finger you may find the lymph nodes in your arm pit swell as they filter the damaged material travelling up the lymph vessels from your injured finger.

As a broad generalisation the immune system consists of two main parts. One half of the system has the uncelebrated but nonetheless important task of keeping the body free of dead, decaying and foreign material. Rather like a vast clean-up crew this aspect of the immune system is permanently working at low intensity even in the most healthy individual. The other, and dynamic 'military', component of the system is designed to recognise living things such as bacteria, viruses, protozoa and fungi — non-living things attract some, but lesser, interest from the military component. Always on standby and possibly engaged in minor skirmishes, for instance pimples and cut fingers, this part of the system comes spectacularly to the rescue in the event of major invasion by pathogenic organisms.

The primary task for the system when confronted with new invaders is to identify the specific proteins or antigens. Speed is necessary but at the same time the 'soldiers' need to take care not to launch an attack on the body's own proteins by mistake. Their task is made difficult by the strategies for avoiding detection and destruction employed by pathogens which live close to or inside body cells. If the immune system succeeds the pathogens will have been killed by a combination of antibodies and special cells. The clean-up crews clear damaged body tissues and the corpses of invaders as the body returns to health.

After a successful campaign the patient will likely be protected; that is, immune from similar infections. Antibodies provide instant protection at the next encounter with the same pathogen, providing that that encounter is close in time. With the elapse of time antibody levels decline. This tends not to be a problem as memory cells persist and are usually able to promptly mount a defence to the next challenge. Importantly immunity to common diseases is maintained precisely because they are common. Small challenges of the immune system occur as a result of frequent encounters with the pathogen and the immune system is thereby kept on alert or boosted.

In naturally occurring infections no one knows how many infectious units gain entrance to the animal thereby provoking disease, recovery and immunity. Since the early days of vaccine research when Louis Pasteur demonstrated the principle of vaccination against anthrax, the subject has become an exact science. (Anthrax in humans is associated with skin pustules and vesicles. Hooved animals are more susceptible, with cattle often succumbing to sudden death.) Vaccine manufacturers now prepare their vaccines with bacterial numbers calculated to provoke an immune response. That number varies according to the particular vaccine. For anthrax ten million spores are needed to vaccinate one cow, and half that number for one sheep.[24] Repeat inoculations with this number of dead spores once each year is sufficient to maintain immunity. If, however, the immune system were to be bombarded with a dose of anthrax vaccine every hour of every day of every year severe immune overreaction would ensue.

We can think of the immune system being bombarded in periodontal disease. The June 1997 *Augusta Chronicle* described peri-odontal disease affecting humans: 'If this oozing mess were out where it could be seen, it would be a bone-deep sore the size of the palms of both hands.'[25] (Dogs, with more teeth and larger jaws, have a proportionately greater oozing mess.) In every milligram of plaque overlying the sore there are 300 million living bacteria — 30 times as many bacteria as in one dose of anthrax vaccine — and as fast as they are removed more take their place.[26] Some bacteria are removed by action of the tongue and salivary glands, but once gums are inflamed, the principal line of defence is the immune system — which works without rest, 24 hours a day, 365 days a year.

It is testimony to the strength of the immune system that it can operate in this fashion despite having evolved for a different role. But just as with a country permanently at war there are costs to be borne. At first the body may meet the energy and raw material costs but in time things go wrong. Maintaining the military analogy, the troops and clean-up crews can become overzealous; in the same way, the immune system can be described as hypersensitive. Some or all of the troops and repair crews can become exhausted or simply lack reinforcements. The immune equivalent is hypo-immunity. In other situations of a country at war there is often collateral damage to the fabric of the country. When the immune system starts to attack not only the dead and dying parts of the body but also the living healthy parts we describe this as auto-immunity.

Hypersensitivity or hyperimmunity

Some people are allergic to peanuts and others thrive on them. Asthma, mostly associated with allergy, is a fatal condition for some people but the same allergens (an extract of any substance known to cause allergy) have nil effect on others. By these examples we can tell that immune responses are not necessarily dose dependent. Sometimes a small dose of an allergen triggers a cascade effect with dramatic outcomes. However it is also true to say that major stimulation over an extended period, for instance by bacterial plaque, is more likely to produce hypersensitivity reactions. Since the immune system operates throughout the body, hypersensitivity reactions can occur anywhere, giving rise to different signs according to the organ affected.

Skin allergy or hypersensitivity disease affects millions of pets. The irritating itch can drive the patient to extremes of self-mutilation and the owner then drives the patient to the veterinarian. Some patients are diagnosed as suffering from allergy to fleas, or environmental allergens such as house dust or pollens. These diagnoses may well be right but are probably only part of the story. The reason being that skin allergies are subject to a 'threshold' effect. This means that while one allergen alone may be enough, often the combined and cumulative effects of several provoke the allergic response. No veterinary textbooks make mention of allergy to overgrowth of oral bacteria

Skin allergy or hypersensitivity disease affects millions of pets. The irritating itch can drive the patient to extremes of self-mutilation and the owner then drives the patient to the veterinarian.

as a source of skin allergy. Circumstantially it would appear that oral bacteria are a significant factor. In my clinical experience animals with clean teeth do not suffer from the range or severity of skin ailments as do the processed food fed, periodontal disease affected majority.

Hyperimmune reactions frequently occur in the tight confines of the capillaries. The capillary walls become damaged and the inflammatory reaction blocks the flow of fluid. Further damage thus occurs in the tissues. If the affected organ, for example heart, lung or joint, has to do plenty of work — even in a damaged state — then further local injury can occur. Dogs and cats suffering from periodontal disease frequently develop signs of heart, lung and joint disease. Once the periodontal disease is treated the joint stiffness and general activity levels of the patient frequently improve. On the available evidence it would be reasonable to suspect that hyperimmune reactions originating in the mouth could be at least partly involved.

The link between hyperimmune reactions and kidney disease is well established for humans and animals. By taking small samples of diseased kidney for histopathological examination it is possible to detect the blocked kidney filtration beds. While any kidney damage harms the patient, the outward signs may not be detectable until more than two-thirds of the kidneys are affected. For this reason many periodontal disease patients have slowly worsening kidneys, but only at the end stage does it become recognised. And this is a common story: either things are not recognised or not investigated.

An obscure hyperimmune-based, generally fatal condition of cats could fit into this category. The disease amyloidosis is associated with deposition of a protein in the tissues, usually the result of chronic infection. In October 1992 Alan Bennet and I attended a lecture by Dr Max Zuber when he discussed his research on 26 affected cats. No mention was made of periodontal disease so, during question time, I raised the matter. Only one of the 26 cats was also affected by periodontal disease, came the reply. When the research appeared in print in the *Australian Veterinary Practitioner* the following year still there was no mention of periodontal disease.[27]

By November 1999 Max Zuber had changed his mind to the extent that he wrote:

Chronic inflammation [for example periodontal disease, is] ... generally thought necessary for the development of reactive amyloidosis...

It has been the author's observation that many affected cats have suffered from relatively severe periodontal disease leading to tooth loss at a young age.[28]

In March 2000 Max Zuber approached me at a gathering in the Great Hall of Sydney University. We were there to honour the retirement of Douglas Bryden as Director of the Post Graduate Foundation in Veterinary Science. 'You must keep stirring ... we need you to keep stirring ... don't stop ... keep going,' urged Max. I was astounded by his generosity, given my earlier published critical comments.[29] Accepting criticism is a scientist's lot; inviting criticism for the greater good goes beyond the call of duty.

In these discussions of possible immune mechanisms of systemic disease I must emphasise that little is proven. But equally it must be asserted that little is disproven either. For the time being it is reasonable and perhaps essential to consider the known immune consequences of chronic infection to be at work in periodontal disease affected animals.

Auto-immunity

The complex notion of the immune system attacking healthy tissues of the body is relatively new to medical science and many answers are still lacking. As with any frontier science the experts often disagree. But you do not need to become an expert in this field in order to draw some valid conclusions as to the likely involvement of periodontal disease in auto-immune processes.

Evidence shows that the disease in the mouth is itself partly due to auto-immune activity as the immune system attacks the collagen supporting the teeth. Naturally enough, antibodies to oral collagen, if released into the circulatory system, continue to do damage to collagen wherever it may be found. Collagen is vital in reinforcement of the body and this tough protein is prevalent in the skin, joint linings and blood vessel walls. As has already been remarked, periodontal disease patients frequently suffer from low grade dermatitis and arthritis. Again this raises the point that disease states are frequently subtle or clinically undetectable.

The horror of auto-immune disease can be seen in debilitating conditions like type one diabetes, auto-immune thyroiditis, nephritis and hepatitis. But even in these defined conditions it is usual to find other organ systems being subtly affected. Systemic lupus erythematosus and rheumatoid arthritis are two conditions where multi-organ signs are common and include weakness, fever and joint pain. Kidney disease is a prominent feature of these conditions and this arises from the blocking of the filtration beds by the endless supply of antigen–antibody complexes.

Numerous factors bear on the development of auto-immune disorders. In humans, where most of the research has been performed, auto-immune diseases affect more females than males. The diseases occur toward the end of life and there is the possibility of an interplay with the mind and auto-immunity. So while there may be an in-built genetic tendency for the disease, a trigger is often required and that trigger is infection. Acute infections can have this effect, as with rheumatic heart disease following a streptococcal sore throat. But chronic infections create a constant stream of the body's own damaged proteins which stimulate the immune system.

Any chronic infection can have this effect but of course we know that periodontal disease is the most prevalent.

A serious and increasingly common condition of dogs (and other species) is auto-immune haemolytic anemia (AIHA). As the name implies, red blood cells are destroyed due to an auto-immune reaction. Unless given prompt and vigorous treatment most sufferers soon die. Research conducted on 58 dogs at the University of Pennsylvania showed a slight increase in AIHA affected animals soon after vaccination.[30] A link was established with the season of the year, suggesting that a number of other factors might well be at work. As the average age of the sufferers was 6.5 years we can assume that the animals were suffering variable degrees of periodontal disease. Unfortunately the researchers overlooked the common disease and concentrated on the unusual but weak association with vaccination.

Another troublesome complaint among dogs of middle to old age is aural haematoma. Due to rupture of blood vessels in the ear flap a large blister of blood accumulates. If left without treatment the blood gradually resorbs into the system and the ear takes on an unsightly crinkled appearance. In humans we say the sufferer has a 'cauliflower ear', most often associated with bouts in the boxing ring. Dogs do not box but they do shake their heads which, undoubtedly due to the centrifugal forces, contributes to the pooling of blood. Investigators found evidence of auto-immune damage to the blood vessels of the ears.[31] Since auto-immunity is frequently associated with chronic infection, and periodontal disease affects the majority of aural haematoma sufferers, then it would be reasonable to suspect a connection.

By now the many interconnections influencing the manifestations of health and disease will be apparent. As a means of handling the information we tend to compartmentalise the subjects and define them according to our liking. But we should be aware that nature does not label or compartmentalise its infinite functions. In considering auto-immunity it is necessary to consider that hyper-immunity plays a part and vice versa. Now as we leave auto-immunity for the intricacies of hypo-immunity it is well to remember that herein lies a paradoxical relationship. Some auto-immune individuals develop immuno-deficiency and some immunodeficient animals become auto-immune.

Hypo-immunity

Dr Niels Pedersen, the co-discoverer of the feline equivalent of HIV, commented:

> With the world-wide HIV pandemic ... immunodeficiency
> has become a byword of the age. Immunodeficiency, however,
> is not just a rare genetic disease or a common outcome of a
> widespread virus infection. Immunodeficiency results from a
> myriad of causes and can range from subtle to catastrophic in
> its clinical appearance.[32]

An animal is said to be immunodeficient if the number or vitality of white cells is reduced or if there is a reduction in antibodies or a combination of these factors. That immunodeficiency is serious is beyond question and the longer the deficiency persists the worse the outcome. Periodontal disease induced immunodeficiency fits into this category and can be said to be responsible for a host of other infections. When infections are unusually severe or hard to treat veterinarians tend to use longer courses of antibiotics at higher doses. When searching for an explanation of the poor results veterinarians often find fault with the antibiotic or blame an unusually virulent bacteria. Although common, veterinarians seldom recognise periodontal disease induced immunodeficiency as the critical factor.

Cancer affects millions of pets. One partial explanation for the development of cancer concerns a failure of the immune system to mount adequate surveillance for damaged cells. If the immune system is depressed, labouring to deal with periodontal disease and a host of other chronic diseases, perhaps we should not be surprised if it fails to recognise mutant cancer cells.

Toxins, cytokines, free radicals etc

Many factors bear on the development of cancers in animals. Genetic susceptibility is a prime factor but after that a range of chemical and physical agents are known to influence the health and structure of DNA, leading to the development of cancer. The longer cells are subjected to toxic chemicals and the greater the number of chemicals the greater the chance of mutations occurring. This is only a common sense observation. But some reactions are not dose dependent. Some toxins are unusually potent and some free radicals breed more free radicals.

The range and quantity of chemicals flowing into the circulatory system from chronic periodontal disease derive either from the bacteria in the gums or from the inflammatory reactions. Endotoxins from bacterial cell walls have profound actions on cells. Exotoxins secreted by bacteria and metabolic end products are a constant feature of periodontal disease and can be expected to exert their influence wherever they go. Some of the actions are direct and some are indirect, as for instance the stimulation of the immune system to produce cytokines and free radicals.

Cytokines are 'local hormone' messengers used by animal cells and bacterial communities for communication. As the chemical mediators of inflammation they have a range of types and functions. A 1998 editorial in the *Journal of Medical Microbiology* gave support to the belief that low level endotoxaemia and cytokines, derived from periodontal disease, are responsible for low birthweight babies and for heart disease in adults — diseases from different ends of the age spectrum.[33] This lends support to the suspicion that other diseases, at any stage of life, are the result of similar mechanisms.

Reactive oxygen species (ROS) or free radicals are potent destroyers of bacteria but also have a range of deleterious effects on contact cells. In the healthy body free radical production is balanced by free radical scavengers such as vitamins E and C and various enzymes such as superoxide dismutase and catalase. In chronic inflammation the rate of production of ROS increases with corresponding likelihood of escape to other areas of the body. ROS are believed to trigger cancer development.[34]

Writing about aging and reactive oxygen species, Stohs stated:

> Oxidative stress associated with production of reactive oxygen species is believed to be involved not only in the toxicity of xenobiotics [foreign chemicals] but also in the pathophysiology of aging, and various age-related diseases, including cataracts, atherosclerosis, neoplastic diseases [cancer], diabetes,

diabetic retinopathy, chronic inflammatory diseases of the gastrointestinal tract, aging of the skin, diseases associated with cartilage, Alzheimer's disease and other neurological disorders.[35]

Periodontal disease patients appear prematurely aged. Could a cascade of reactive oxygen species arising from inflamed gums provide part of the explanation?

Collagenases, ellastases and other enzymes

Collagen is vital in reinforcing the body, accounting for 6 percent by weight of the body and 30 percent of the total protein. This specialised protein and its closely related connective tissue proteins impart strength and elasticity to the body, act as a template for the production of new bone and provide the matrix for the construction of all other tissues. Flexible, strong connective tissue is a feature of youth with the converse being stiff, brittle connective tissue of old age. The outward signs, wrinkles and thinning, are seen in the skin which represents 12 percent of the body and is largely made up of collagen. As anyone who is old will attest, joints and muscles also begin to stiffen and ache. Old age brings subtle changes in the tissues and an overall loss of function and departure from the rude good health of youth. Arteries which lose their elasticity carry less blood and are subject to rupture. Kidneys become hard and fibrous and loss of elasticity in lungs can give rise to emphysema.

The aging process is hard to combat but it is a pity when that unavoidable process becomes accentuated by preventable disease. On the available evidence this seems to be what happens as the immune system begins to identify self collagen as foreign and develops auto antibodies. Reactive oxygen species attack collagen. Importantly, it would appear that there is a surfeit of enzymes, for example collagenase and ellastase, deriving from chronic periodontal disease which have the same effect. The source of those enzymes is the periodontal bacteria themselves and also the damaged gums where, as part of the inflammatory process, collagenases and ellastases are produced.

The full ramifications of this scenario are not yet known. However, it would seem that chronic periodontal disease patients have a constant shower of collagenases affecting the body reinforcement, similar to perpetual acid rain affecting the structure of an industrialised city. Where a city can trace its pollution to its industries, the pollution of the body can be traced to the periodontal disease and then back further to the inadequacies of an artificial diet. This failure can be summarised as a failure of the physical cleaning system. But the physical form of the food goes hand in hand with the correct chemical constituents. Natural food provides optimum cleaning and chemicals, whereas artificial food does not.

Patients tormented by lifelong diet-induced periodontal disease invariably have to contend with inappropriate chemical constituents of artificial food, the focus of the next two chapters.

4

———⟫●⟪———

Raw vs cooked food

Chemicals are important. Utilising experience in combination with the five senses of taste, touch, sight, smell and hearing we can distinguish many chemicals and combinations of chemicals. Most often we do not know the names of the chemicals, but we can tell subtle differences in formulation or concentration. Take tomatoes. Unripe tomatoes are green in colour, feel unduly firm and the chemicals they contain fail the taste test. Ripe tomatoes by contrast have an agreeable odour, pleasing bloom to the skin and the sound of the knife slicing the flesh suggests a suitable chemical combination which the taste test confirms.

I mention these things because I want you to trust your senses and intellect when assessing information on complex biochemicals. Of course it is important to acknowledge limitations and admittedly chemistry can be a difficult subject. As we progress through this chapter we shall consider some of the 'difficult' chemicals in 'difficult' combinations. In coping with what may be unfamiliar, try ranking the concepts by drawing on what is familiar in your life experience. Consistent with this let's take a slight detour via the fuel requirements of a car.

If the maker's instructions are followed when fuelling a car, good engine performance can be expected. The engine should sound healthy and give off the expected colour and volume of exhaust fumes. Depending on the model of car, there are expectations about the power output. A small car should be lively under acceleration, compared with the smooth acceleration and power of a family saloon car. If a car sounds 'healthy' and performs with 'vitality' under average driving conditions then this is usually reflected in the 'longevity' of the engine.

If, like me, you have scant idea about petrochemicals and the refinery business or how lead acts as an anti-knocking agent then you are at no particular disadvantage. Nothing needs to be exact because car makers allow for impurities and octane variations in the fuel used in their cars. However, adding large amounts of water to the fuel or putting diesel in a petrol-driven car has immediate effects on the 'health' and 'vitality' of the engine. Due to the effects being readily detectable and the fact that engines do not have a self-cure mechanism, the advice of a mechanic is usually sought before long-term damage is done. Things become more complicated when the fuel is only slightly adulterated because the 'ill health' of the engine and the poor power output may not be noticed and long-term engine damage may occur. Even so, as engines are relatively simple mechanical devices, the range of outcomes are fairly predicable and detectable.

Chemical effects of raw food

When we start to consider the chemical fuel needs of our carnivore companions the equations become more complex. The 'fuel' or food needs to provide the energy and raw materials for growth, maintenance and repair. If the quantity, quality and frequency of intake of the chemical constituents are optimal this will be reflected in optimum health, vitality and longevity. There are of course tolerance limits but even when the quantity, quality and frequency of intake are significantly altered there may not be any immediately obvious outcomes. For, unlike the motor car suffering fuel-related problems and needing the services of a mechanic, an animal can employ a vast range of compensatory mechanisms which obscure from the outside observer the true state of health.

the food of a species is defined by that which is consumed in nature. For carnivores this means almost any mammal, amphibian, reptile, fish or bird capable of being overpowered and killed.

In the midst of scientific uncertainty and our own limitations as chemists you may be wondering how we can be confident of the chemical requirements of carnivores. The answer is straightforward and can be summarised as 'nature knows best'. From the origin of life, more than 3.5 billion years ago, through the evolution of mammals, about 200 million years ago, up to the present time, the food of a species is defined by that which is consumed in nature. For carnivores this means almost any mammal, amphibian, reptile, fish or bird capable of being overpowered and killed.

Wild dogs and cats like to eat rabbits. In the act of tearing and bolting chunks of rabbit some herbage and soil may be ingested, however the bulk of the meal consists of meat, bone and offal (the internal organs including the heart, lungs, liver and intestines). Rabbits mostly eat herbage which after maceration (softening by soaking) with digestive juices passes through the intestines as a substance with a milky consistency called chyme. Rabbit chyme gets eaten along with the intestines but the more fibrous material found in the stomach is often ignored, as is the colon and its contents. Both cats and dogs will scavenge carrion (the putrefying flesh of animals that have recently died). Even the maggots emerging from a carcass may be eaten by dingoes and foxes as live prey. Some herbage may be chewed and in certain instances members of the dog family, but not members of the cat family, eat ripe fruit. Faeces may occasionally be consumed.

As to the number of biochemicals and their relative proportions in the whole raw rabbit, no one knows. When nutritionists attempt to analyse the intricate chemical makeup of the rabbit they strike obstacles which render the task impossible. Put simply, biochemicals are destroyed by the analytical processes of heating and solvent extraction employed by scientists. Carnivores do not need to know. Instinct and learning are combined and the five senses assist in achieving the correct balance of quality and quantity.

It would be an error to see whole rabbits as the appropriate food for carnivores without giving some thought to the context. It is in context that interactions and processes come alive and gain significance. Feeding behaviour is itself important in establishing optimum digestion. Typically, carnivores gorge to the point of severe abdominal distension. Tearing and bolting large lumps of food is done with gusto and accompanying growls. Food for wild carnivores is never continuously available and so they have evolved to consume large amounts infrequently. Complementing the behavioural mechanisms is an anatomy well suited for the purpose.

Retractable lips move easily out of the way of large dagger-shaped teeth. From killing to skinning and crushing the bones there are teeth designed for the purpose. Carnivore jaws hinge wide, allowing food to be passed to the back of the mouth where crushing pressures are maximal. Masticatory muscles (muscles used for chewing) attached to the skull create a powerful scissor action. Leaving the mouth, food passes in large pieces down the distensible oesophagus to the elastic stomach. Next comes the muscular small bowel leading to the colon and finally the rectum.

Physiological mechanisms are equally evolved for the purpose. Digestive juices are regulated, both in quality and quantity, to suit the food passing through the digestive tract. X-ray pictures of a stomach full of bone serves as a reminder of the strength of stomach acids, which reduce that bone to a granular slurry. Raw meat subjected to the churning action and body heat in the stomach begins to dissolve under a process known as autolysis — much like a piece of steak left out on a kitchen bench on a hot day. On leaving the stomach, enzyme-rich pancreatic fluid and bile from the liver mix with the food. By the time the food reaches the colon it is unrecognisable as the once raw rabbit. Water and water-soluble vitamins are absorbed and the ingesta passes into the rectum prior to being voided as small faecal pellets. Since the meat, skin and organs are almost completely digested the faecal composition is mostly fur and powdered bone.

At the biochemical and cellular level the system is highly efficient. Lean rabbit carcasses are mostly made up of protein and fat. The composite peptides and fatty acids are absorbed into the lymph and blood stream and transported to the liver. The liver, as the factory for processing fuel and building-blocks necessary for maintaining the health of the animal, possesses a rich store of enzymes. Biochemicals arriving at the liver in appropriate quantity, quality and frequency are easily handled by the enzymes. While most molecules journey from the bowel to the liver, some are ingested by white cells and macrophages which line the intestine. Cells of the immune system monitor the passage of ingesta generally and of course are at the ready to deal with harmful bacteria.

Beneficial bacteria live at all levels of the gastrointestinal tract, including in the acid environment of the stomach. (Stomach acids help to combat foreign bacteria contained in food.) Further down the bowel, in the colon and rectum, a large and helpful population of bacteria assist with the final stages of digestion. Maintenance of the health of the bowel lining, production of fatty acids and vitamins B and K are some of the benefits provided by bacteria.

Chemical effects of cooked food

Tolerance limits exist for all parameters within a healthy system and of course individual animals have widely differing needs. For these reasons it is not possible to be prescriptive as to the exact or even optimum needs of individual carnivores. It is much easier to say what is not appropriate. By way of introduction to this concept we shall start with a cooked as opposed to a raw rabbit. Cooking alters both the physical and chemical makeup of a food. Where the raw item provides the correct quantity and balance of proteins, fats, carbohydrates, vitamins, minerals and micronutrients, the cooked version does not. In general the greater the heat and the longer the duration of heating the greater the damage to the fragile biochemicals. Damaged or altered biochemicals are not as 'bio-available'. That is to say that the physiological and enzymatic systems are not able to make as much use of the altered chemical.

Heated proteins coagulate and the constituent amino acids are frequently destroyed. Absence of vital amino acids can be fatal, as was discovered when heat-treated cat foods were found to be deficient in taurine. Taurine deficiency gives rise to heart muscle disease and blindness, neither of which can be reversed. As well, proteins are the main source of allergens and with change in chemical structure comes changed allergic profiles. Interestingly, one of the first experiments on protein allergies was carried out in 1921 by Heinz Kustner, who found that he was allergic to cooked fish but not raw fish.[1]

Cooked fats become significantly altered at the biochemical level even to the extent of becoming toxic. The correct balance of short and long chain fats is essential to good health but once the rabbit is cooked the balance of fats changes.

Complex carbohydrates such as starch are not part of the chemical makeup of prey animals. Neither are grains a significant part of the food of rabbits. So, whether the rabbit be eaten cooked or raw, carbohydrates hardly feature.

Of more significance is the effect of cooking on the delicate vitamins and micronutrients. The B group vitamins are particularly sensitive to heating and a great many micronutrients including anti-oxidants are thereby destroyed.

Even the bio-availability of minerals in cooked rabbit is altered. Carnivores which have evolved to feed on whole carcasses have adapted to the high levels of calcium in the bones. This source of calcium is balanced by the high phosphorus content of raw meat. However once bones are cooked the availability of the calcium is reduced and of course the brittle bones can penetrate the bowel or get stuck — anywhere from the mouth to the anus.

Perhaps one of the most important but poorly understood aspects of cooked food is the absence of biologically active cellular enzymes. All cells, whether plant or animal, contain enzymes. When raw cells are crushed and the enzymes released into the tissues rapid chemical digestion takes place reducing complex proteins, fats and carbohydrates to their constituent parts. Thus the raw rabbit being churned in the warm, watery environment of the stomach undergoes considerable digestion prior to being exposed to the pancreatic enzymes in the duodenum. With much of the digestion already done the pancreas need not produce as much digestive juice and digestion is soon complete.

> Cooking kills cellular enzymes and puts an end to the auto-digestion of the food.

Contrast this situation with that prevailing when the rabbit is cooked. Cooking kills cellular enzymes and puts an end to the auto-digestion of the food. While cooking may reduce some proteins to their constituent amino acids, the process does not continue in the stomach to any great extent. When the food arrives in the duodenum the pancreas has a much bigger job to do, providing enzymes that are otherwise absent from the food.

Clearly there are many factors at work, all of which change the microenvironment in the bowel and thus the rate of digestion. Slowly or poorly digested material tends to damage the bowel lining. Damage can occur by direct physical or chemical action of the food on the bowel. More commonly the damage is due to a change in the resident population of bacteria as a result of the poorly digested material. Harmful bacteria and their toxins affect the lining of the bowel, and if absorbed into the blood stream are harmful to other organs. With an increase in harmful bacteria there is a corresponding decrease in helpful bacteria. The perception that raw food is somehow dirty and bacteria laden while cooked food is clean and safe represents a complete reversal of what happens in the bowel. Thousands of pets eating cooked food suffer a condition known as SIBO, small intestinal bacterial overgrowth.

Supplements can't save spoiled broth

Many people believe that chemicals denatured or absent from cooked food can easily be replaced. This view is understandable given the constant bombardment with advertising messages supported by university teaching which says that adding vitamins and minerals sufficiently fortifies pet diets. Unfortunately this is false on many levels and the consequences are insidious and hard to detect.

Vitamin supplements

The chemical formula for a range of vitamins is known and there is a vast industry devoted to their production. If a hypothetical manufacturer of cooked-rabbit pet food were to try vitamin supplementation of the food, they would be taking a gamble on getting it right. And of course the manufacturer would not know if the gamble had succeeded. Dr Ian Billinghurst in his book *Give Your Dog a Bone* describes the five possible levels of vitamin supplementation.[2]

Level 1 Absence of or barely sufficient level.
Theoretically diets can be severely deficient but this is rare in practice due to modern supplementation with crude artificially produced vitamins. Vitamins are also available in other food sources — bowel bacteria are a rich source of vitamins B and K and exposure to sunlight

produces vitamin D in the skin. Clinically detectable deficiency of vitamin B_1 does occur in both cats and dogs where the sufferers have seizures and may die. (Some prepared sausage and raw meat preserved with sulphur dioxide may be deficient in vitamin B_1. This latter form of treated raw meat has an unusually red appearance.)

    Other factors can exert an influence on the effective vitamin levels. Storage can bring about deterioration as can the presence of heat and air. Vitamin E requirements are dependent on the amount of fat in the diet. More fat or rancid fat means a greater vitamin E requirement.

Level 2   Minimum levels of vitamins.
At this level there is an absence of frank signs of deficiency but optimum health is unachievable.

Level 3   Presence in abundance.
This is the level at which all vitamins occur in the diet of wild animals. Supplementation by manufacturers may occur at this level.

Level 4   Pharmacologic level.
At this level high doses are employed to treat disease.

Level 5   Toxic level.
High doses of vitamins sufficient to poison an animal are rare. High doses of vitamins B and C are excreted in the urine. Vitamin A and D are sometimes associated with toxicity. This occurs when diets are already adequate but owners continue to feed vitamin supplements. In the case of cats fed an all liver diet vitamin A toxicity occurs.

Other problems can arise due to the inability of vitamin manufacturers to make the correct three dimensional structure — this structure being crucial to the vitamin's effect. (On a familiar scale, your left and right hands look and act quite differently. Try picking up a cup with your left hand in exactly the same way that you use your right hand.) In nature vitamins exert their influence in conjunction with micronutrients which, we have to accept, are absent or badly damaged in cooked food.

Mineral supplements

If the rabbit canner believes the cooked rabbit has inadequate mineral levels there are several options for supplementation. Powdered bone meal, itself cooked, and the salts of various minerals could be estimated and added, but it would be a gamble. When considering minerals the American National Health and Medical Research Council listed a number of concerns:

> It is common practice to include all the minerals shown to be required by other mammals in the formulation of dog [and cat] diets, even though the quantitative requirements for all minerals have not been established experimentally for this species. The mineral concentration used in dog [and cat] diets are usually based on estimates extrapolated from the requirements of other species; from data obtained from studies that involve dogs and that, although not designed to establish nutrient requirements, nevertheless yielded nutritional information; or from experience with diets that have resulted in acceptable performance in dogs [and cats].
>
> Limited controlled published data on quantitative mineral requirements of dogs is not the only complication in making an estimate of mineral requirements for dogs [and cats]. The interaction between dietary mineral concentrations, availability of minerals in different compounds, and the breed of dog involved are factors which may modify individual mineral requirements... Perhaps the factor of most concern regarding the controlled data available for estimating the mineral requirements for dogs [and cats] is that a large percentage of the research was conducted two or three decades ago.[3]

Thus the rabbit canner should be justifiably nervous as to how to proceed. While mineral deficiencies are undesirable the serious and detectable signs of mineral excess may be worse. And perhaps the operative word here is 'detectable' for even severe mineral imbalance is often hard to identify in adult animals. Puppies and kittens are more vulnerable during their growing phase and consequently can show clinical signs of mineral imbalance. But even in this situation interpretation of signs is far from easy. When a group of nutritionists looked into the effects of over-nutrition they managed to produce Great Dane puppies with obvious skeletal disease. Unfortunately they were unable to tell if the changes were brought about by excess levels of calcium, phosphorous, magnesium or vitamin D.[4]

Other researchers have commented that young puppies do not have a mechanism to protect themselves against excessive calcium intake.[5] (They were researching the effects of artificial calcium supplementation. It seems that calcium in raw bones does not have the same adverse effect.) The result of this imbalance is most often seen in the puppies of giant breeds which develop bent legs. And to make matters worse well-meaning owners and even some veterinarians attribute the leg deformity to insufficiency of calcium and accordingly increase the level of calcium supplementation. Excess inorganic calcium also has the effect of reducing the availability of other minerals such as iron, copper, iodine and zinc. As long ago as 1963 researchers demonstrated how too much calcium provoked zinc deficiency problems.[6] Affected puppies may have crusty scabby skin around the face, elbows and hocks. More commonly the affected pups and kittens just have a dull coat, appear less active and fail to grow well.

A major problem faced by owners and veterinarians is that there are plenty of other reasons why pups and kittens fail to grow well and suffer from dermatitis. A common assumption is that the young animals must be deficient in some essential vitamin or mineral and consequently high levels of supplementation are often tried as a first line of treatment. While this shotgun approach to medicine often fails or makes things worse, the corresponding exact scientific method is no better. In commenting on the assessment of zinc levels in the blood of affected animals a leading authority on the subject states: 'proper analysis for zinc is difficult and may be unreliable due to contamination of samples by zinc in glassware, rubber stoppers, and other items.'[7]

But I'm not selecting facts just to torment our much maligned rabbit canner. The reality of life for all animals raised and maintained on cooked food is that their mineral requirements are haphazardly met by either too little, sometimes adequate or often excessive levels.

A pet food company newsletter makes a telling point:

> A balanced Ca:P [calcium: phosphorus] ratio does not offer protection from a high level of calcium in the diet. Many pet foods in Australia, even some especially formulated for puppies, contain higher levels than this new recommended maximum for calcium of 2.5% (according to their own guaranteed analysis). Check these for yourself and see![8]

Micronutrient supplements

My veterinary dictionary defines a micronutrient as 'a dietary element essential only in small quantities'. But while these elements may be essential, we, and especially pet food manufacturers, have a problem. For we do not know the number or range of micronutrients in raw food. Finding out is nigh on impossible too, as heating or solvent extracting the complex biochemicals affects their structure and quantity.

Not so long ago vitamins and minerals were in the same category as micronutrients — while essential they were not known and therefore not included in artificial diets. But the health problems affecting animals consuming vitamin and mineral deficient diets were often severe and detectable. Micronutrient deficiencies, by contrast, exert subtle and long-term effects which are hard to detect. (Animals continue to live and breed but perhaps at a sub-optimum level.) Pet food manufacturers manage to avoid responsibility for subtle and hard-to-detect deficiencies — consequently, when cooking their broth, they add few if any micronutrient supplements.

In the final analysis, nutrients, whether macro or micro, need to be raw. Only then may animals enjoy appropriate good health.

5

What's in the can?

What about the real world?, you may ask. Surely the situation can't be so bad? Well, from our current perspective on chemical constituents, I have to say that the situation is very much worse. In popular books and articles dealing with the noxious substances found in the can and packet the starting point is often the flavourings, colourings and preservatives. Undoubtedly these factory-made products are foreign to the digestive system of carnivores and are bound to have deleterious effects. However, the chemicals in greatest quantity, and generally contributing the most harmful effects, are those provided by the main food ingredients (carbohydrates, proteins, etc).

Note that there are so many different formulations and feed types that it's not possible to comment on them all. And in any case different batches of cans or packets will differ according to the raw materials available on any particular day. The US National Research Council (NRC) lists 165 common feed ingredients of dog food and 147 for cat food, which provide the manufacturers with a wide choice.[1] At the extreme ends of the range manufacturers bake wheat biscuits for dogs and can whole fish for cat food. Both of these products have their own particular drawbacks. However our purpose is to look at the generality of processed foods fed to the majority of pets and which carry the 'complete and balanced' claim. Manufacturers encourage the exclusive feeding of these products for long periods of time. While good for profits, long-term use means long-term side effects for the animals.

Carbohydrates

Cereal grains are the chief ingredient in most dry and semi-moist pet foods. Canned foods often contain cereals too. The absurdity of this situation is summed up by Professor David Kronfeld's facetious question: 'Have you ever seen a dog attack a wheat field?' Cat behaviour, anatomy and physiology are even less well adapted to a grain-based diet. As the taste test tells you, there are differences between oats, corn, wheat, barley, rice and rye, but they are all utilised primarily for their carbohydrate content. If whole uncooked grains are fed to carnivores they pass through the digestive tract unchanged and thus confer no nutritional benefit. Milling and cooking the grains breaks down the cell structure and renders the starches more bio-available. Superficially this serves to make a cheap food source available to pets but in fact it serves to store up trouble.

Dogs have little evolved need for carbohydrates and cats have no need for this source of energy.

Dogs have little evolved need for carbohydrates and cats have no need for this source of energy. Consequently these species produce low levels of digestive enzymes required to deal with the high starch content. As we have seen in the previous chapter, undigested food arriving in the bowel provides nutrients for a teeming population of harmful bacteria. But the carbohydrate problems associated with grains are just the beginning. Grains contain protein too. David Kronfeld says:

> ... the protein [in cooked grains is] low in quality to begin with, then further degraded to a variable degree by cooking [from 5 to 50 percent biologically unavailable[2]]. This destroys methionine and histidine, and combines proteins with starch to form indigestible brown polymers like caramel — a nice color and flavor but otherwise useless.[3]

Proteins

Plant proteins

Although plant proteins start out as inferior and then become further denatured by the manufacturing process, they usually feature in the total protein percentage listed on the outside of pet food packets.

Manufacturers realising the limitations of grain-derived protein seek to offset some of the limitations by including soy meal in their recipes. Soy protein may be of reasonable quality and cheaper than animal protein but other aspects are less welcome. Soy-fed animals are prone to diarrhoea and of course the room-clearing properties of their flatus is legendary. The chemical explanation of this latter phenomenon is centred on the bacterial action on soy sugars in the lower bowel. Another undesirable component of soy is a substance called phytin. This material has the effect of combining with calcium, thus requiring increased calcium supplementation of grain and soy-based diets. Too much calcium creates other mineral disturbances and so the vicious cycle continues.

Animal proteins

Most of the animal proteins incorporated into processed pet foods, at least in the raw state, would be suitable for pets. Even whale meat, listed by the NRC as item 142 on the dog food list and 125 on the cat food list, might be consumed by wandering carnivores if they came across a beached specimen. But just as manufacturers do not can whole rabbits they don't can whole whales either. Instead they make use of a range of animal products and by-products. Some examples are blood, cattle lips, livers and udders, whole fish and fish meal, day-old chickens and poultry viscera. The NRC lists a number of milk and milk products including buttermilk, cheese and whey. A range of mammals, fish and birds end up at the rendering plant and the resultant meat meal and rendered fat become incorporated in pet foods.

Noting the competing protein claims between rival products, David Kronfeld investigated three best-selling brands and five so-called high quality brands.[4] All products were found to be deficient in at least one essential amino acid when compared to the established standard. Professor Kronfeld had difficulty interpreting his findings due to the variable digestibility of the proteins. When compared to the cost of eggs, the benchmark protein source, Kronfeld had no difficulty. He priced eggs from the supermarket and found that the protein in seven of the eight artificial products cost more, in one case eleven times more, than the equivalent egg protein.

While Professor Kronfeld's findings point to the nonsense of manufacturers' competing claims, we need to exercise caution — the reality is probably worse than a 'scientific' investigation can reveal. Kronfeld, in speaking about the complexity of body processes, observes: 'The whole is exceedingly complex, but we are driven to think simply, so our knowledge is usually a pale image of the real thing... Those strivers for simplicity and order, called scientists, like to study how each substance is handled on its own.'[5] What if liver made up most of the protein in the products? Vitamin A and purine excess would have been a possibility. If milk or milk products featured then problems could have arisen due to the indigestibility of lactose, the milk sugar. Kronfeld neither posed these questions nor provided the answers because as a scientist he needed to keep things manageably simple.

Fats

It is a pity that Professor Kronfeld did not go on to test the eight products for fats and degradation products of fats. The likely outcome of such an investigation is that the products, from a bio-available fat point of view, would not meet the NRC-established criteria. If those same products were then compared with the fat profile of our whole raw rabbit we could expect to find multiple failings.

Rabbits and other prey species are almost never fat animals. Life in the wild is too hard for herbivores to lay down substantial reserves of fat. Nevertheless all animal tissue contains fat in varying percentages. In 100 grams of rabbit meat 71.1 percent is water, 20.8 percent protein and 6.6 percent fat.[6] (The figures for whole rabbit were unavailable.) When the fat content of rabbit meat is expressed as a percentage of the dry matter (that's with the water removed from the meat) the figure is 22.8 percent. The following table shows the comparable percentage of fat in four types of commercial food, as published by the British Small Animal Veterinary Association.[7]

FAT AS A PERCENTAGE OF DRY MATTER

FOOD TYPE	COMMERCIAL DOG FOOD	COMMERCIAL CAT FOOD
Dry complete	11.0	7.5
Semi-moist	9.0	7.5
Moist (canned) meat-based	35.0	28.0
Moist (canned) ration (animal by-products and cereal)	8.0	30.0
Fat as a percentage of dry matter in rabbit meat	22.8	

In the table two cat diets and three dog diets have a fat content significantly below that of rabbit meat. The other three classifications have fat appreciably in excess of the estimated fat content of rabbit meat. Perhaps in the short term such imbalances may not create health hazards. It's in the long term that imbalances give rise to problems. Just as the occasional hamburger is tolerated by the average person but a regular high fat diet predisposes people to diabetes, obesity and heart disease.

Quantity of fat is not the only consideration; quality is of vital importance too. Chemists speak of fats being saturated, mono-unsaturated or polyunsaturated. This concept refers to the number of hydrogen ions attached to carbon in the fatty acid chain. Unsaturated fats are, in general, easier to digest and there are three polyunsaturated fatty acids (PUFA) which must be supplied in the diet. Game animals, fish and birds contain high levels of PUFA which are appropriate for cats and dogs. (Some fish contain too much PUFA. A theoretical problem arises if these fish are fed to cats in large quantity.) Even though most commercial pet foods claim to meet the minimum PUFA requirements there is widespread and justifiable belief that this is not the case. Diets deficient in or with inappropriate proportions of PUFA — for example many dry foods — are known to predispose animals to varying degrees of dermatitis and hair loss.

The quality of the fat in manufactured pet foods primarily depends on the source of the fat and subsequently on the manufacturing and storage conditions. In the extreme it is known that burning or charring fat creates a range of carcinogenic chemicals. Animal fats incorporated in pet foods are usually extracted by rendering. Rendering is a process which depends on heating animal products for extended periods at high temperatures. The biological value of fats decreases and the toxic degradation products can generally be said to increase with greater time and temperature. These chemical changes continue during storage of the products, especially if the fat is exposed to air.

Exposure to air is most problematic for the grain-based kibbles, which are coated with fat in order to increase palatability. Even though anti-oxidants are incorporated in the final mix, oxidation and therefore rancidity are inevitable. Pet food companies may have evidence of the harm done to animals which eat those 'spoiled' products. The lack of experimental evidence should not be a bar to our declaring the practice unhealthy.

'Digest' and other protein additives

The 'shock horror' style of reporting invites condemnation of manufacturers that include chicken guts, and the bodies of pet dogs and cats in artificial pet foods. While we may not relish the thought — especially the idea of one's own pet rendered and in the can — it is important to separate objectivity from emotion. In the raw state chicken entrails provide an excellent food source for carnivores. Packs of dogs are known to kill and eat cats, and wolves engage in cannibalism during times of food shortage.

If we concentrate on the health implications of adding exotic proteins to pet food then we need to be concerned at the degradation of the nutrients during processing. We should also give some thought to the extraneous chemicals which might be included. 'Digest' is the euphemism for products of bacterial fermentation of chicken guts and other offal used as a flavour and palatability enhancer. Since chicken guts contain any chemicals recently fed to the birds, those chemicals also become incorporated in the mix. In early 1996 an outbreak of paralysis in cats in The Netherlands and Switzerland was traced to poultry guts used in commercial cat food. The guts contained Salinomycin, a poultry medication. (Coccidiosis is a problem for intensively raised chickens and the chemicals used to control the disease are often toxic for other animals.)[8]

In an article in the *American Journal of Veterinary Research* the authors estimated that more than 40 percent of pets put down in large US cities are rendered for meat and bone meal and fat.[9] The barbiturate used to kill the animals was found to survive the rendering process, but not a great deal found its way into individual pet diets. That does not rule out, however, that under special circumstances barbiturates could be included at higher concentrations. The researchers were careful not to commit themselves as to contamination by insecticides and other chemicals. Since insecticidal flea collars are worn by some pets, inclusion in the resulting rendered products may add to the total burden of artificial pet food induced toxins.

Fibre

Fibre is a buzzword in human nutrition. Fibre is mostly carbohydrate material, such as cellulose, which escapes digestion in the stomach and small intestine. High fibre breads, breakfast cereals and fruits are recommended by all those concerned with the promotion of human health. Since fibre enjoys a favourable image, pet food manufacturers have had no difficulty utilising the image for their benefit. And not without good reason, since their grain-based products are inevitably high in fibre.

Pet carnivores, unlike humans, have not evolved in ways that allow them to consume large quantities of plant fibre. Physically the material absorbs water like a sponge, shortens the transit time of foodstuffs through the bowel and distends the colon. Within the colon a wet, nutrient-rich microenvironment facilitates the growth of bacteria. It would be reasonable to assume that these additional bacteria are not of benefit to the pet and are most likely harmful.

In an attempt to offset the harmful effects of colonic bacteria (which in humans are said to include diarrhoea, constipation, infections, liver damage, cancer and encephalopathy) pet food companies have experimented with modification of the fibre fed to animals. A substance called fructo-oligosaccharides (found naturally in leek, onion, wheat, garlic, chicory root and artichoke) is credited with binding bacterial toxins and is included in some proprietary foods. In order to extol the benefits of its wizardry Uncle Ben's of Australia, a division of the Mars Corporation, suggests that fructo-oligosaccharides 'may have a role in the nutritional management of similar [disease] conditions in companion animals'.[10] I remain skeptical.

Professor Kronfeld describes racing sled dogs which were fed huge amounts of dry food and which in the course of racing bled from the anus. Overextension of the bowel due to the high fibre content of the food was presumed to be the source of the problem.[11] White sled dogs bleeding onto white snow would be noticed by spectators and officials at a race meeting. Unfortunately the average domestic dog resting in the lounge room does not demonstrate such signs and the effects of a monotonous high fibre diet go undetected.

In the absence of information to the contrary we can assume that cats suffer from high fibre diets in much the same way as do dogs. A particularly distressing form of constipation, known as megacolon, affects some middle-aged cats. Just as a balloon, once overinflated, loses its elasticity, the same appears to be the case with an affected cat's colon. Unfortunately veterinary texts speak about surgical removal of the colon but make no reference to artificial food. Instead they refer to megacolon as being idiopathic — meaning that the cause is unknown or that the condition arises spontaneously.

High fibre and the phytates (phosphorous-based chemicals) in plant-based diets have another drawback: they interfere with mineral absorption. Calcium and trace elements become biologically unavailable with potentially serious and detectable consequences, especially for growing pups. In order to compensate, some manufacturers supplement their products with additional calcium. High levels of calcium may then inhibit the uptake of copper, zinc, iron and iodine. These latter minerals are essential to good health, but hard-to-detect deficiencies may go unnoticed and therefore untreated.

Dogs and cats have little option but to eat the food they are given and then suffer the consequences. If the diet is high in fibre, akin to the diet of a herbivore, the waste products must also resemble those of herbivores — high in volume, frequency and odour. Dog turds pollute private gardens and public parks. Cats seek to cover their embarrassment and contain the odours as they scrape in the kitty litter, but to no avail. Human responses to the processed food excrement problem include leash laws, pooper scoopers, kitty litter deodorisers, even dung beetles to chew up the dung. But like a turd on the sole of your shoe the problem persists.

By contrast with grain-fed pets, those eating a natural diet based on raw meaty bones produce small quantities (about a third the volume of processed food fed pets) of relatively odour-free faeces. These pellets of powdered bone turn chalky white after a couple of days in the sun. Fly maggots and dung beetles find no sustenance in natural dog turds. Neither does the natural product have much affinity for the sole of your shoe.

Vitamins and minerals

Vitamin and mineral supplementation is complex. Manufacturers of 'complete and balanced' products may attempt to overcome problems by over-supplementation. They take a gamble that major detectable abnormalities will not occur and subtle changes will be overlooked. The British Small Animal Veterinary Association's comments on the mineral selenium illustrate the potential problems of over-supplementation: 'Highly toxic in large doses; the difference between the recommended allowance and the toxic dose may be quite small.'[12]

The average pet suffering borderline insufficiency or excess of a particular mineral or vitamin over an extended period is unlikely to reveal identifiable signs. The situation becomes more acute in the case of rapidly growing puppies and kittens, pregnant and lactating females, racing and working dogs. In these cases the food intake can be up to five times the quantity of the average resting adult. Five times the usual intake of any toxic element in the food, for example vitamins A and D, calcium and iron, can impose an excessive burden.

It is worth reminding ourselves that the problem of vitamin and mineral imbalance is almost entirely a function of artificial feeding. Pregnant and lactating wolves and cats simply eat more of the same wholesome food without risk of toxicity.

Sodium chloride

One much used and abused mineral is sodium chloride, more commonly known as table salt. This mineral is essential for life and needs to be kept in fine balance in relation to water content and other minerals, particularly potassium, within all living cells. Various body pumps regulate the levels of sodium chloride in different cells and secretions of cells. For instance tears and sweat are salty but saliva is not. In nature salt derives from the diet and water supply. If animals experience a need greater than that provided in their diet they frequently seek out brackish water or salt-rich earth. It is for these reasons that salt licks provide good big-game viewing areas in parts of Africa. The animals craving the salt are mostly herbivores — their diet tends to be deficient in salt. The carnivores suffer no such problem and come to the salt lick to ambush the herbivores.

The meat of herbivores contains about 0.4 percent salt on a dry-matter basis and this sets the optimum for our carnivores. By comparison dry processed pet foods often contain greatly elevated levels. According to the label on three separate dry cat foods the levels were 1 percent, 1.5 percent and 2 percent salt. Three brands of dry dog food carried label claims of 1 percent, 1.7 percent and 'not more than 3.5 percent'.[13] Sea water, by comparison, is about 2.6 percent sodium chloride and as the rhyme from the *Ancient Mariner* has it, 'Water water everywhere and not a drop to drink'.

We need to know why it is that diets are supplemented at this high level with the real risk of chronic or acute salt toxicity. Is salt included at up to 8.5 times the natural level for the benefit of the animals or for other reasons? According to Hill's Pet Foods: 'Some pet food manufacturers use sodium chloride and other inorganic salts to increase the palatability of their foods.'[14] Another reason may be that salt is a cheap and effective preservative. Manufacturers appear to be aware of salt toxicity risks and that these risks can be diminished if fresh water is made constantly available — pet food labels often carry big warnings to this effect.

The long-term consequences of chronic salt intoxication are difficult to determine and are a matter of divided opinion in the scientific community. Cattle and sheep maintained on a high salt diet suffer from weakness and occasional diarrhoea and pigs develop brain oedema (accumulation of fluid).[15] A consensus is forming that high salt intakes predispose humans to develop high blood pressure with adverse effects on the heart, kidneys, brain and eyes. The effects on dogs is not so clear cut, but what is generally agreed is that once blood pressure is increased salt intake should be restricted.

Hill's Pet Foods say that, in respect to salt content and high blood pressure, pet owners and veterinarians have two options:

- Wait until signs of underlying disease or end-organ [e.g. heart, kidneys, etc] damage become obvious and then avoid excess dietary salt.
- Or, because high blood pressure and its underlying conditions can be hidden, and avoiding excess salt is perfectly safe, always feed foods that do not contain excess amounts of salt.[16]

But of course the safest low salt food is the natural alternative — whole carcasses or raw meaty bones. This is equally true for sick pets suffering from kidney disease or diarrhoea. The salt needs of these animals are likely to vary enormously and cannot be safely met by the fixed amount of salt in artificial food. I recommend low salt natural food and, in keeping with the 'salt lick principle', I recommend that salty water be made available alongside a supply of fresh water. Sick dogs and cats will usually select from the bowl that better satisfies their need for salt. (To make salty water: in two pints (1200ml) put one level teaspoon of salt and half of one level teaspoon of bicarbonate of soda.)

Additives

In 1997 the US Animal Protection Institute published a long list of food additives.[17] (See accompanying box.) Most are foreign chemical compounds not normally encountered by animals living in the natural state. Some additives act as preservatives by reducing oxidation, enhancing colours and preventing microbial spoilage. Some sugars and gums provide nutritive value to the pet but in general additives confer no advantage on the animal.

ADDITIVES IN PROCESSED PET FOOD

Anticaking agents, Lubricants, Antimicrobial agents, Antioxidants, Nonnutritive sweeteners, Nutritive sweeteners, Colouring agents, Oxidising and reducing agents, Curing agents, pH control agents, Drying agents, Processing aids, Emulsifiers, Sequestrants, Firming agents, Solvents vehicles, Flavour enhancers, Stabilisers, Thickeners, Flavouring agents, Surface active agents, Flour treating agents, Surface finishing agents, Formulation aids, Synergists, Humectants, Texturisers, Leavening agents.

It is true that mouldy or rancid food is toxic and that food additives are generally less toxic at the dosage present in food. But that is not to say the additives are without harmful effects as long-term constituents of a pet's diet. Just how harmful they are is difficult to gauge for most of the constituents, since little or no long-term research is available. Consequently we are required to make a judgment on the basis of partial information, even for the best known chemicals.

Colouring agents

Research on colouring agents is limited but the US National Research Council had this to say:

> Information on the effects of food additives in cats is scarce because routine toxicity testing is rarely conducted on this species... Avoidance of the cat as a test animal is probably partly due to its reputation as a finicky eater. More important, however, is the cat's unusual sensitivity to some chemicals because of the differences in the pathways of metabolism of these compounds in the cat compared with other animals. Consequently, results obtained from screening tests might not be readily applicable to other mammals (including man) and

could give an unrealistically severe assessment of the toxicity of an additive.[18]

Regulators operating in an environment of uncertainty employ acronyms divorced of meaning — ADI stands for Acceptable Daily Intake or GRAS for Generally Recognised As Safe. Additives are GRAS, 'simply because they have been used for many years with no established evidence of ill-effects on humans'.[19] In other words the colours are 'acceptable' or 'recognised as safe' until someone, by chance, demonstrates otherwise. Some azo dyes have been withdrawn from use in developed countries on account of their cancer-producing properties. Others known to cause cancer in laboratory experiments are still permitted.

Erythrosine dye is used to impart a rich red colour to artificial pet foods. Rats fed a high oral dose developed thyroid cancer.[20] When Brazilian researchers tested the effects of eleven common food colours, erythrosine was found to have the most potent effect on delicate cellular enzymes.[21] Erythrosine is deceptive in other ways. On analysis, erythrosine and food containing erythrosine are shown to be rich in iodine. Unfortunately that iodine is biologically unavailable to the animal.[22]

Before leaving the issue of food colourants we should give some thought to the context. Whole raw rabbits contain no artificial colourants, but artificial products contain varying concentrations in varying combinations — and animals often eat nothing but artificially coloured food. These colour combinations may add to the eye appeal for consumers, but the benefits for pets are either negative or non-existent.

Humectants

Chemical humectants absorb moisture and thus dehydrate spoilage bacteria and fungi. They also impart the semi-moist characteristics of some pet foods. Since these chemicals are not a natural feature of carnivore diets they may have various adverse consequences. The severity of the effects depends on factors such as concentration of chemical and frequency of intake. In 1996 the British Small Animal Veterinary Association sounded a warning when it said semi-moist diets preserved with propylene glycol are not recommended for kittens as the chemical affects the red blood cells.[23] In the same year the US Food and Drug Administration removed propylene glycol from the Generally Recognised As Safe category.[24]

Antioxidants

All fats, particularly polyunsaturated fats and fat soluble vitamins such as A and E, when exposed to air, become oxidised and rancid. The loss of nutrient value, bittertaste and buildup of toxins is of especial concern in dry and semi-moist products. To offset these effects manufacturers include antioxidants, both natural and synthetic, in their formulations.

Unfortunately the natural antioxidants such as vitamin E are subject to oxidation themselves and are less potent than the synthetic substitutes. Consequently manufacturers rely upon ethoxyquin, butylated hydoxyanisole (BHA) and butylated hydroxytoluene (BHT) and other such chemicals either singly or in combination. Curiously, these compounds have been shown to inhibit some cancers while simultaneously promoting others. Despite their known carcinogenic properties these products continue to be employed in foodstuffs for pets and people.

The concentrations in human processed foodstuffs are low — the US Food and Drug Administration (FDA) limits ethoxyquin to five parts per million of human food — and in any case humans do not eat out of one packet to provide all of their daily needs. Many modern pets consume the same dry food on a daily basis and that food could contain ethoxyquin at 150 parts per million. When laboratory marmosets were accidentally fed ten times the usual amount of ethoxyquin for a five day period deaths started within two days and continued for three weeks.[25] Merely coming into contact with ethoxyquin-preserved animal feeds has provoked severe contact dermatitis in people.[26] Unfortunately the effects of direct contact on the lining of the digestive tract of pets is unknown — pets never complain of stomach ache. Some people believe that a range of skin and fertility problems are directly attributable to ethoxyquin. Again, incontrovertible direct evidence is unavailable.

On any realistic assessment it would be reasonable to expect long-term adverse consequences of high levels of ethoxyquin. In 1990 Dr David Dzanis, Veterinary Nutritionist at the FDA, disagreed. Speaking at a pet food industry symposium, he reassured the audience:

In summary, there is insufficient scientific evidence to show that ethoxyquin is unsafe when used at approved levels or to warrant action against its use in pet foods. As an agency charged with ensuring the safety of foods, FDA is most unwilling to review new scientific data on ethoxyquin that would confirm or detract from this conclusion.[27]

But seven years later Dr Dzanis's conclusion was overturned by the FDA. Reacting to a report from Monsanto, the manufacturers of ethoxyquin, pet food companies were asked to reduce by half the levels of ethoxyquin in their products. The FDA stated that 'the 150 ppm level may not provide an adequate margin of safety in lactating female dogs and possibly puppies'.[28]

The pet food industry is reported to be investigating the effects of ethoxyquin at lower levels and the FDA is 'monitoring the progress'. Perhaps we should be monitoring the progress of the FDA, their involvement with the pet food industry and their unwillingness to review new scientific data.

Miscellaneous preservatives

Chemical preservatives are added to processed food to kill or inhibit micro-organisms. At high dosages the chemicals exert varying toxic, mutagenic and carcinogenic effects on mammalian cells. However, when tested individually and at low dosage the chemicals are generally found not to have demonstrable adverse effects. The World Cancer Research Fund stated:

> ... firstly, there are no reliable data on dietary exposure levels and secondly ... the relevant expert committees and regulatory bodies concerned with toxicity of food preservatives have concluded that, in the current state of science, food preservatives, when regulated and monitored, do not significantly affect human cancer risk.[29]

It may be true that, as with human food, preservatives pose the least hazard in the overall diet of pets. But until there is evidence to the contrary it would be safer to assume that preservatives have significant health impacts for pets. I do not suggest that pets are in some way more sensitive to preservatives but that it is more to do with the pattern of exposure. For many pets every mouthful of food is laden with chemical preservatives, the actions and interactions of which are poorly understood — even by the experts.

> **For many pets every mouthful of food is laden with chemical preservatives, the actions and interactions of which are poorly understood — even by the experts.**

Professor Kronfeld admitted that he was at a loss to understand the impact of acid preservatives until an article on acids in pet foods 'opened a door in the fortress of [his] mind'.[30] He investigated further and was astonished to find that even dry food, with low risk of bacterial spoilage, may be acidic. Potential adverse consequences of acidic food include etching of teeth and irritant effects on the bowel. Enzymes in the lower intestine need an alkaline medium in which to work. It could be that acidic food affects digestion and absorption of nutrients. Ultimately the acid needs to be excreted by the kidneys with likely accompanying loss of important minerals.

As with other aspects of pet nutrition the issue of preservatives raises more questions than answers. In finalising our position we need to depend on instincts and first principles; which must inevitably lead to the conclusion that food without preservatives is best. Coincidentally, and judging by the numbers of products claiming to be preservative free, there are many who already share that view.

Prescription and special diets

For the reasons already set out, plus a whole lot more, the so-called 'complete and balanced' artificial pet foods are both physically and chemically unsuitable for their declared purpose. No doubt manufacturers of these products will disagree. But in this they will encounter many difficulties, not least that they themselves have been criticising the 'complete and balanced formula' since 1948. In that year an American veterinarian, Mark Morris Snr, founder of Hill's Pet Foods, created the category of 'therapeutic nutrition'. In 1998 the company boasted that it produced 21 individual products. Other companies such as Mars and Iams have similar ranges of so-called therapeutic products.

In such a crowded field the jumble of claims can be confusing, but as a common denominator they either claim an increase in, or reduction of, certain food ingredients — some claim the inclusion of a special or trade mark protected ingredient. For instance the claim might be one of 'low salt' or 'increased fat' or 'selected protein' or 'special fibre'. Now, it may indeed be beneficial for animals to have a low salt and selected protein diet (as with a whole raw rabbit) but the problem for the manufacturers is how to sustain the credibility of their 'complete and balanced' claims for other products in their range.

A favourite game of the big companies is to trumpet their own products as compared with lowly 'grocery store' brands. However, this strategy breaks down as soon as they compare their specialty products against their own standard line. The Mars Corporation fell into this trap with the launch of their PAL Professional Formula. Label claims on regular cans and packets of PAL promise 'complete and balanced' nutrition, implying optimum health and well-being for pets. Of course, it is absurd to suggest that PAL Professional Formula could be more 'complete' or more 'balanced'. On its own terms and on its own evidence Mars makes a tacit admission that either one or both of its PAL products is inadequate.

Blanket condemnation of other products occurs as a result of the Hill's company's promotion of its tartar control diet. This diet of dry kibble vies with others on the basis of physical texture as opposed to chemical composition. An advertisement in the *Journal of Veterinary Dentistry* boasts: 'The only complete and balanced pet food that's part of a daily dental care program for your feline patients.'[31] If correct then all other so-called 'complete and balanced' products, including those produced by Hill's, are deficient in respect to daily dental care. However, when compared with a whole raw rabbit the product cannot be considered either complete or balanced, and in my view makes an insignificant contribution to a 'daily dental care program'.

As the companies and their allies scramble to promote their competing products in the marketplace, they will likely generate more categories carrying inflated but conflicting claims. 'More "Senior pet" dietary products are, nevertheless, likely to appear in the future and will undoubtedly have a useful role in the feeding options for aging dogs and cats', cooed the British Small Animal Veterinary Association, despite noting:

> It is not surprising that there are few products designed specifically for old dogs and cats since there are few or no consistent data on their nutrient requirements. The old dog or cat may be characteristically obese or thin, it may have renal, hepatic or cardiac dysfunction. It may be losing lean tissue mass and/or it may be retaining fluid, salt, phosphorus or nitrogen. The dietary indications for many of these conditions are conflicting.[32]

Smoothing over inconvenient but conflicting dietary requirements cannot be condoned. Pets, both young and old, encounter ill health and suffering regardless of whether they eat from specialty or regular cans.

6

⟹⟹⟹⟸⟸

Unpleasant diseases; painful death

It is not a matter of whether artificial pet foods and food-induced periodontal disease give rise to ill health; it's more a matter of which disease, when and how.

Puppies and kittens develop an interest in solid food at the same time they cut their deciduous teeth. In nature the first solid meal would likely be a small prey animal, for example a rabbit. (Puppies in the wild eat regurgitated foodstuffs from the mother's stomach for a couple of weeks until strong enough to chew on whole carcasses.) Chewing on whole prey takes time. Gums and erupting teeth are massaged and polished in a flow of antibody-rich saliva. The main point at issue for competing wild litter mates is whether they each receive enough raw food.

For pets raised on artificial food, biologically appropriate nutrients are, alas, in short supply. Feeding is accomplished quickly with minimum flow of saliva. Teeth are never cleaned. The situation steadily worsens with a crisis period, between four and six months of age, when the permanent teeth erupt. During this time of rapid growth the immune system is still not mature and immunity gained from the mother's milk declines. Conditions tip in favour of plaque organisms and the risk of infectious viral and bacterial disease increases.

Even if the young animal does not show outward signs of ill health, it is reasonable to assume that many diseases of old age have their genesis at this time. Early intense pressure on the immune system is a likely prelude for hyper, hypo and auto immunity of later life. Artificial dietary chemicals and periodontal toxins perfuse the major organs with likely long-term effects. The same pertains for young people who consume too many cigarettes and beers. In each case disease processes are triggered early but manifest themselves as organ failure in old age.

Before proceeding to a discussion of individual diet-related diseases I would like to raise a couple of points of clarification. Not all pets eat processed food 100 percent of the time. Nevertheless, processed food represents the bulk of the diet for most pets. Not all pets have periodontal disease. However, as pointed out in the Mars Corporation magazine *Waltham International Focus*, 85 percent of pets over the age of three years have the disease at a level warranting medical intervention.[1] Of the other 15 percent most have a mild form of the disease, or can be said to have suffered from periodontal inflammation during teething.

> **It is not a matter of whether artificial pet foods and food-induced periodontal disease give rise to ill health; it's more a matter of which disease, when and how.**

In general we can assume that periodontal disease and the foreign nutrient profile of artificial foods have a synergistic effect in the body. There are times when one ingredient of a diet is the determining factor giving rise to manifestations of disease. If a case of enteritis or a skin condition disappears with a change from one processed food to another, only to recur when the first food is reintroduced, then we can say that the disease was probably due to ingredients in the first food. Toxic and immune consequences of periodontal disease would likely remain the same on both diets and could therefore be discounted as the specific problem affecting the animal. (Periodontal disease continues at more or less the same level on all artificial diets.)

The following sections represent a guide to some common or important adverse consequences of artificial diets for pets.

Unwell

'Unwell' is a quaint and hard-to-define concept covering a multitude of ailments. When humans are unwell they may be aware of pain or lassitude and be able to tell others of their symptoms. Pets cannot articulate inner feelings and we need to be alert to subtle signs which indicate a departure from health and vitality.

Reluctance to move, stiff gait, dull coat, reduced appetite or loss of sparkle are just some of the telltale signs. Often it is only after a change of diet, and in retrospect, that owners become aware that the previous artificial diet was harming their pet. Scores of testimonial letters echo the following sentiments.

> I would agree that the dental hygiene of our dogs has improved enormously — particularly our old Australian terrier bitch who is a changed dog since we gave her bones and table scraps rather than tins of pulp.
>
> Her dental hygiene and lack of 'dragon breath' is a joy to behold. She enjoys her six kilometre walk every day on her tiny little legs and has a new zest for life.[2]

In our culture it is customary to blame a virus or other micro-organism when either we or our pets are unwell. Microbes may play a part, but frequently only as a result of stress and lack of immunity. Scrawny puppies and kittens, when presented at the veterinary surgery, are likely to be prescribed antibiotics. The patient usually improves and antibiotics gain the credit. But antibiotics kill microbes whether they be diet-related periodontal organisms, bacterial overgrowth in the bowel or other microbes taking advantage of the immune-compromised, immature pet. And thus the stage is set for a lifetime reality of repeat visits to the vet.

Sometimes young animals are more than just unwell but face a life-threatening viral disease. Parvo viral enteritis is one such disease of young dogs where overgrowth of bacteria in the puppy's bowel coupled with a precipitous fall in white blood cells leads, in many instances, to a nasty death. Precautions can be taken against the disease. First, maintain good hygiene to keep the virus away; second, vaccinate susceptible puppies; and third, feed a natural diet. Natural food ensures an optimum population of microbes in the bowel and a healthy immune system.

Behavioural and neurological abnormalities

Probably the most common behavioural abnormality of diet-affected pets is lassitude and prolonged sleeping. Owners do not consider this to be a nuisance, or sign of ill health, and consequently seldom seek advice.

When cats and dogs are constantly pacing, vocalising and exhibiting aggression, owners frequently take a different view. Unfortunately anti-social behaviour often leads to the pets' early death. Each year, whether at welfare shelters or veterinary clinics, millions of unruly pets are put down by injection.

> **Probably the most common behavioural abnormality of diet-affected pets is lassitude and prolonged sleeping. Owners do not consider this to be a nuisance, or sign of ill health, and consequently seldom seek advice.**

In the beginning, when I started to change animals to a natural diet, I was surprised when owners reported that previously agitated aggressive animals had become contented. (Some owners worry, unnecessarily, that pets with a taste for raw food might become savage.) On reflection one should not be surprised if artificially fed animals, in chronic pain, appear cantankerous by comparison with their naturally fed counterparts. Gnawing on bones keeps mouths healthy and pain free. It's possible gnawing exercise releases endorphins in the carnivore brain giving rise to a natural high. In humans evidence is being accumulated that some dietary chemicals, dubbed 'nutriceuticals', travel directly to the brain and thereby improve neuronal activity including ability to memorise facts.[3] Could there be 'nutriceuticals' in the natural food of carnivores?

Back in London in the 1970s I remember an outbreak of 'frenzied cats'. The demented creatures would growl and hiss and race around madly as if pursued by a thousand demons. When it was discovered that not demons but benzoic acid preservative in the food was the cause, the problem subsided almost as quickly as it arose. Modern additives may be having similar if not such dramatic effects. It is now well accepted that food additives can play a part in hyperactivity and Attention Deficit Disorder in young children. Since many pets consume still higher levels of the same additives, similar effects can be expected.

Corn (maize) is the principal ingredient in many processed foods. Tryptophan, an essential amino acid, is in short supply in corn protein and the vitamin niacin is largely unavailable.[4] Tryptophan is a precursor of the important brain chemical serotonin and people lacking niacin suffer a disease known as pellagra, the signs of which include dementia. In 1983 Professor David Kronfeld speculated that peculiar pet behaviour may be attributable to the high corn levels in processed food.[5] He also reported that one large pet food company was testing diets for their behaviour impact.[6] In 1986 the animal behaviourist Roger Mugford spoke about aggressive Golden Retrievers at a Waltham Symposium.[7] Some of the dogs, despite being members of a breed usually noted for docility, had inflicted serious wounds on their owners. When Mugford changed the dogs' diet from commercial to home-cooked food he observed some dramatic improvements.

This raises important questions:
- What further improvement would have been detected in the Golden Retrievers if Mugford had tried a natural diet?
- Since 1983, when Kronfeld said companies were researching behavioural aspects of diet, what have pet food companies discovered?
- Are pets being unnecessarily destroyed due to diet-induced aggression?
- What are the health, financial and amenity costs of food-induced aggression?
- Are manufacturers legally liable for pain, loss and suffering arising from the sale of their products?

One, admittedly isolated, example of an apparent direct connection between diet and brain function occurred when a little 'white shaker' came into my general veterinary practice. White shakers tend to be white, for instance Maltese or West Highland White terriers, and they suffer from the uncontrollable shakes. The textbooks locate the problem in the brain but do not offer much help on an effective cure. Knowing these facts it was easy to propose a diet change for the patient — there appeared to be little to lose and everything to gain. Within a couple of days the shakes had gone. It is to be hoped that others will obtain similar good results with so little effort.

The 'body' of evidence

Malnutrition, literally meaning bad nutrition, is the reason why so many pets lack muscle and possess too much fat.

Too thin

Some pets slowly starve in the presence of plenty because the food is not sufficiently nutritious. Affected animals have distended abdomens, wasted muscles and spindly legs reminiscent of human famine victims. Rapidly growing puppies, pregnant and nursing bitches are the most commonly affected. Manufacturers recognise this problem and there are now various kitten and puppy 'growth formulations'. These products contain higher levels of animal protein and less grains and fibre than other 'complete and balanced' products. Natural food is, of course, ideal for all stages of growth.

Too fat

They are sick that surfeit with too much,
As they that starve with nothing.

SHAKESPEARE, *Merchant of Venice* I II

Obesity is the most commonly diagnosed nutritional problem of modern pets. While fat animals often take little exercise, lack of exercise is not the reason for obesity. The British Small Animal Veterinary Association suggested that around 25 percent of cats and dogs are obese.[8] Others have estimated that 25–44 percent of dogs and 6–12 percent of cats are affected.[9] It's true that naturally fed animals can be too fat, but it is a rare occurrence. Once their hunger is satisfied dogs often bury their bones. Artificial food does not seem to have the same ability to satisfy the appetite and pets seem to crave more. If too much food is offered, either at meal times or by being made constantly available, the net result is a fat pet. Once obese, the affected animal is at greater risk of a range of problems including diabetes, heart, liver and musculoskeletal disease.[10]

Too flaccid

Where naturally fed animals are trim, taught and terrific, artificially fed animals sometimes feel 'doughy' to the touch. While they may tip the scales at the optimum weight they cannot be considered healthy. Their skin feels inelastic, the muscles lack tone and the animals have a disproportionate amount of body fat. In due course someone may develop a flaccidity meter, but for now we must depend on our finger tips.

Gastrointestinal tract disorders

Natural food passing down a healthy carnivore's digestive tract undergoes a remarkable transformation. The soft parts of the prey are almost completely digested and the faecal residue consists of powdered bone with some hair. By contrast, processed pet foods are poorly digested and have the potential for damaging the gut in numerous ways. Unfortunately most damage remains hidden and difficult to investigate. Outward signs of gut disturbance include diarrhoea and vomiting, which are also difficult to investigate due to the range of dietary, parasitic and other causes.

> Natural food passing down a healthy carnivore's digestive tract undergoes a remarkable transformation . . . By contrast, processed pet foods are poorly digested and have the potential for damaging the gut in numerous ways.

Diarrhoea and vomiting

It is a matter of common human experience that food reactions often result in diarrhoea and vomiting. Chemical irritation, allergy and bacterial overgrowth all produce the same general outcome. It is the duration and degree of signs that vary. In the extreme situation cats and dogs can die of acute toxic shock. More commonly the problem is intermittent and lingers for a protracted period. And the longer the problem persists the greater the potential for irreversible bowel damage to occur.

When the bowel is inflamed the lining swells, causing gaps to occur between the protective lining cells. Other materials, especially micro-organisms and proteins, can slip through the gaps. Micro-organisms can do damage within the body, but it is the proteins that can give rise to lasting problems. Once the body mounts an immune response to a protein, then each time that protein is fed there is a risk of further gastrointestinal signs.[11]

There are veterinarians who are reluctant to acknowledge that artificial pet foods are a prime reason for diarrhoea in pets. But as soon as diarrhoea manifests itself in a dog or cat the same veterinarians may recommend removing the commercial food and changing to home-cooked food as part of the treatment. The British Small Animal Veterinary Association support this approach, saying: 'Dietary modification is probably as important as pharmacological intervention in the treatment of most GI [gastrointestinal] diseases and indeed may be the only treatment necessary.' They list a number of home-cooked chicken, turkey and venison recipes.[12] Of course, it is often too late when diarrhoea becomes chronic. By then even a natural raw diet may not help.

Both veterinarians and pet food companies may suffer private guilt over the implications of recommending that commercial products be discontinued as soon as a problem arises. However, in the game of protecting pet food sales, recommending home-prepared (but cooked) foods serves two useful purposes. First, if the diarrhoea persists, even on a home-prepared diet, then possible criticism of the original commercial diet can be deflected. Veterinarian and owner alike can both make the easy, but not necessarily correct, assumption that something other than diet must have been the underlying problem. Second, as allergy to food ingredients may develop during prolonged diarrhoea, from the manufacturer's point of view it is better that any allergies develop to the home-prepared food. 'Feeding a novel food [when treating diarrhoea] may avoid the development of an acquired allergy to the patient's staple diet' suggests the British Small Animal Veterinary Association.[13]

Canine gastric dilatation-volvulus (GDV)

'I found my six-year-old dog dead in his kennel this morning. Can you do a post-mortem examination for me?' These are the style of words used by countless pet owners as they telephone for help.

Nothing will bring the pet back to life, but with some answers the owner's pain and sense of guilt can be assuaged.

If the owner discloses that the dead pet was a large breed of dog, usually fed on commercial dry food and was OK when last seen at night, then the consulting veterinarian will already be making a preliminary diagnosis of bloat or GDV (these terms are used interchangeably although the stomach can bloat without the twist or volvulus). On examining the tightly distended abdomen, which resonates like a drum, the veterinarian will be expecting to find evidence of a catastrophe involving the stomach. Bloody fluid in the abdominal cavity, and a blackened stomach wall, confirm that the dog suffered in agony until death came as a welcome release.

Bloat/GDV facts:

- It is estimated that 60,000 cases of bloat occur in the US annually.[14]
- Of these cases about two-thirds, if detected early, can be saved by heroic surgery and intensive care.
- None of the factors, nor the relevance of each one involved in this disease, are well understood.
- The disease is believed to be rare in nature and to be associated with domestication.
- Professor Kronfeld states: 'Bloat has been observed occasionally in dogs fed table scraps or mixtures of meat (or meat by-products) and cereals. But by and large, bloat is usually associated with commercial dry dog foods.'[15]
- On the available evidence a natural or near natural diet will minimise the risk of bloat in susceptible dogs.
- Some pet food company funded research projects seem designed to obscure rather than illuminate the situation — they don't use naturally fed control groups. Given the seriousness of bloat I believe that research projects should be well designed and well conducted.
- Where product safety issues are at stake — for instance defective motor cars — the onus of proof usually resides with the manufacturer. Now that suspicions exist regarding the safety of processed pet food in respect to bloat, I believe that pet food manufacturers have similar obligations.

Intussusception

Intussusception is a nasty affliction of the bowel which affects kittens and puppies around six months of age (older animals may be affected). The sufferers appear wretched and refuse to eat. Sometimes diagnosis is difficult but usually gentle palpation of the abdomen serves to locate the problem as a turgid 'sausage' between the finger tips. The 'sausage' is in fact a length of bowel telescoped inside itself. (Try telescoping your sleeve to better understand the concept.) The turgidity and swelling are due to restriction of blood supply to the bowel wall.

Veterinary articles devote time to explaining surgical techniques for revitalising the bowel but have little to say on why the bowel telescopes. An article published in the British Small Animal Veterinary Association *Journal of Small Animal Practice* regarding twelve cats with intussusception promoted treatment without adequately dealing with cause or prevention.[16] In an attempt to stimulate debate among the membership I submitted a letter entitled 'Revitalising veterinary science' and drawing attention to the following:

> The relevant clinical data contained no reference to oral hygiene and it would be valid to assume that the cats were not fed a natural diet. Excluding a twelve-year-old cat suffering from lymphosarcoma, the other eleven averaged 6.4 months of age. It should be borne in mind that kittens shed their primary and simultaneously gain their secondary dentition between four and six months of age. If raised on artificial food during this physiological upheaval they lack the essential gum massage and oral cleansing, and suffer a resultant gingivitis. This should be perceived as a significant insult to the immature immune system and the collagen supporting the teeth. Cats fed a 'natural' diet pass small amounts of virtually odourless faeces in contrast to the copious, malodorous stools of artificially fed cats. If the eleven kittens suffered these diet-induced burdens, it would be reasonable to expect their collagen-rich bowels to behave in an aberrant fashion.[17]

At first the Journal procrastinated, then one day a fax arrived: 'The editor has now accepted the letter for publication and this should appear in our January '95 issue.' An event to look forward to, I thought. But my joy and the hopes of sick kittens were shortlived. Within a month the assistant editor wrote again:

> Further to my fax of November 24, the question of your letter was referred to the Board of Management who, after discussion, decided that it would not be in the interests of the Journal, or in compliance with its policy, to publish.

Reversals are hard to accept even though they often prove to be of long-term benefit. That there had been a power struggle within the British Small Animal Veterinary Association on this issue appeared likely — none of the Board members could feel proud about revoking the editor's written undertaking. I wrote again asking for 'constructive thought to be applied to the current problems', but to no avail.

In the escalating paper war I accused the Journal of 'actively suppressing information, in what I believe to be the cruel infliction of disease upon an entire population of domestic pets'. Eventually I lodged complaints with the Royal College of Veterinary Surgeons and the Ministry of Agriculture — both bodies having responsibility for the conduct of the British veterinary profession. Predictably, perhaps, they showed no willingness to look into the matter. As a last resort I referred the matter to the Patron of the Royal College of Veterinary Surgeons, Her Majesty the Queen. With regal courtesy the Palace replied that Her Majesty was unable to become involved in the matter and that my letter had been forwarded to the College!

Coprophagy

Coprophagy — the eating of faeces — is not due to a disease of the bowel or even a bad habit. However, we shall discuss the matter now since most people view the activity as one of the least appealing aspects of a pet's digestion.

But we need to keep things in context. Carnivores which consume whole prey animals eat the faeces along with the animal. Nursing dogs and cats keep the nest clean by avidly licking the faeces of their young at the moment it is passed. (Licking stimulates urination and defaecation and should be mimicked — with a moist wipe — when raising orphan puppies and kittens.) Steaming horse and cattle poo seems to be a favourite and the poo from domestic cats is much sought after. On our daily walks my female dog searches for and unearths the deposits of our neighbourhood cats. I don't seek to dissuade her, as I know she is obtaining benefit.

Herbivore and omnivore faeces — and faeces from cats and dogs fed grain-based artificial food — is enzyme rich and teeming with micro-organisms. Microbial enzymes when consumed by a dog contribute to its digestive efficiency. The microbes are a source of live prey. On contact with stomach acids they soon perish and their proteins, fats, carbohydrates, vitamins and micronutrients can then be absorbed. In fact eating poo may be the only source of micronutrients for artificially fed pets.

By contrast with herbivores and grain-fed animals, excrement from naturally fed carnivores is without nutrient value, being predominantly powdered bone. Never have I seen a dog show the slightest inclination to eat this material. The answer to undesirable coprophagy would therefore seem to be simple — feed whole carcasses or raw meaty bones.

> Animals which have always been fed a natural diet, and therefore enjoy a healthy mouth, retain a youthful appearance until late in their lives.

An additional benefit, remarked on by owners of female dogs, is that urine scorch marks are less visible on the lawn when animals are fed a natural diet.[18]

Collagen and old age diseases

'Like a puppy/kitten again', say elated owners of older animals after dental treatment and diet change. Providing oral hygiene and a natural diet are maintained the newfound vitality persists. Animals which have always been fed a natural diet, and therefore enjoy a healthy mouth, retain a youthful appearance until late in their lives. What does this mean?

Everyone is aware of the features of youth that are absent in the old. Zest and vitality are obvious and reflect the functioning of all body systems. Mental acuity, muscle tone, heart output and a host of other functions could be listed. Importantly the young have a youthful appearance and this brings us to the central issue. Collagen, the reinforcing material of the body, loses its tough elastic properties with age. At the same time there is a reduction of collagen in the tissues. In effect the bloom of youth is to do with healthy collagen, and hence the modern preoccupation with collagen treatments for maintaining a youthful appearance.

While collagen is made within cells it performs its useful function outside the cells in bundles of collagen fibres. The combination of fibres and the cells producing the fibres is known as connective tissue. As the name implies it provides a connecting framework, thus preserving shape and function. In blood vessel walls the arrangement of fibres is designed for flexibility. In tendons and ligaments tensile strength is the main requirement. In bone, collagen combines with calcium salts to provide both toughness and rigidity. Joint cartilage contains high proportions of collagen and the resultant material is able to withstand impact and wear. In the cornea the arrangement of collagen molecules permits the passage of light.

When collagen loses its properties the organ dependent on the collagen starts to deteriorate too. In the case of collagen supporting the filtration apparatus of the kidney, deterioration may be slow and the signs of kidney failure equally slow to develop. Heart and lung disease associated with a deterioration in collagen fibres tends to develop slowly — even when weakened those organs can continue to function. In the case of tendons, ligaments and bones the deterioration of the collagen may be slow but eventual breakage is usually a sudden event.

Cruciate (cross-shaped) ligament injury — a common knee injury in sports players — also occurs in dogs. Usually the canine patient has periodontal disease and consumes artificial food. Some old dogs suffer from perineal ligament breakdown allowing the bowel, and sometimes the bladder, to bulge through the skin under the tail. Treatment involves pushing the organs back inside the abdomen and then sewing up the wound. Surgical treatments for diseased collagen are always expensive but not always successful. Medical treatments for pets with muscle stiffness and arthritis support a multi-million dollar drugs industry. Instead of blithely treating diseased collagen, veterinarians could begin to question the need for treatment.

Since the general health and apparent collagen health of patients improves dramatically after dental work and diet change it would be reasonable to suspect either or both are in some way responsible. It could be that improved chemical nutrition, for instance chondroitin sulfate and glucosamine contained in natural food, supports the improved cellular synthesis of collagen. Proceeding from first principles, my favoured explanation concerns the rate and degree of collagen damage. It is well known that periodontal disease involves the destruction and loss of collagen connective tissue. It would be reasonable to expect that the collagenases — the enzymes responsible for the destruction of collagen — flowing from the gums would dissolve collagen wherever it is found. Since collagen in connective tissue lies between, as opposed to within, cells it comes into intimate contact with circulating collagenases.

Robert Hamlin of Ohio State University has speculated about periodontal disease induced collagen disease and the idea is well supported by some Australian veterinarians.[19] At this stage the evidence provides a workable hypothesis for premature aging in dogs and cats. While drug and surgical treatments are costly and often unsuccessful, the natural preventative approach is easy, economical and effective.

Skin diseases

Most pet diseases are suffered in silence. Skin disease is different. Millions of pets are troubled by persistent irritation to the point of self-mutilation. Pet owners are troubled by the fusty smell, the sight of excoriated skin and the sound of incessant scratching. Due to the constant reminders owners actively seek out treatment. In the first instance this may be in the form of remedies from the pet store or supermarket, or employing the services of a pet groomer. Ultimately owners end up at the veterinary clinic where perhaps one-third of patients have similar skin problems.

Veterinarians depend on thick dermatology textbooks, lectures and the Internet for information on skin diseases. Antiparasitic, antibacterial and anti-allergy preparations are recommended as the self-evident treatments of choice. With the ready demonstration of fleas, mange mites, bacteria and allergy profiles this approach appears to be justified. And of course the pharmaceutical industry is there to lend a hand — promoting the notion that all will be well once better products are made available. But is this search and destroy strategy appropriate for organisms that have always been part of the web of life? Does this siege mentality suit our situation?

While there can be no denying that fleas, mange mites, bacteria and allergies can be problematic, the evidence is now accumulating to suggest that they are not the main cause for concern. As with so many other diseases the evidence is that unnatural diets predispose animals to unnatural outcomes. In some instances the disease signs are directly resulting from the diet. In other cases the diet renders the animal more sensitive to the fleas, bacteria and allergens that share this world. Although one aspect may be of prime significance, the other factors usually combine to make matters worse.

Where is the evidence, you may ask, for suggesting that diet is the main issue? The accumulated experience of countless animal owners and a solid circle of vets can testify. Healthy puppies and kittens raised on natural food do not exhibit the range and severity of skin diseases of their artificially fed cousins. Frequently owners, who have grown resigned to the skin complaints of their pets, are delighted to find that a change of diet seems to work miracles. In seeking an explanation we do not need to look far. The skin provides a manifestation of the general health of the animal. Since the skin and hair coat are constantly being renewed, any imbalance due to poor organ function can show as unhealthy skin and a dull sparse coat.

Frequently owners, who have grown resigned to the skin complaints of their pets, are delighted to find that a change of diet seems to work miracles.

The skin accounts for 12 percent of body weight and is the barrier with the outside world. Skin contains large amounts of collagen which impart strength and elasticity and immune cells guard against invaders. If collagen health and the immune system are impaired by diet and periodontal disease, then skin health will also be impaired. A cascade effect can then get under way. Bacteria can colonise unhealthy skin more readily. Bacterial toxins damage the skin further and set up local allergic responses. Even fleas seem to prefer unhealthy animals. Dr Tom Hungerford, the grandfather of the Australian veterinary profession, reported that his dogs fed on raw meaty bones did not harbour fleas.[20] In households with several animals I have seen the pets with the worst teeth harbour the most fleas, but when their oral hygiene was improved their flea burden decreased.

Sarcoptic mange is another condition of dogs, foxes and wombats which seems to have a link to general and immune system health. When the animal is in good condition the mange mites inhabiting the skin are kept under control. When the animal is stressed or inappropriately fed, the mites can multiply and create a severe and ultimately fatal disease. Immune-related skin disease is common in cats too. The textbooks and veterinary Internet discussions adopt a pessimistic outlook for diagnosis and treatment. In treating a couple of skin conditions known as 'scabby cat disease' and 'rodent ulcer' I hit on lasting success based on dental treatment and a change to more natural feeding.

Rodent ulcers, which at first sight look like skin cancer, affect the lips of cats. Sometimes similar ulcers affect the inside of the mouth and tongue. Ming, a seven-year-old female cat, was suffering from an extreme form of the condition when she came to see me. Ming's owner gave consent for pathology samples — I wanted to be certain of the diagnosis — to be obtained at the same time that Ming underwent surgery on her teeth, gums and ulcers. Conventional treatments for such patients involve long-term medications. In Ming's case I administered a short course of penicillin and some anti-inflammatory hormones. Ming thoroughly enjoyed her new diet of raw meaty bones and within a month her mouth was completely healed. In the case report published by the Sydney University Post Graduate Committee I concluded:

> Never before have I insisted on a total dietary change, nor have I seen such a rapid recovery. It will take me years to accumulate a series of such cases [they are quite rare]. If other practitioners try this approach we can quickly determine if there is a diet, periodontal disease, eosinophilic granuloma nexus.[21]

Plasma cell pododermatitis, an ulcerative condition of the foot pads of cats, is an even rarer condition. First signs may be blotches of blood on the vinyl as the cat makes its way across the kitchen floor. Despite the oozing craters in the pads patients do not seem to feel much, if any, pain. However treatment is essential, if only to safeguard the furniture. Textbooks report that some cases spontaneously heal, but for many the outlook is poor despite elaborate long-term therapy. In 25 years of practice I have only seen two plasma cell pododermatitis cases and both received my standard treatment for cat skin diseases. First perform dental treatment under anaesthetic, thereby removing a source of inflammation and immune insult. Then change the animal's diet to raw meaty bones. In addition, for the two foot pad cases, I placed temporary bandages on the feet and administered a short course of antibiotics. Healing was rapid and permanent.

Keen to share the benefits of this simple approach with a wider audience of veterinarians, I wrote a paper for publication. I explained why I thought gum and foot pad disease are connected:

> The early histological feature of periodontal disease within the gingiva is a vasculitis [inflammation of blood vessels] with loss of perivascular collagen. Scott [renowned US dermatologist] has remarked that in two of his series of five cats the concurrent plasma cell stomatitis was histopathologically and immuno-pathologically identical with the foot pad lesion. It may be contemplated that an immune and chemical response creating a vasculitis in the gingiva can also bring about similar changes in the vasculature generally. Foot pads are subject to constant deformation. Even slight vascular and perivascular collagen disease within pads could be expected to become magnified in time... Degeneration over time is a feature of many collagen and immune system dysfunctions, which it has been suggested may form a necessary regulatory role in carnivore population dynamics.

Previously, in 1990, the *Journal of the American Veterinary Medical Association* published a report by two veterinarians who used long-term corticosteroids to treat two foot pad cases.[22] This, I thought, established a precedent for publication and in 1996 submitted my manuscript to the Journal. Alas the editor and referees thought otherwise and rejected the article. Owners and veterinarians may like to make up their own minds — whether the article is worthy, and whether the treatment described offers a better option for cats with foul-mouth and foot pad disease. The full text can be viewed on the Internet.[23]

Liver disease

Commenting on the effects of alcohol, the World Cancer Research Fund stated:

> Excessive alcohol consumption, generally speaking, results in 'alcoholic liver disease' which proceeds through three progressively severe stages: fatty liver, alcoholic hepatitis, and cirrhosis ... ultimately leading to liver cancer by mechanisms not yet understood.[24]

From this statement we can deduce that despite the vast sums expended on research, the scientific authorities do not possess all the answers on alcohol-induced liver disease. Since little research is conducted into the effects of artificial pet foods on the livers of domestic pets, information is virtually nonexistent. Nonetheless a range of liver diseases, which seem to be artificial diet related, affect cats and dogs. (Fewer animals are fed natural food but, in those animals, liver disease appears to be rare.) In particular we should note that the liver is sensitive to the flow of toxins emanating from the bowel and periodontal disease affected mouth. Liver disease is frequently associated with immune disturbances and loss of collagen between the liver lobules, both likely consequences of an artificial diet.

Since liver disease tends to be a disease of older animals already suffering a multiplicity of ailments — and since liver disease can be difficult to diagnose and treat — the situation becomes complicated. In conventional veterinary practice animals showing signs of liver disease may be subjected to a range of expensive and inconclusive tests. The concurrent periodontal disease often remains untreated and the regular artificial diet changed for a prescription artificial diet purported to be of benefit. In my practice we placed the emphasis on correcting the patient's diseased mouth, changing to a natural diet and monitoring the liver disease. When animals regained weight and vitality — as was frequently the case — we were provided with strong circumstantial evidence that the liver disease was a secondary consequence of the diet.

Cancer

In 1981 Richard Doll and Richard Peto published *The Causes of Cancer*, a report commissioned by the US Congress. The authors estimated that about one-third of human cancers were due to smoking and one-third due to diet.[25] A variety of factors including viruses, genetics, environment and unknown causes accounted for the remaining third.

In 1997 the World Cancer Research Fund experts drew heavily on Doll and Peto's evidence and stated: 'Cancer is largely a preventable disease; the incidence of cancer can be substantially reduced by means of diet.'[26] The panel explained that 'there is no absolute proof' but that their opinions were firmly based. They said: 'The strongest evidence indicating that food and nutrition modify the risk of cancer comes from a combination of different types of epidemiological enquiry, supported by experimental findings, and by identification of plausible biological pathways.'[27]

At this stage the US Congress has not commissioned a study into the dietary impact on cancer in domestic pets. This, however, should not stop us from interpreting the available evidence in order to broadly assess the situation. If we remove smoking from the equation — some pets smoke passively, none smoke actively — and if we remove viruses, genetics and the environment as being factors common to both people and pets, we are left with diet as the principal factor. But where people obtain dietary carcinogens from many sources including the butcher's shop, liquor shop, fast food outlets and several aisles at the supermarket, pets tend to receive theirs direct from a single supermarket aisle.

Knowledge of plausible biological pathways supports the diet/cancer connection. For instance we know that the pointless, persistent proliferation of cancer cells is frequently triggered by the effects of unusual chemicals on DNA. Artificial pet foods contain a mass of unusual chemicals which, when cooked together, create still more unusual chemicals. The inflammation and bacterial activity of periodontal disease create a further chemical load, including free radicals, which could be carcinogenic.

Cancer is thought to occur when the usual repair functions of the body are in some way disabled. At the cellular level there are enzymes designed to repair damaged DNA and thus prevent mutations. Besides removing dead cells, the immune system is believed to have a surveillance function monitoring and removing early cancer cells. When diet is sub-optimum both enzyme health and immune system health are impaired. A further problem with artificial diets is the lack of anti-cancer compounds such as the naturally occurring antioxidant vitamins.

'Prevention is better than cure' is especially apt when considering cancer. While it is true that cancer mostly reveals itself in later life, it is generally believed that the first changes to DNA can occur many years earlier. Thus for prevention to stand the maximum chance of success it needs to be commenced early. Similarly treatment of any cancer is facilitated by early detection. Though I cannot say that introducing a natural diet has produced remission of cancer in my patients, it nonetheless makes good sense to ensure that the diet and oral hygiene of all patients is optimal.

Unless and until research demonstrates that carnivores benefit from a high vegetable diet it would be wise to follow closely the natural diet of free-living wild carnivores — whole carcasses of raw meaty bones.

Preventive dietary strategies for human cancer are now beginning to be understood. In its simplest form this entails choosing a predominantly plant-based diet — rich in a variety of vegetables and fruits, legumes and minimally processed starchy foods. When considering an anti-cancer diet for carnivores it is unwise to make too close a comparison with the human anticancer diet. Unless and until research demonstrates that carnivores benefit from a high vegetable diet it would be wise to follow closely the natural diet of free-living wild carnivores — whole carcasses of raw meaty bones.

Cat diseases

Cats deserve our special sympathy for the severity of common diseases which appear to be directly related to artificial feeding. But sympathy is not much good to the patients and treatment frequently does not work. For some cases the kindest treatment may be euthanasia. In these circumstances at least there is a restoration of dignity for the animal and an end to the cruelty and suffering.

The following are some of the more dramatic ailments of cats.

Tooth rot

Both cats and dogs are equally at risk of the broad range of periodontal-induced diseases, but only cats suffer the agony of 'feline neck lesions' — a form of tooth rot involving the neck of the tooth at the level of the gums. One or many teeth may be affected. As the condition advances, the nerve in the pulp cavity of the tooth becomes exposed. Ultimately teeth so weakened break off at the crown, leaving damaged roots buried in the gums.

Surveys conducted in the United States, Australia and the United Kingdom have shown that between 52 and 65 percent of domestic cats are affected.[28] Perhaps you wonder if the cat sitting beside you has rotten teeth, and if so how you would know. Unfortunately, in most cases, cats endure in silence even when the problem is acutely painful. Careful observation may reveal sufferers showing an irritative gnawing motion when chewing.

Vets can overlook the condition especially when the cavities are small. Large cavities may be obscured by overgrowth of the gums and of course diseased roots can only be demonstrated on an X-ray. Conscious cats flinch in pain when a probe is gently introduced into a cavity — let me assure you that this is not a usual response to the probing of healthy tissue. Even under gaseous anaesthetic, cats' jaws chatter in pain as the dental probe explores the cavities.

Screaming cat disease

Another disease peculiar to cats and associated with much pain arises secondary to periodontal disease (a virus is also said to be involved). Commonly the sufferers have teeth affected by neck lesions, but the characteristic signs are areas of angry red inflammation affecting the soft tissue of the mouth. A number of names are used for this vile affliction — the commonest being lymphocytic-plasmacytic gingivitis-stomatitis, an amalgam of words describing the immune cells present in the gums and mouth. Screaming cat disease might be a better name reflecting the noise these patients emit when having their mouths examined.

The sequence of events often starts with an owner noticing the cat approaching the food bowl as if hungry, lingering in the vicinity for a while and then backing away. After a few occurrences of this behaviour the cat might be seen to reluctantly take in food but experience difficulty eating. The first thing the vet does when presented with such a case is open the cat's mouth to inspect. Many cats snatch away and seek to escape, and when this is attended by a bone-chilling scream the message is clear.

Providing a cure for these wretched animals is, in my experience, often impossible and the best that has been achieved, at vast expense, is some relief. Treatment usually starts with administration of antibiotics, corticosteroids and painting the gums and mouth with anti-inflammatory and antibacterial solutions. After several weeks obtaining dismal results the vet usually recommends removal of all teeth with the exception of the canines.

Removal of the teeth tends to be a major undertaking. Even tiny root fragments need to be removed — which often requires an X-ray to confirm successful removal. And after the surgical intervention the cats usually need intermittent antibiotic and corticosteroid treatment. (Two veterinarians reported improved results using a babies' teething gel.)[29] Owners and vets alike experience nagging concern over these unfortunate animals and their cruel condition.

At the primary level the animal is affected by periodontal disease; at the secondary level it suffers the effects of the stomatitis; at the tertiary level there is the impact of the treatment — perhaps as a fourth level the owner's and clinician's feelings of anguish should be considered. This fourth level of concern is made the more poignant by the likelihood that the whole sorry saga could have been prevented by an appropriate diet.

Iliac thrombosis

Domestic cats usually sit quietly in their carry basket on visits to the vet. When, instead of silence, mournful cries rend the air, clearly something is seriously wrong. If the stricken animal wears a terrified expression, pants and drags its hind legs then iliac thrombosis is a likely diagnosis. This medical crisis occurs when a clot travels from the heart to lodge at the end of the aorta, blocking the iliac arteries at the point where they branch into the hind limbs. Starved of blood the muscles become stiff, cold and useless. Treatment is expensive and almost certain to fail.

The offending clot usually originates from the lining of a diseased heart. And the most likely explanation for the diseased heart is bacteria and bacterial toxins from a foul mouth, which is usually diet related.

Feline Lower Urinary Tract Disease (FLUTD)

Every year about 0.6 percent of the cat population suffers from FLUTD and about 10 percent of cats visiting veterinary clinics have the disease.[30] Clearly the problem is reasonably common and certainly nasty. In the mild form of the disease both male and female cats suffer from increased frequency of urination, blood in the urine and difficulty passing urine. Male cats are at risk of blockage of the urethra and resultant inability to pass urine. David F Senior stated at a conference sponsored by the pet food industry:

> Cats become progressively more depressed, then comatose, and finally die if left untreated after about 2–4 days. Death is due to dehydration, hyperkalemia, metabolic acidosis, and accumulation of metabolic waste products.[31]

Veterinarians employ various intricate treatments, but with mixed results. Many cats suffer for years, and some have repeated blockage of the urethra. As a treatment of last resort, amputation of the penis can be performed. However, an unacceptably high number of cats suffer from complications following the operation. The climate of uncertainty regarding treatment is matched by the uncertainty of the mechanisms which precipitate the disease. Some scientists postulate that high levels of magnesium in the diet, alkaline urine and problems of the bladder lining trigger the disease. Others blame the crystals in affected cats' urine. But crystals occur in the urine of healthy cats too.

Dry cat foods and the chemical alteration of diets are solidly implicated in the epidemic of FLUTD. Dr C A Buffington commented on how manipulating diet, by reduction of magnesium and increase in acidity, to control struvite urinary crystals increased the risk of oxalate crystals developing. Dr Buffington's only confident recommendation was for more water to be added to the diet.[32] Pet food companies do not even bother to deny the connection between their dry products and FLUTD. Alison Lambert, Veterinary Business Manager for Pedigree Petfoods, a division of the Mars Corporation, states:

> We are pleased to announce that our understanding of the risk factors associated with feeding dry cat food has allowed us to develop a product which helps minimise the risk.[33]

When we consider the suffering, and in many cases death, arising from this disease, a product which 'helps to minimise the risk' seems inadequate. For those of us interested in protecting our pet cats from the ravages of FLUTD, avoidance of artificial pet foods would be a better approach.

Potassium depletion

The direct connection between diet and struvite crystal related FLUTD is well recognised. Manufacturers have sought to overcome the problem by making their product acidic. Acidification has potential side effects for all cats consuming the product, not just those susceptible to FLUTD. Potassium depletion is one potential side effect. Chronic renal disease, which is especially common in periodontal disease affected cats, can also give rise to potassium depletion.

Signs of potassium depletion vary, but in the severe form cats exhibit profound weakness and collapse. Various tests for the disease are inconclusive so vets rely on trial and error treatment. If a patient recovers on potassium supplementation the clinician is likely to assume that potassium loss was the main problem. Unfortunately success of potassium supplementation often serves to obscure the fundamental dietary connection, resulting in the diet and oral disease remaining untreated.

Hyperthyroidism

Since 1979 hyperthyroidism has come to prominence as a major disease of old cats.[34] The thyroid gland located in the neck is responsible for producing the regulatory thyroid hormones which generally have a stimulatory effect on other organs. When the gland produces too much hormone a variety of confusing signs can occur. Most commonly the affected animals suffer from weight loss, increased appetite, hyper-activity and irritability and have an increased heart rate. On the other hand some animals display a decreased appetite and appear lethargic.

Characteristically, the veterinary textbooks are vague on the under-lying causes of hyperthyroidism. Since thyroid hormones contain iodine, the iodine content of commercial cat foods was investigated for clues. A 30-fold variation in iodine content was discovered.[35] While this seems to make a nonsense of manufacturers' claims for a 'balanced diet', no connection could be established between dietary iodine content and hyperthyroidism. But as we know, after a lifetime consuming commercial food, old cats suffer from periodontal disease. Diet and periodontal disease seem to have a bearing on most old age diseases of domestic cats. Until ruled out by further research, hyperthyroidism appears to belong on the list.

7

———➤✦◄———

Foul-mouth AIDS

Some consequences of artificial pet foods are more insidious than others — Foul-mouth AIDS comes close to the top of the list. As with HIV AIDS in humans, pets suffering Foul-mouth AIDS are vulnerable to a range of cancers and infections. Our pet carnivores and our finances have felt these consequences for a long time, but it was only by luck that I recognised the condition and gave it a name. Naming things is often the first step on the road to coherent discussion and resolution of problems — once HIV AIDS was named medical researchers could focus on and deal with the threat. By contrast veterinary authorities have either ignored or sought to suppress information on Foul-mouth AIDS.

The August 1991 Waltham Symposium, Clinical Nutrition in Practice, triggered my thoughts (see Chapter 1). I noted that the pet food company speakers and their veterinary audience shared a belief in grain-based, factory-made products. Proponents of natural feeding, from the opposition camp, appeared to suffer problems of New Age mystification.[1] When discussing the needs of pet carnivores they spoke of pureed vegetables and porridge oats processed in the kitchen mixer. Raw bones — raw meaty bones — needed putting back into the debate, supported, if possible, by hard numerical evidence.

Five days after the Waltham Symposium, providence smiled when the opportunity arose to conduct a small experiment. Mr and Mrs Zubrycki visited the veterinary hospital with their terriers Blossom and Tuffy. The Zubryckis doted on their pets. Only the best was good enough — regular worming, vaccinations and a diet based on My Dog, the most expensive canned food from Uncle Ben's. Unfortunately, despite the owners' commitment and extensive veterinary attention the dogs often suffered vague illness, lethargy and dermatitis. Tuffy was prone to bouts of neurotic scurrying as if fleeing some unknown threat. Over the years my associates and I had been asked for diagnosis and treatment but always without success. On this occasion the dogs were presented for routine vaccination — the owners no longer sought advice regarding vague ailments which they had come to accept as normal.

Despite past disappointments the Zubryckis listened as I explained a plan to perform thorough dental treatment on both dogs, following which there would be a *committed* change to a diet of raw meaty bones — previous attempts had been rather half-hearted. While I hoped for a demonstrable improvement in the general health of the pets, I was also keen to conduct tests to measure the numbers of blood cells before and after dental treatment. This was to be the hard numerical evidence.

> While I hoped for a demonstrable improvement in the general health of the pets, I was also keen to conduct tests to measure the numbers of blood cells before and after dental treatment. This was to be the hard numerical evidence.

In the event things went almost too well. The treatment under anaesthetic — each animal had several tooth extractions — and blood tests were performed and the patients returned home to convalesce. By the time of the immediate post-surgery checkup Tuffy's scurrying attacks had disappeared. Over subsequent months a contentment settled on the dogs and their coats developed a new lustre, such that the owners could see no reason to return for blood tests.

Luckily I ran into Mrs Zubrycki while out shopping. Brimming with enthusiasm, she told me of the almost magical change in the dogs. I was keen to see for myself and also to perform the follow-up blood tests. 'Perhaps there will be some changes in the blood which reflect this newfound health' I said.

Next day the Zubryckis brought their pets for blood testing. One millilitre samples were taken from each dog and dispatched to the laboratory by courier. By morning we had our answer, exactly in line with predictions. There in black and white the faxed results revealed that Tuffy's white blood cell count had risen by 67 percent and

Blossom's count had risen 58 percent. Just as one swallow does not make a summer, two blood tests do not prove a hypothesis. However, if these results could be repeated the implications for pet health, veterinary practice and the artificial pet food industry would be overwhelming. I rushed into print under the heading 'Raw meaty bones promote health'.[2]

In the article I mentioned how a range of chronic ailments disappeared and were replaced by signs of vitality and apparent good health. I postulated that poisons flowing from the mouth provided the likely explanation for the initial depression in blood cell numbers. In fact there are probably a number of factors which contribute, but at that time the predominant belief among veterinarians was that a deficient immune system allowed periodontal disease to develop. My article, instead of blaming a faulty immune system, reinterpreted the evidence to say the reverse: that periodontal disease depressed the immune system. Such contradictions of orthodox opinion often produce spirited rebuttals from the establishment. No such thing occurred, which I suspect was due to recognition of the validity of the findings.

One response to the article confirmed that members of the veterinary establishment were watching — 'Raw Meaty Bone Lobby' became their term of disparagement for veterinarians who promoted health through feeding. Those of us in the so-called lobby are not disparaged but wear the label with honour. Mrs Zubrycki, while delighted with her pets' progress, was angry with the makers of My Dog. She penned a letter of complaint to Uncle Ben's of Australia. Walter Swanson, Customer Relations Manager, replied:

We are sorry to learn that your dogs have experienced trouble with their teeth, necessitating several trips to the veterinarian at great expense to yourself. It is always distressing to see our canine companions suffering… Uncle Ben's also has complete scientific research support from the Waltham Centre for Pet Nutrition in the United Kingdom which is recognised as the world authority on pet care and nutrition… It would appear that, although complete consensus has not been reached, the majority of veterinarians would recommend that dogs are fed raw meaty marrowbones once or twice a week. Uncle Ben's of Australia is in complete agreement with this recommendation.

Whether Uncle Ben's was previously aware of the immune compromise resulting from consumption of its products I cannot be sure. However, it was not long before I noted the appointment of Professor Neil Gorman, Britain's foremost veterinary immunologist, as Head of Research at the Waltham Centre for Pet Nutrition.

The research

Further investigation was needed but the way forward appeared uninviting. Clinical experiments are costly, time consuming and often fraught with frustration. Besides, writing a scientific paper and gaining publication in a journal would, I thought, be nigh on impossible. But these negative thoughts were themselves a cause for concern. They needed to be dispelled and I resolved to make a start. In the first instance I called on the generosity of Drs Bruce Duff and David Snow at the local pathology laboratory. Without hesitation they agreed to provide free laboratory blood testing for those animals undergoing investigation. Clients were similarly understanding and cooperated in the research.

I kept the research tasks simple: first assess the connection between immune deficiency, periodontal disease and diet; then assess the ability of the immune system to recover once periodontal and dietary insults were removed. With owner consent the pets, both cats and dogs, under-going dental surgery for a foul mouth were blood-tested. The animals recording a low blood count at the time of dentistry were rebooked for testing some weeks later. Owners participating in the investigation under-took to change their pets' diet to raw meaty bones and a few table scraps.

The results

Blossom and Tuffy and six other patients were included in the survey. All made a good recovery and demonstrated subjective good health. During the investigation Tess, a twelve-year-old Maltese, became a TV star. She was filmed undergoing dental surgery and then three months later, on a celebrity talk show, she leapt off the presenter's lap to attack raw chicken wings on the studio floor. Despite her age, mammary cancer, heart condition, liver problems and few teeth she gained a 20 percent increase in weight on a raw chicken wing diet. Tess's white cell count rose 105 percent and the average increase for all patients was 77.7 percent.

Four of the cases, including the Zubrycki terriers, deserve mention because their owners did not attend the veterinary surgery for perceived problems. In fact they considered their pets to be healthy or normal — only in need of vaccination and a checkup. This group showed an average 55 percent increase in white cells after dentistry and diet change.

> In science, as in life, we are called upon to make judgments about isolated events or general trends in the absence of complete information.

Care needs to be exercised in the interpretation of any experimental results. In this survey the animals were in a clinical setting and there could be no standardisation of the investigation. Equally there was only a small number of participating animals and follow-up testing was performed once only after a non-standard interval.

Increased white cell counts can also signal problems. Upward variation from an animal's base reading may indicate the presence of inflammation, infection or dead tissues. Attaching too much importance to the numerical values can be a trap in itself. After all it is the health of the white cells, not just their number, which determines their value to the body — military analysts do not count troops as the sole means of assessing a country's defences.

In science, as in life, we are called upon to make judgments about isolated events or general trends in the absence of complete information. For this reason much of modern science is conducted via statistical analysis. When working with small numbers of cases, changes, which at first sight appear significant, may not be supported by statistical theory. I needed advice and consulted two colleagues well versed in medical statistics. Both were of the opinion that, statistically speaking, the blood cell changes were either 'significant' or 'highly significant'.

Several conclusions flow from the results:

1. The eight animals were suffering a form of acquired immune deficiency syndrome (AIDS) attributable to a foul mouth or an artificial diet or both.

'A' is for 'acquired'. Some forms of immune deficiency are inherited and not easily reversible. Most immune deficiency syndromes are acquired as a result of infection, environmental factors, toxins, diet or other stresses. Removal of trigger factors can, in certain instances, reverse acquired immune deficiency — as was shown with the eight cases — thus confirming the deficiency I was dealing with as being acquired not inherited.

'I' is for the 'immune' system. Any component of the system may be affected. In HIV AIDS the T cell subset of lymphocytes are reduced in number. The eight Foul-mouth AIDS patients suffered from a reduction in both lymphocytes and neutrophils.

'D' is for 'deficiency'. Deficiencies may be mild or severe. After treatment, and in retrospect, the eight patients could be seen to have suffered a severe deficiency of immune cells.

'S' is for 'syndrome' — i.e. 'a combination of clinical signs resulting from a single cause or so commonly occurring together as to constitute a distinct clinical picture'.[3] In the case of Foul-mouth AIDS the syndrome appears to be acquired as a result of periodontal toxins and other dietary factors. These factors are not infectious so please do not worry about the risk of catching AIDS from your pet.

Note: Feline AIDS derives its name from the Feline Immunodeficiency Virus (FIV) which affects cats but not humans. Researchers at North Carolina State University point out that in FIV-infected cats 'clinical AIDS ... is predominantly associated with secondary infectious diseases.'[4] Perhaps oral bacteria, not FIV, are the principal agents which give rise to the condition called feline AIDS.

2. The acquired immune deficiency could be reversed by dental and dietary changes.

At the moment, HIV AIDS, once contracted, cannot be reversed. Lacking an adequate immune defence sufferers fall victim to infections, cancer, weight loss and death. In the terminal stages expensive drugs can be used to limit pain and slow progression of the disease but ultimately these drugs fail. Foul-mouth AIDS sufferers encounter similar wasting diseases. However, my small research project showed that without recourse to drugs, but with timely dental and dietary change, such patients can be saved. It follows that by institution of a natural diet and the maintenance of clean teeth Foul-mouth AIDS can be prevented.

3. The 'normal' reference ranges used by veterinarians for white cells (and other parameters) must be considered unreliable.

While the increase of 77.7 percent in white cell numbers was dramatic, in some cases the increase occurred within the published so-called normal range for white cells. (University of Guelph 'normal' figures are: cats: 5.5 to 15.4 x 10^9 WBC/litre, and dogs: 6.1 to 17.4 x 10^9 WBC/litre.)[5] Imagine having your legs chopped off and then being told your height is still OK and within the 'normal' range — the 'normal' range having been established using pygmies and American basketball players. You would rightly feel indignant being compared with either a pygmy or a basketball player instead of your individual 'normal' height. The same occurs when we consider white cell numbers. We each have an optimum and 77.7 percent variations must be significant.

If the so-called 'normal' range of white cells is so unhelpful we need to ask why? Did the investigators use Chihuahuas and Great Danes to obtain the reference ranges and thus obtain figures which are either too low or too high for most dogs? No, is the answer. They did much worse than that — they used diseased animals. So-called 'normal' ranges are based on blood samples obtained in two ways. The animals providing samples are either kept in a research colony or are pets presented at a veterinary surgery for non-medical reasons, for example vaccination.

Colony-raised animals fed artificial food are notoriously badly affected by periodontal disease. Similarly the majority of cats and dogs attending veterinary surgeries are fed artificial food and suffer from the disease. When researchers establish 'normals' they take samples from 40 or 50 animals in order to discover the span of values. In that number of periodontal disease affected animals the likelihood is that some will have been suffering a depressed white cell count.

Others, in such a large group of periodontal disease sufferers, would likely be experiencing an inflammatory spike with an unduly high number of white cells. Instead of setting a *reference range for health*, it appears that the researchers have merely established the broad range of white cell values encountered in disease.

4. When the 'pet food curtain' disintegrates we can expect a rush of new scientific research and discovery.

Following the collapse of the Iron Curtain there was a rush of social, political and economic readjustment. By daring to peep behind the pet food curtain my simple research project provides a glimpse of the future. In the first instance the research will need to be repeated and expanded to reveal the full implications for pet health and haematological reference values. In the likely event that my findings are confirmed, information, dependent on flawed reference values, will need to be reevaluated. More detailed research will surely follow.

By daring to peep behind the pet food curtain my simple research project provides a glimpse of the future.

5. Inappropriate diet, periodontal disease and immune depression exert combined adverse effects on individual animals. In nature, things that adversely affect some may benefit others.

Inappropriate diet, including starvation, leads to periodontal disease and immune depression. Chronic infections, for instance periodontal disease, also depress the immune system. Those suffering immune depression, whether animals or people, are at greater risk of developing periodontal disease. (Dentists treating severe periodontal disease in humans may, where appropriate, recommend that patients obtain an HIV test.) Since periodontal disease and immune deficiency each worsens the other, a downward spiral ensues. Other organs are likely to become involved — for instance heart, liver and kidneys — in a complex interactive sequence. At first clinical signs may be subtle and overlooked, but ultimately manifest as severe disease — which coincides with and is often mistaken for the signs of old age.

Periodontal disease, immune depression and death may seem to be an undesirable endpoint for an animal. But in a natural setting death of one carnivore means less competition for food among the remainder — for them a positive effect. Similarly the prey of a pack of wolves or pride of lions gain some respite when a predator dies. Contemplation of the mixture of negative and positive effects led me to postulate a uniting hypothesis of periodontal disease, the subject of Chapter 14.

Getting published

Packaging this information in an acceptable fashion for the editor of a scientific journal was the next challenge. The raw experimental results had to be collated, reference material sourced and the manuscript typed. Even for experienced and respected researchers, gaining publication can be something of a lottery. Prestige United States and British journals pick and choose from a wide selection of submissions. By aiming a little lower I hoped to improve my chances. With trepidation and a trace of optimism I submitted the manuscript, entitled 'Foul-mouth AIDS — a dietary disease', to the *Australian Veterinary Journal* in July 1993.

Rejection

Prior to coming to his decision on whether to publish I knew that the editor would seek the opinions of referees. Referees are people with recognised expertise who volunteer their time to review new work. While my name, as author of the paper would be known to them, they would always remain anonymous to me. Within two months their verdict arrived in the post.

Each of the three referees found much to criticise and recommended that the paper be rejected. One of them opined: 'Even after the paper is extensively revised and condensed, I doubt that it will be suitable for publication in the Journal.' He or she went on to defend the current system: 'The population of "normal" animals used to establish laboratory reference values should be as similar as possible to the population of animals which are seen in veterinary clinics. It is therefore appropriate that commercial foods are fed to the latter animals, if they are the diets being fed to most dogs and cats which veterinarians treat.' A second referee stated: 'Most of the animals used as examples in this study have "normal" haematological values and the variation quoted is also within "normal" limits.'

As we shall see in Chapter 11, referees often see their role as defending the status quo, not, as you might expect, the facilitating of useful new discoveries. These particular referees seemed to endorse the use of a biased system to derive biased 'normals', then to use biased 'normals' to justify a biased system. Clearly I had failed to persuade them of the faulty logic of this circular argument. But despite the gulf between us I accepted that many of their criticisms were valid. Dealing with those criticisms and also the despondency I felt were in the first instance too difficult. I closed the file and focused on other projects.

Success

Time heals and events unfold such that two years on I was ready for another round with the publishers. I forced myself to think as a conventional researcher and rewrote the paper according to the model used in the *Journal of Small Animal Practice* (*JSAP*). A prestigious journal, it had already published a letter from me on the effects of artificial diets on cats' lower urinary tracts.[6] I thought this augured well, and besides I was still a member of the British Small Animal Veterinary Association (BSAVA), publishers of the *JSAP*.

Rewriting the manuscript took time, references needed collating and sentences needed adjustment. Simultaneously I continued correspondence with the *JSAP* editor regarding the infamous intussusception article involving the telescoping bowels of young cats. The editor agreed to publish my observations in the journal and then without warning reneged on the agreement. As described in the previous chapter, I lodged complaints against the editor and the BSAVA, first with the Royal College of Veterinary Surgeons and then with the Queen as Patron of the College. Suddenly my chances of gaining publication of the Foul-mouth AIDS paper in the *JSAP* seemed remote — until fate lent a hand.

The long-time editor of the *JSAP* departed and was succeeded by Dr Frances Barr. It was to her that I sent a revised paper under the new title 'Periodontitis and leucopenia'. Leucopenia means low white cell count — a less emotive term than AIDS — but in the covering letter I mentioned my belief that 'veterinary surgeons and those researchers investigating human AIDS would be well served by publication of this paper.' Just what passed through Frances Barr's mind when she received the manuscript I don't know. But perhaps she was fearful that if she didn't give it favourable treatment I might report her to the Queen!

Within three months the paper, with minor modifications, was accepted for publication. After another three months, in December 1995, it appeared in print.[7] It was a moment of pure elation, but no time for celebration. It was clear to me that the material would simply moulder in the archives if left to the usual forces. What was needed was a media campaign to stimulate interest.

Informing the community

Two things were prominent in my thinking. First, that the pet food industry and the veterinary profession continued to downplay the extent and severity of periodontal disease. This needed to change. Second, the community needed to know that artificial diets lead to many noxious diseases including a form of diet-related AIDS. But breaking the news had to wait for Christmas and the January summer holiday period to pass. When a general election was called for the month of February I knew that my media campaign would have to wait still longer.

By March 1996 the timing and preparation were as good as it gets. I had consulted fellow Raw Meaty Bone lobbyist Breck Muir as to the suitability of the proposed media release. Breck gave his approval of the wording and the veterinary meanings implied. But since truth alone might not be a sufficient defence in defamation proceedings, the legal position needed to be established. My legal adviser, who had provided advice throughout my struggles with the pet food industry and allied voices in the veterinary profession, read the draft. He corrected a spelling error, inserted one word and otherwise approved the draft.

Monday 18 March 1996 was chosen as the day when the electronic and print media were widely circulated with the media release:

——— *Media Release* ———

MANY PETS NOT OLD BUT STRICKEN WITH
DIET-INDUCED AIDS

Modern processed diets are known to be responsible for periodontal or gum disease which affects more than 85% of domestic cats and dogs. Foul breath odour is an early sign suggesting that more severe heart, liver and kidney disease may follow.

An article published in the December 1995 issue of the *British Journal of Small Animal Practice* confirms that processed pet foods produce periodontal disease which often leads to an AIDS-like condition in affected animals. (*JSAP* 1995, 36, 542–546)

Dr Tom Lonsdale of Riverstone, NSW, author of the paper, admits that he, along with almost everyone else, used to recommend processed pet foods. "Previously we thought animals were suffering the effects of old age when in fact they were wasting away with periodontal disease and diet-induced AIDS.

"Now we treat the periodontal disease and provide the pets with a natural diet. The removal of the poisons allows the immune system to recover and owners frequently report that their old pet is like a puppy/kitten again.

"I believe that this information should have been available to Australian vets and their patients in 1993. The *Australian Veterinary Journal* refused to publish the research findings.

"In my view a committee of inquiry should be established. Diet-induced AIDS of pets is just as nasty as HIV AIDS for humans. In France HIV AIDS experts suppressed information for a mere two months and as a result were prosecuted and some gaoled for 'complicity in poisoning' (*Science*, vol 268, 16 June 1995)."

Dr Tom Lonsdale and other concerned veterinarians continue their campaign for the banning of what they consider to be misleading pet food industry advertising. "Pet owners should be informed that feeding processed pet foods is likely to lead to ill health, suffering and unnecessary vet bills."

Circularising information to the media is usually an unpredictable activity. Even the most interesting information can be overlooked, especially if other big stories break at the same time. But on this occasion high level impact was guaranteed as a result of a leading science journalist's involvement. Two years previously Julian Cribb, Science Editor for *The Australian* newspaper, had run a story on the devastating effects of artificial pet foods.[8] When offered the opportunity to break the news on the AIDS connection he cautiously accepted. Julian satisfied himself of the validity of the claims prior to arranging for a photographer to take a photo of myself examining a dog's mouth. The article and photo appeared in the 16 March 1996 weekend edition of *The Australian* under the heading 'AIDS-like disease threatens family pets'.[9]

Denial and rebuttals

The *Australian* enjoys kudos throughout the Australian newspaper industry and consequently our story quickly gained momentum. In the following days numerous articles appeared in the press and on the radio. The pet food industry kept a low profile, but the Australian Veterinary Association responded with a media release:

> Dr Pam Scanlon, president of AVA, sought to reassure pet owners that there is absolutely no evidence that periodontal disease causes anything remotely like "AIDS".
>
> "To claim that it does is alarmist and irresponsible and will cause caring pet owners unnecessary concern about the well being of their pet", she said.
>
> "I am disappointed that a newspaper of the high quality of *The Australian* would publish such a story without also seeking and reporting a second opinion. Dr Lonsdale apparently bases his claim that processed food causes an AIDS-like disease on the observation that the white cell count of a few dogs with periodontal disease may be reduced. To claim as this story does that this therefore indicates an AIDS-like syndrome is present is nonsensical and without any rational or scientific foundation", Dr Scanlon said.

Being used to having its views accepted without question the AVA was concerned that on this occasion its press release was widely ignored. As messenger bearing the Foul-mouth AIDS message I came under personal attack — mostly within the veterinary profession and away from public view. Professor Wayne Robinson of the University of Queensland was commissioned to 'review' the original *JSAP* paper and subsequent newspaper reports. Professor Robinson's argument ran to four pages and included the statement: 'Dogs with periodontal disease do not have clinical signs or disease processes that could be construed as being AIDS or even AIDS-like.' The professor concluded: 'I am afraid that I have little to offer in the way of suggestions to combat such behaviour of a member of the veterinary profession.'

The professor's letter, on University stationery, was addressed to the President of the Australian Companion Animal Council (ACAC).[10] ACAC circularised Professor Robinson's letter and other documentation to Australian veterinarians, 'in the interests of providing informed comments'. On closer inspection ACAC turned out to be an umbrella group of veterinary, pet industry and pet food organisations operating from the AVA offices in Sydney. AVA members received the eight pages of documentation during the 1996 AVA elections in which Breck Muir and I were candidates.

Dr Roger Clarke, an AVA heavyweight, wrote a letter of criticism to the *JSAP*. With the reputation of the journal and its referees under attack, the editor asked me and one of the referees — who had applauded the original manuscript — to respond to Dr Clarke's letter. We quickly dispatched our replies in anticipation of open debate. But instead of publishing the letters for all to see, the editor, in consultation with the editorial board and officers of the British Small Animal Veterinary Association, had a change of heart and 'decided to publish no correspondence'.

The British veterinary publishing industry seems to experience difficulty coming to terms with the concept of a diet-induced acquired immunodeficiency syndrome. Dr Frances Barr, editor of the *JSAP*, tells people she regrets publishing the original article. Clause two of the *JSAP* copyright agreement states: 'In assigning your copyright you are not forfeiting your right to use your contribution elsewhere. This you may do after seeking permission from the *Journal of Small Animal Practice...*' Three times I wrote to Dr Barr seeking permission to publish the paper at my web site and each time she sidestepped the agreement. Her final words were: 'I therefore reiterate that I, on behalf of the BSAVA [publishers of the *JSAP*], do not give permission for reproduction of your paper, originally published in the *JSAP*, on your site on the Internet.'

Martin Alder, editor of *The Veterinary Record*, journal of the British Veterinary Association, was similarly obstructive. He claimed that on legal advice he was obliged to erase the words 'including an AIDS-like condition' from my 1998 Royal College of Veterinary Surgeons election manifesto. When pressed to reveal the origin of the legal opinion Mr Alder became evasive but was adamant that he would not publish the offending phrase.

Back in Australia veterinary dentist Dr David Clarke was critical of the *JSAP* paper. He promoted the view that a natural diet does not protect cats against periodontal disease and that 'commercially available canned and dry foods have not been the sole cause, nor increased the prevalence, of periodontal disease in the domestic cat'.[11] Dr Jill Maddison, a lecturer at the University of Sydney and consultant to Friskies, the Nestlé pet food company, said on television:

> The theory that it [natural diet] promotes better overall health and prevents a wide variety of diseases from cancer to heartworm is not based on truth — and the claim that it prevents the AIDS-like syndrome is totally wrong. Because the AIDS-like syndrome doesn't exist.[12]

While the pet food industry and its defenders exist I worry that pets will continue to suffer the catastrophe of Foul-mouth AIDS. As an activist I can be accused of bias so I leave the last word to the feline immunodeficiency virus expert quoted in Chapter 3, Dr Niels Pedersen:

> With the world-wide HIV pandemic ... immunodeficiency has become a byword of the age. Immunodeficiency, however, is not just a rare genetic disease or a common outcome of a

widespread virus infection. Immunodeficiency results from a myriad of causes and can range from subtle to catastrophic in its clinical appearance.[13]

8

———➤꣠꣠꣠ぽ◐꣠⇐———

The right diet

Diets of wild small carnivores

A jungle cat sleeping off a meal in the shade of an equatorial tree has features in common with a recently fed pack of wolves sheltering from a blizzard. With freshly cleaned teeth and distended stomachs the somnolent creatures digest their food and replenish reserves in readiness for the next hunt. Circumstances may appear different for the house cat hiding under the mahogany sideboard or family dog resting under the Scandinavian pine table, but appearances can be deceptive. The inner needs of cats and dogs are the same as those of their wild counterparts.

While few pets justify their existence by catching their own meals, the meals they consume should ensure optimum health and vitality. Establishing with precision the appropriate diet for wild and therefore domestic animals is not easy. Carnivores are frequently shy, nocturnal creatures living in remote areas. Food quality, quantity and frequency may vary with the season, the prey supply and the needs of offspring. Since round the clock monitoring is impossible, biologists employ indirect methods to derive dietary information. Each method has limitations.

Radio tracking of pack animals to locate their kill does not reveal the proportions of each organ consumed by individual members of the pack. Examination of scats (faecal deposits), using a combination of experience, physical and chemical means, may be used to identify components of a carnivore's diet. Better information can be obtained by examining stomach contents of dead carnivores, although this method also has drawbacks. Finding random road kills is at best haphazard and shooting endangered species for minimal biological information is no longer acceptable.

An exception occurs in Australia where dingoes, medium-sized feral dogs, are regarded as pests. Scientists working to protect the livestock industry have examined dingo stomach contents and this inform-ation is of use to us in assessing canine dietary needs. In 1977

> While few pets justify their existence by catching their own meals, the meals they consume should ensure optimum health and vitality.

Whitehouse reported on the contents of the stomachs of 160 dingoes trapped in the range lands of Western Australia.[1] More than 70 percent of the identified remains were derived from kangaroos. Domestic stock formed only a small part of the diet and 6.5 percent of the ingesta was rabbit, after which came birds, reptiles and insects.

In a survey of 530 dingo stomachs removed from animals trapped in south-eastern Australia 89.3 percent of the contents were from native marsupials.[2] A wide variety of mammals, birds, reptiles, fish and insects made up the remainder, with rabbit forming 7.8 percent. Where maggots were found in the stomach this was taken as an indication that the dingo had eaten carrion (dead putrefying flesh). Another possible explanation, which I favour, is that the maggots were preferentially eaten as live prey. I say this because a colleague reported seeing a fox bury some meat and then some days later a fox, presumably the same one, returned to lick up the maggots.[3]

Interpretation of survey results is always open to question. However, it is notable that cereal grains were never recorded in dingo stomachs although some contained sticks, stones and dirt. Both surveys demonstrated that dingoes prefer lean game animals in preference to domestic cattle and sheep. This ties in perfectly with a story told to me by an old dingo trapper who was fond of dingoes and reluctant to kill them unnecessarily.[4] A particular family of five dingoes lived on a sheep station. The property owner wanted the animals killed even though they ignored his sheep. When two were shot the remaining three began killing sheep. The apparent explanation was that sheep are easy to kill, whereas it requires a full pack to hunt and kill kangaroos.

Since European colonisation of Australia, more than 200 years ago, populations of domestic cats have established themselves in the remote outback. The shift in ecological balance between native animals and invaders has been considerable. Past actions cannot be reversed but efforts are under way to understand and correct imbalances. In an Australian survey of 128 feral cat stomachs, rabbit remains and small mammals comprised 88 percent of the contents.[5] Birds, reptiles, frogs and insects were of secondary importance, amounting to 5.2 percent of the volume. Vegetation made up 1.5 percent of the total and much of this derived from the trapped animals biting madly at the surroundings as they tried to escape.

Diets of captive wild carnivores

Twenty-five years ago I first met Peter Litchfield, at a time when he was in charge of the animals in a safari park and I was a junior veterinarian. Peter, I soon discovered, is an astute searcher of the truth and I came to depend on his judgment whenever health maintenance and disease prevention were on the agenda. While researching for this book I consulted Peter — now Animal Manager at John Aspinall's two zoos in Kent — for information on captive carnivore diets. Captive carnivores must eat what they are given but in this regard John Aspinall's zoos are world leaders. By ensuring diets and conditions are as close as possible to those found in the wild, the two zoos conduct successful breeding programs for several endangered species.

Peter referred my enquiry to Neville Buck who cares for the Aspinall collection of small carnivores. The notes Neville sent to me on the feeding preferences of three wild dog species and six species of small cats are reproduced in full in Appendix B. All animals were fed whole carcasses and ate most of the internal organs, meat and bones. None of the animals ate faeces, either their own or the faeces of other animals. Most animals ate grass and bush dogs ate some fruit.

Wolves and African hunting dogs chose not to eat the rumen and colon contents of large herbivores. Neither did they eat heavy bones, hooves and horns. This, I believe, reflects nutritional needs and behaviour of animals in the wild. For them, pulling down large prey involves effort and risk of injury. That some parts may be discarded, despite the costs of acquisition, indicates those parts have little or no nutritional value. Captive wild cats showed a similar dislike for the stomach and colon contents of their prey. Their refined feeding habits included plucking the fur from small rodents and careful avoidance of the gizzards of day-old chicks. Why an aversion to gizzards with the attendant effort required to dissect out these tiny organs? I don't know, but nature knows and knows best.

Quality

During seasonal or temporary food shortages wild animals often change their diet as a means to survival. Wolves in the Arctic feed on the summer mice plagues and coyotes in the Nebraska farmlands eat the ripe fruits of autumn.[6] However, the real suitability test for a diet is not whether it permits temporary survival but whether it can support the demands of reproduction in a harsh natural environment. It is worth noting that if the environment is to some degree protected then the quality, quantity and frequency of feeding can drop and yet still support reproduction. Diseased, malnourished populations of dogs and cats scavenging on Third World garbage tips provide testimony to this fact. Similarly millions of puppies and kittens are born to animals maintained on low quality commercial food. However, our purpose is not to devise the lowest diet consistent with survival but to discover the optimum.

(Note: The concept of food is usually viewed as that material ingested by and sustaining the weight of individual animals, whether wild or domestic. I believe this concept permits distortion and error — seriously inadequate food can sustain individual animals locked in a cage. As a solution I propose that food for carnivores could be defined as: *That ingesta which shows direct correlation with, and facilitates the increase in, wild population numbers.* Such a concept would represent a move away from the individual animal being seen as the unit of consideration and in its place the population would be seen as the viable unit over time. It would also serve to emphasise that the suitability of a food depends on both its chemical constituents and physical form.)

The Australian dingo and feral cat surveys and the feeding practices at John Aspinall's zoos provide a clear guide to the chemical and physical quality of carnivore food. In each instance the diets are based on whole raw carcasses of a range of animals. The size of those carcasses broadly correspond with the hunting ability of the carnivore. For instance feral cats caught a preponderance of rabbits, while dingoes preferred kangaroos. It seems reasonable to me that domestic pets living in zoos without bars should be treated at least as well as captive wild animals. Responsible zoo keepers feed their carnivores on whole carcasses *all* of the time. Since most of us only have a couple of tame carnivores living in our households it ought to be possible to feed whole carcasses *some* of the time.

Raw meaty bones and table scraps

Farmers, hunters and fishermen may already be able to provide whole carcasses for their pets and those of us who travel the country roads can pick up road kill. For the majority, these are not realistic options and the next best alternative needs to be found — pending the development of a natural pet food industry. By analysing what carnivores derive from whole carcasses we can make some generalisations:

- The food must be raw.
- Meat on bone should provide the bulk of the diet.
- The bones must be of a suitable size to permit consumption — large bones are unsuitable.
- The pieces should not be small and susceptible to being swallowed whole but should require concentrated chewing.
- Ripping, tearing and gnawing at carcasses takes time: time needed to scrub, clean and polish the teeth.
- Muscle meat and internal organs have approximately the same high nutritional value.
- Liver, a rich source of vitamins and minerals, comprises between 2 and 6 percent of the carcass weight of prey animals.[7]
- Intestines are consumed together with their contents of part-digested herbage.

At the culmination of a successful hunt wolves start with the soft parts of the carcass before settling down to the main meal of meat and bone — as if saving the best until last. In Aesop's fables the dog carrying a bone over a bridge notices his reflection in the stream below, growls with envy and so drops the bone in the stream. Tom Hungerford, grandfather of Australian veterinary science, wrote from personal experience when he said:

> At the culmination of a successful hunt wolves start with the soft parts of the carcass before settling down to the main meal of meat and bone — as if saving the best until last.

Rightly or wrongly, I regard the feeding of raw bones daily as being one critical factor in the health of dogs. Why is this? The crunching of the bones may clean the teeth. The enormous dental pressures of crunching bones may cause great circulatory changes in the jaws and gums. The primitive euphoria generated by the crunching of bones is obvious. To tease my dogs and take away their food is nothing, but to tease them and take away the bones causes a very definite reaction. The canine joy of crunching up bones is a daily feature of exhilaration and well-being which may have a bearing upon their immuno-competence and their immune system.[8]

In his book *Give Your Dog A Bone*, Dr Ian Billinghurst tells us: 'The vast majority of healthy dogs that I have known professionally and otherwise, were bone eaters. No matter what else they ate, the central theme of their diet was raw meaty bones. By contrast, most of the sick dogs I have known, rarely if ever ate bones.'[9] Other Raw Meaty Bone Lobby veterinarians agree and so do their delighted clients and healthy pets. If whole carcasses are not available, I recommend that the diet for dogs should comprise at least 70 percent raw meaty bones from a variety of animals. (Some apparently healthy dogs eat nothing else but raw meaty bones.) In Australia chicken carcasses (after the meat has been removed for human consumption) form the staple diet for many pets. Australian dogs also commonly eat beef brisket bones, kangaroo tails and lamb bones.

In recognition that wild carnivores consume the intestinal contents of their prey it seems that some vegetable matter, besides grass, may play a useful part in canine nutrition. Accordingly I suggest that the remainder of the diet for dogs should be cooked and raw table scraps — the food of human omnivores. That our digestive juices are not added to the scraps does not seem to seriously impair the usefulness of the food. However, in order to more closely mimic the intestinal contents of prey animals, food scraps can be pulped in the kitchen mixer.

My recommendations for domestic cat diets are similar. In the absence of whole carcasses a diet based on raw meaty bones provides good health. At least 80 percent (up to 100 percent) of the diet should be made up of chicken wings, necks, rabbit, fish, quail or similar. As with dogs the remainder can be a combination of cooked and raw scraps from the table.

Supplements

Raw carcasses provide the bulk of the dietary needs of wild carnivores with minor contributions from other sources. Soil and herbage stick to raw meat and are swallowed with the main food. Grass is actively consumed by many animals and some eat fruit and vegetables. These latter items are not available to dingoes in the Australian outback or wolves in the Arctic. For them survival in harsh environments depends on an adequate supply of raw carcasses. But since raw meaty bones are a second best option many people have an understandable desire to supplement their pet's diet because they reason 'something must be missing'.

Until scientists provide conclusive evidence demonstrating inadequacies of a raw meaty bone and table scrap diet, I believe that the temptation to add supplements should be resisted — though perhaps the addition of liver and fruit is useful. Liver is part of every carcass and can form a valuable part of a carnivore's diet. But not too much, for excessive liver in the diet can lead to an oversupply of vitamins A and D. And this highlights the dangers of dietary supplementation — it is too easy to overdose on vitamins and minerals. Many puppies are crippled by injudicious use of vitamin and mineral supplements.[10]

Ripe raw fruit, especially stone fruit and melons, is eagerly consumed by many pet dogs. Billinghurst promotes fruit for dogs. But in answer to the question, 'Is it essential that dogs eat fruit?', he states:

> No, definitely not. All of the nutrients present in fruit can be obtained from other sources. However, by adding fruit to your dog's diet, you do one more thing to ensure it is fed a a wide variety of foods. This gives it the greatest chance of receiving a balanced diet with plenty of those longevity and immune promoting nutrients.[11]

As to how much is too much remains a moot point. Some dogs eat copious amounts of raw fruit without apparent ill effect — but the stones (pits) can give rise to bowel blockage with serious consequences.

When doctors advise on human nutrition they recommend more and better quality natural food ingredients, not the addition of artificial supplements. Exactly the same criteria should apply to animal diets. Unfortunately many recipes for purportedly natural diets start with grains and vegetables — owing more to vegetarian cookery than the needs of carnivores — which must then be supplemented with vitamins and minerals. Obtaining a correct balance of vitamins and minerals, under these circumstances, becomes nigh on impossible. Some grain and vegetable advocates recognise the need for dental hygiene and recommend their diets be supplemented with large marrow bones, cow hooves and cow hide chews — the very items discarded by captive wolves.

Other supplements, for instance apple cider vinegar, kelp and garlic, are recommended ingredients in some so-called natural recipes for pets. While these may be wholesome ingredients of a human diet, other foods contain the same range of vitamins, minerals and micronutrients. In summary, there is no need to spend time in the kitchen preparing exotic mixes for your pets. Raw meaty bones and a few table scraps provide an acceptable alternative to first quality raw carcasses. More details are located in Appendix C.

Quantity

Having addressed issues of quality we now need to give some thought to the quantity of food to be offered to our tame carnivores. In this regard, study of wild animal food intake is not a particularly helpful guide. There are good reasons for this disparity. No two animals have the same metabolic rate, body size or environmental conditions. A striking example is provided by Fuller and Keith who calculated the summer food requirements of adult wolves at 1.7 kg per adult wolf per day. In winter requirements increased to 5.5 kg of food per wolf per day — keeping warm and running through snow takes up more energy.[12] When we take into consideration the fact that rapidly growing pups may require several times more food than a comparable adult and lactating females also need large quantities, then firm pronouncements become even more difficult.

Dogs

The artificial pet food industry encounters similar difficulty in making recommendations on quantity. Uncle Ben's of Australia, in a feeding guide for the PAL brand of dog food, states:

> Individual dogs may require as much as 25 percent more or 25 percent less. This reflects the variation between dogs, and other factors such as the environmental temperature and the base level of activity of the dog.[13]

The Iams Corporation recommend that a medium-sized dog receives between 215 grams and 350 grams of their dry food daily depending on whether the dog engages in low or high activity.[14] In my view this is something of a hit and miss affair, with the owner ultimately having to make judgments.

In an attempt to take the anxiety out of this vexed question I point out that no one tells mothers how much to feed a family and yet everyone gets fed enough. (This is true in the Western world, however overfeeding can be a problem.) Similarly when feeding the family dog or pack of dogs people usually get it right without resort to weighing scales and pocket calculators. People judge according to whether the dog:

- is big or small
- is lively
- is eager for food
- quickly consumes food or leaves some uneaten
- buries bones in the backyard (a sign of overfeeding)
- is too thin or too fat.

Experience acquired in feeding dogs over a period of time — whether personal experience or that gained from watching a parent or friend — also helps owners gauge the amount to feed the dog.

The best way to assess if an adult dog is too thin or too fat is to run the finger tips over the ribs. If there is a pleasing layer of flesh covering the ribs, but the ribs can be counted, then the weight is about right — for comparison try counting your own ribs. In short-coated breeds the outline of the lower parts of the ribs should just be visible.

For pregnant bitches and growing pups it is best to feed to appetite. Only if a pup shows evidence of becoming overweight should the rations be reduced. This policy of erring on the high side is to be recommended when feeding adult dogs too. It is always better to slightly overfeed and then to cut back later, rather than risk leaving an animal with insufficient to eat.

The longer pets spend ripping, tearing and gnawing at their food the cleaner their teeth will be. For this reason, wherever possible, feed the raw meaty bone ration in one large piece.

The longer pets spend ripping, tearing and gnawing at their food the cleaner their teeth will be. For this reason, wherever possible, feed the raw meaty bone ration in one large piece.

Thus far I have avoided specifying quantities in either kilograms or pounds weight — dependence on exact numbers is best avoided. However I shall modify this stance and say that my own two dogs each weigh approximately 25 kg (55 lb). Each day they each consume about 500 grams (1 lb 2 oz) of raw meaty bones which is approximately 2 percent of their body weight. In addition they receive leftover scraps from the table or scavenged on our daily trips to the neighbourhood park. Dr Alan Bennet feeds his overweight 30 kg Golden Retriever 300 grams of raw meaty bones daily (1 percent of body weight) and his trim 10 kg terrier eats 200 grams daily (2 percent of body weight). Both dogs eat table scraps and cat faeces. Small dogs often require proportionately more food — about 20 percent of body weight per week or 3 percent per day of raw meaty bones plus additional table scraps.

Cats

The quantity of food required by pet cats also varies according to individual need and environmental conditions. Feral cats in Sweden were found to consume an average 294 grams (10 oz) of rabbit daily.[15] Most domestic cats attending my veterinary practice eat a little more than 1 kg (2 lb 3 oz) of food weekly (usually based on chicken necks or wings). On a daily basis this approximates to 150 grams (5 oz) of food — one large chicken wing or neck. Pregnant and nursing mothers always consume more, as do rapidly growing kittens.

Frequency

Dogs

The appropriate frequency of feeding depends on the quality and quantity of food offered. In nature, wolves (the progenitors of domestic dogs) vary the frequency of feeding depending on the food supply. When dependent on mice they eat numerous small morsels. When preying on large herbivores there is usually an interval of several days between kills. Fuller and Keith found that the wolves in their study killed a moose every 4.7 days.[16] During the initial feeding frenzy wolves gorge on the softer parts of the prey and are estimated to be able to consume up to 9 kg (20 lb) of food in the first one and a half hours.[17] Wolves usually remain in the vicinity of a kill until all edible parts are gone. Fuller and Keith reported that a pack stayed an average 2.5 days at the site of an adult moose kill, but only 1.5 days at the site of a moose calf kill.[18]

Wolves seem equally well adapted to fasting for extended periods. McCleery fed his wolves every five days in winter and every five to ten days in summer.[19] Mech estimated that wolves could spend several weeks without feeding and suffer no ill effect.[20] The same is true for obese domestic dogs which, according to a pet food company vet, can fast for five weeks.[21] Body weight losses of around 23 percent occur without incurring any serious consequences.

In adapting these findings to the normal domestic setting my recommendation is to feed domestic dogs once daily in the evening. Depending on body condition and state of health it seems a good idea to fast adult dogs on one or two days each week. Most zoos fast their carnivores occasionally and this practice seems justified in light of wild carnivore feeding behaviour.

In the case of young pups and pregnant and nursing females I generally recommend free access feeding of appropriate foodstuffs. Females seldom overeat in this situation and pups spend much time playing and sleeping between times of gnawing at their food.

In the wild the first solid food offered to young pups is that regurgitated by the mother. Domestic dogs cannot be relied upon to perform this task and it is better to mince the food offered to pups between three and six weeks of age. Chicken carcasses, once the meat has been removed for human consumption, are suitable for mincing. At the same time whole pieces of food, for instance chicken carcasses, can be made available and by about six weeks no further mincing is required. While pups should be well fed they should not be fat. From four months of age puppies can be fed twice daily. From seven months of age once-daily feeding is suitable for most puppies.

Besides correct feeding, rest and play are important contributors to the healthy development of pups.

(Note: Besides correct feeding, rest and play are important contributors to the healthy development of pups. Wolf cubs raised in the wild spend time sleeping when they are not playing with their litter mates. In adolescence they begin to venture out behind the main pack. Forced exercise is avoided and for good reason since growing bones are prone to stress injuries. In the case of large domestic breeds it is important that puppies are kept slim, well rested and not forced to undertake vigorous exercise — even though the puppies may appear to be having fun. From nine months of age exercise can be increased moderately and by twelve months the young adult can run freely, but never to the point of exhaustion.)

Cats

Cats dependent on their hunting skills for survival can tailor their meal frequency to the prey available. When mice are numerous cats take many small meals, but when depending on rabbits fewer large meals are eaten. In the domestic situation a satisfactory compromise is to feed the rations in the evening. In the cool of the night when flies are not troublesome cats can consume their food at leisure. Where there is competition from other cats the meal may be eaten at one sitting. Otherwise the food may be taken in several small meals throughout the night.

Healthy cats are able to fast for considerable periods without seeming ill effect. Tales abound of cats being locked in rooms or cupboards or simply becoming stranded in tall trees. If temperatures are moderate they are able to go without food and water for many days. Undoubtedly this ability stems from their ancestry as desert dwellers dependent on unreliable food sources. Contrasted with this resilience, fat cats which are suddenly subjected to a severe fast can succumb to an unusual form of liver failure. Affected cats refuse to eat and even with treatment most do not recover. For this reason, unless under veterinary supervision, it is wise not to withhold food from cats for more than a couple of days.

Obesity is a problem among cats fed an artificial diet but cats fed a natural diet seldom overeat. This is especially so for lactating and pregnant females and growing kittens. From three weeks of age kittens need their food minced but by six weeks they can usually handle whole pieces of raw food.

Changing to natural food

In order to ensure a smooth transition to the feeding of a more natural diet a few advance preparations are advisable. In the first instance it is useful to think of yourself as an enlightened, responsible zoo keeper intent on providing the optimum for your modified wolves and cats in a zoo without bars.

1. At least one large bowl of drinking water should be permanently available. No bowl is necessary for raw meaty bones or carcasses.

Hungry carnivores soon drag their food to a safe spot where they can settle down to the important task of devouring the feast. Table scraps are best fed from a stainless steel or plastic bowl.

2. Pet food needs to be bought in bulk in order to avoid repeated shopping trips. Small carcasses and raw meaty bones can be stored frozen — place each day's allowance in a separate container or plastic bag — but an old refrigerator may suffice for shorter periods. Freshly frozen food is almost as good as fresh food and much better than spoiled food.

There is no need to thaw frozen carcasses or raw meaty bones prior to feeding. In this way smells and mess are kept to a minimum and the food is maintained at peak freshness. Providing the environmental temperature is above freezing the food will thaw on the ground. Cats usually wait for the food to thaw but dogs will readily eat frozen food.

Large carcasses suffer decomposition and spoilage if frozen and then thawed. If large numbers of animals are to be fed with large carcasses it is best that the food be fresh. Alternatively carcasses can be eviscerated (internal organs removed) and kept cool.

> Finding dependable suppliers is crucial to the success of the enterprise. Pet stores, supermarkets, butchers and fish shops are all potential sources of food.

3. Finding dependable suppliers is crucial to the success of the enterprise. Pet stores, supermarkets, butchers and fish shops are all potential sources of food. It may be necessary to make prior arrangement with the shopkeepers. Once a good relationship is established then encourage your friends to make use of the same source. In this way a good turnover and therefore freshness of stock can be maintained. Food freshness is a major consideration when feeding cats, but dogs will accept food which is beginning to decompose.

4. Given the way carnivores jealously guard their real food it is wise not to risk fights or human injury at feeding time. Especial care needs to be adopted with small children, and dogs and cats may need to be separated. Common and predictable feeding routines can help to avoid conflict and

training is always advisable. My own two dogs permit me to remove bones from their mouths. They realise that I both supply the food and remove it — at times of my choosing.

Given the way carnivores jealously guard their real food it is wise not to risk fights or human injury at feeding time.

5. You may wish to keep this book close at hand for reference — a 'Diet guide' is located in Appendix C. In the early days you may feel insecure, but with time you should gain confidence. Clients of mine tell me of their satisfaction in watching and hearing their pets consume real food.

6. Even if everything goes according to plan it can still be a lonely experience if you do not have an understanding veterinarian at call. You would be wise to seek out a veterinarian who supports your attempts to care for your pets as nature intended. If you and your veterinarian are both newcomers to the principles of natural feeding — and we were all beginners once — it may be helpful to support each other during the early stages. (When I commenced natural feeding I was fearful of the potential risks. Discussion with trusting clients and veterinary colleagues helped place things in perspective.)

Problems and solutions

Often the first benefit pet owners perceive when feeding natural food is the changed faecal output of their pets. Pets fed raw meaty bones produce one-third of the volume of faeces that processed food fed animals do. The faeces does not stink and after a day in the sun the pellets of powdered bone turn chalky white.[22] For apartment dwellers who must rely on a pet litter tray, the lack of odour is a distinct advantage. In Australia a raw meaty bone diet costs less than processed food, with further savings on veterinary bills.[23] Apart from the monetary savings it makes for good conscience to know that one's pets are not suffering from diet-induced disease.

But as with any complex system, the feeding of natural foods can give rise to problems. The sometimes dramatic problems are insignificant when compared with the ailments arising from processed food. Nevertheless problems associated with natural food are best studied with a view to minimising their impact — whether it be impact upon the animals or their human carers.

> But as with any complex system, the feeding of natural foods can give rise to problems. The sometimes dramatic problems are insignificant when compared with the ailments arising from processed food.

Refusal to eat

Puppies and kittens raised on natural food soon learn how to tackle raw food. Processed food raised animals may not recognise carcasses or raw meaty bones as being their biologically correct food. A couple of days fasting is all it takes to persuade most dogs to accept raw meaty bones. When feeding whole carcasses, sometimes it is necessary to make the first knife cut, past the fur or feathers, in order for dogs to realise there is good food inside.

Adult cats are frequently addicted to processed food and resist a change to a natural diet. Patience and the application of a few tricks are usually required in order to gain compliance — not an easy task for owners used to feeding their pet's addiction. Often a local veterinarian — committed to natural feeding and aware of the wiles of cats — is the best person to solve the impasse.

In the first instance the patient needs to be kept hungry under hospital supervision. Sometimes hunger alone is sufficient inducement to persuade a cat to eat raw chicken necks or whole fish. At other times mincing the food helps, as does force feeding a few mouthfuls until the cat acquires the taste for the new food. Another trick is to mix small amounts of the previous commercial diet with the new food, or alternatively smear the old foodstuff on a chicken neck or the cut surface of a wing. Lightly grilling the skin, but leaving the meat and bone raw, on chicken wings sometimes proves appetising to cats. But some cats can be very stubborn and for these I use a small dose of tranquilliser prior to feeding.

Stale food must be discarded and fresh food, at room temperature, offered each day. In all cases I maintain an accurate daily weight recording to safeguard against rapid weight loss. Fasting combined with rapid weight loss can lead to fatal liver disease. Most cats will eat chicken necks after three to four days of fasting and force feeding, although one particular cat held out for ten days. Such battles of will are enervating and it is easy to admit failure and give up. Once cats are converted to eating chicken I recommend the introduction of other foods, for instance fish, rabbit and quail. I know of many apparently healthy cats addicted to raw chicken bones, but food from a variety of sources is always better.

Owners nominally control what their pets eat, but only nominally. The pressures abound to slip into unhealthy ways. At the supermarket the cheap, easily available meat is often hamburger mince or liver. When fed to pets these items are gulped down with gusto and with no immediate ill effects. Simultaneously owners, only half aware of any discrepancies, find justification for their modification to the natural diet. Some maintain that this is a necessary adaptation for their lifestyle. Others reason that since hamburger mince is fresh raw meat it must be close enough to the ideal for all practical purposes. The scene is now set for a decline into habituation for both owner and pets. The busy owner rushes home with the shopping bags to be met by the pets drooling a greeting. Minutes later the pets are licking the bowl clean and the owner's feelings of satisfaction peak at the completion of another task.

Unfortunately this scenario and its variations are much too common and result in severe pet ill health. I encourage owners to resist. The best antidote that I know entails the constant repetition of the dietary habits of wild carnivores. In essence this means feeding whole carcasses of a range of animals or, at the very least, raw meaty bones derived from a number of sources. As previously remarked there are plenty of pets fed exclusively on raw chicken carcasses without apparent ill effect. In contrast, I've heard of New Zealand sheepdogs being fed exclusively on sheep carcasses and suffering from unthriftiness and a poor hair coat.[24] My guess is that those dogs suffered from too much saturated sheep fat and too little selenium and vitamin E.[25] By adding raw chicken carcasses and a few table scraps to the diet such problems can be solved.

Anatomical and physiological problems

In the early days of the Raw Meaty Bone campaign the pet food industry and its helpers used many scare tactics to confuse the debate.

A popular argument launched by them was that domestic dogs were so modified both anatomically and physiologically that they cannot handle raw food. Circumstantial evidence indicates that some dogs experience difficulties, but sound objective facts are scarce. One puppy treated by me had gorged on chicken necks and suffered a resultant rectal impaction of chicken vertebrae. When fed on larger pieces requiring more chewing the puppy suffered no further problems.

It is true that dogs with flat faces such as Bulldogs and Pekingese may experience a degree of difficulty with chewing and swallowing. Due to their misshapen jaws these dogs need more, not less, chewing in order to cleanse the oral cavity. And in any case it has taken several hundred years for these breeds to be developed from the parent stock of wolves. Throughout that period the diet was often based on meaty bones with assorted table scraps. For these reasons I don't believe flat-faced dogs should be denied the benefits of a more natural diet. However where increased risks exist increased vigilance is required.

Carnivores readily vomit food and most pets suffer occasional bouts of diarrhoea. Providing the occurrences are neither severe nor frequent, there is no need for concern. I have heard tell, but have no immediate experience, of animals which regularly vomit or have diarrhoea after being fed beef or chicken. Allergy, or a population of intestinal microbes that is slow to adapt to the natural food, may provide an explanation for such unwanted episodes. If the problem persists then alternative food sources must be found, for instance rabbit, fish or turkey.

Talk of anatomical and physiological problems associated with the consumption of carcasses or raw meaty bones has not been supported by sound evidence. My guess is that evidence will not be forthcoming, since large artificial pet food companies now recommend or endorse the feeding of raw bones.

Stuck bones

Older dogs used to canned food and with a flaccid, weak bowel sometimes become constipated when fed a large meal of raw bones — especially if those bones have little meat attached. In fact all dogs and cats tend to strain when passing the dry, crumbly faecal residue of raw meaty bone digestion. This appears to be normal and not attended by any hazard — more a sign of the digestive tract receiving a good physical workout.

Raw bones can and do get stuck anywhere between the mouth and the anus. In my own practice I had the unpleasant task of performing post-mortem examinations on two small dogs which had attempted to swallow pieces of ox tail. In both instances the bone had been fed as a bite-sized chunk and when the stringy fascia caught around the teeth the bone could not pass further than the pharynx and the dog choked to death. Other dogs have suffered indigestion as sharp bone fragments passed down the intestine. Sometimes bone spicules cause pain on passing through the anus.

Even wild animals experience problems with their diet. Two events stick in my mind from the days when I was a part-time zoo veterinarian. On one occasion a tigress became impacted with bone which necessitated an operation for removal of the blockage. When a piece of sawn ox vertebra penetrated the bowel of a lion the discovery was only made at post-mortem inspection. Some accidental blockages are inevitable; for instance, Neville Buck reported that a bush dog choked on rabbit skin.[26]

In attempting to reconcile ourselves to these fatal or near fatal accidents we should bear in mind that most blockages in pet dogs are caused by a range of foreign objects, with corn cobs and peach stones high on the list. Rather than recriminations we need understanding of the risks and benefits of our decisions and a resolve to be ever watchful.

Broken and worn teeth

It is possible but highly unusual for teeth to break when eating raw meaty bones. In general the bones which create problems are large ox bones — especially when sawn lengthwise to extract the marrow.[27] Brittle cooked bones and cow hooves are also a potent source of trouble and should never be fed.

Carnivore teeth last a lifetime without appreciable wear if pets consume a natural diet — minerals in saliva constantly replenish surface enamel. Worn teeth are often found

Carnivore teeth last a lifetime without appreciable wear if pets consume a natural diet

in dogs which chew balls or bricks or, most commonly, nibble at their own skin. It may surprise you, but dog hair has a more abrasive effect on teeth than a diet of raw meaty bones.

Parasitic bacteria, protozoa and worms

Processed heat-sterilised food is free from bacteria, protozoa and worms. By contrast natural food always contains bacteria and sometimes contains protozoa and worms. The risks inherent in this situation can best be assessed by reference to the facts.

The first thing to consider is that parasites have been around for as long as pets and humans. Currently those same parasites are brought into the kitchens of the world in meat intended for human consumption. Pets currently gain access to meat scraps and bones and yet there is no major scare regarding either human or pet health. Whether the risks will increase with a rise in natural food feeding is hard to predict and dependent on numerous factors. Meat handling regulations are in place in most countries and are designed to minimise risk.

Meat and bones passed as fit for human consumption are considered to be fit for animals. Pets in general are resistant to bacteria and can be fed meat salvaged from diseased, debilitated, dying and dead stock (4D stock). The Chief Veterinary Officer of Victoria conducted an appraisal of the knackery industry in 1997 and reported:

> The hazard considered to represent the major risk to pets from the consumption of pet meat is barbiturate poisoning associated with meat derived from an animal which has been euthanased with a barbiturate.
>
> There are very few reports of infections being spread to pets through pet meat in Australia. Pet meat does not need to be sterile because carnivores, such as dogs and cats, have evolved eating meat from diseased, debilitated, dying and dead animals. The acid barrier in the stomach of carnivores appears to provide adequate protection against food-borne pathogens for the immunologically competent dog or cat. Cooking would reduce potential risk to a negligible level.
>
> There is a report of anthrax being spread through pet

meat to dogs from a knackery at Echuca in 1972 where anthrax was not recognised as a cause of deaths in cattle. Apart from this incident there are no other records of anthrax being spread through pet meat in Victoria.

The adverse consequences of defective handling practices for pet meat, poor personal hygiene and temperature abuse of pet meat do not appear to have led to outbreaks of food poisoning in dogs or cats.

The Chief Veterinary Officer went on to say:

> There are no reports of cross-contamination between pet meat in household refrigerators and food intended for human consumption that have led to outbreaks of food poisoning.[28]

Salmonella and Campylobacter

Several forms of bacteria can infect animals and humans but two groups deserve special mention. Salmonella and Campylobacter both occur commonly in cats and dogs. Usually the animals are free of signs of disease but may suffer from diarrhoea. In humans the signs of infection may be severe and involve acute diarrhoea and even death. Locating the source of infection is not always successful. Occasionally a pet is held to be the source and sometimes children pass the infection to the family pet. More commonly the source is found to be contaminated poultry meat.

In March 1998 the American Consumers Association published the results of its investigation of almost 1000 chickens intended for human consumption and bought from grocery stores in 36 US cities. As expected the level of contamination was high and the report stated:

> We found campylobacter in 63 percent of the chickens, salmonella in 16 percent. Eight percent of all chickens had campylobacter and salmonella. Only 29 percent were free of both.[29]

With this level of contamination it is best to assume that all raw chicken, whether for human or pet consumption, is affected. Pork and beef can also be a source of infection even though the meat has been cleared for human consumption. Exercise caution whenever handling raw meat. Surfaces, utensils and hands should be well washed after contact. Young children should be encouraged not to put their fingers in their mouths after handling the family pet or its food.

Toxoplasma

Toxoplasma gondii is a protozoan parasite which primarily infects cats but also occurs in a range of other species including man. There are complicated aspects of the life cycle of the pathogen which need not concern us here. What we should be aware of is the sometimes severe disease which occurs in cats, dogs and human foetuses. A range of organs may be affected including the eye, brain, lungs and liver. Transmission is thought to occur as a result of eating or handling raw meat. The faeces of infected kittens is also a potent source of infection. Adult cats do not pose the same hazard, with less than 1 percent shedding the infective oocysts in their faeces.

Due to the risks to the unborn child, non-immune pregnant women need to take especial care when handling raw meat or the cat litter tray. Wearing rubber gloves and using hot water sterilisation of surfaces is a good idea. More detailed advice is available from doctors and libraries.

While it is helpful to know of potential hazards there is no need to panic. Surveys of dogs in Western Europe revealed a picture of high exposure but low prevalence of clinical disease.[30] In some human populations 'up to 90 percent of individuals have serological evidence of previous exposure', but clinical disease is rare.[31] Future monitoring will be necessary but, on current evidence, raw meaty bone feeding does not create unacceptable risks of toxoplasmosis.

Sarcocystis

Sarcocystis species are protozoans which occur as cysts of varying size in meat and when consumed by carnivores undergo the remainder of their life cycle in the intestinal wall. Dogs and cats do not appear to suffer disease consequences but humans handling infected raw beef or pork may be affected. Once again the usual hygiene recommendations apply.[32]

Neospora

Neospora caninum is another protozoan which is only slowly becoming recognised as a parasite of cats, dogs and cattle. In California there is evidence of widespread infection in dairy cows.[33] The main problems associated with Neospora in cats and dogs is abortion and progressive paralysis in kittens and puppies. Current opinions indicate that the female consumes infected meat and then transmits the infection to the foetuses in the uterus.

In early 1998 Bernstein, a Florida veterinarian, researched the available evidence on Neospora. He found a low incidence of reported disease and concluded that freezing meat was the best way to eliminate the parasite and at the same time preserve the nutrient benefits of fresh meat.[34]

Worms

As a school student I was fascinated by the preserved worms on display in the biology lab. Spaghetti-like round worms scarcely had room to move in their watery tomb. Tapeworms developed lifelike undulations as their bottle was rotated — which added to the mystery. If the exhibits had a ghostly air of unreality the facts behind their existence only served to heighten that unreality.

To my schoolboy mind it seemed extraordinary that these creatures could spend their adult life lying in the intestines of humans and other animals. Apart from the fact that they could resist the digestive juices they also had to resist being ejected along with the faeces. More extraordinary were the reproductive cycles, especially those of the tapeworms. In most cases, we were told, worm eggs are passed in the faeces which under the influence of sun and wind turns to dust. In this way the eggs are scattered over a wide area. Some eggs settle on grass consumed by herbivores and thus find their way into the intestines of their intermediate host. In the warm watery environment the eggs hatch and the larvae make their way to the muscles of the host. There, encysted, the larvae quietly wait for the host to be eaten.

In the case of the beef tapeworm we were told how millions of people throughout the world are infected by eating undercooked beef and the meat of other herbivores.[35] The pork tapeworm, as the name implies, is contracted by people eating worm cysts buried in under-cooked pork. This same tapeworm sometimes lodges in humans as the intermediate host. If these cysts lodge in the brain, serious effects, including death, can occur. My veterinary textbook says 300,000 Latin Americans are affected annually and that a survey revealed that about 2 percent of Mexicans are infected.[36]

The message is clear. If carnivores, including dogs and cats, eat their natural raw diet of meat, fish and bones they will be likely to contract parasitic tapeworms. Some round worms can also be transmitted to cats and dogs via small rodents. However in the domestic situation there is no cause for alarm. Raw meaty bones cleared for human consumption contain few if any worm cysts. Similarly, low numbers of adult worms do not create health problems for carnivores. The few worms that do develop can be controlled by regular use of modern anthelmintics (worming medicines). And daily removal of faeces helps to limit the spread of worm eggs.

There is one important exception, involving the hydatid tapeworm, which necessitates extra precautions.

Hydatid tapeworm

The hydatid tapeworm *Echinococcus granulosus* needs to be singled out for special consideration, not because of its effects on pets but because of the dangers for humans.

The adult worms are tiny, measuring only 2-7mm, and live in the intestines of domestic dogs, dingoes, wolves, coyotes, jackals and foxes.[37] In common with other tapeworms the eggs are passed in the faeces and scattered on the herbage. If those eggs are eaten by a suitable intermediate host the larvae proceed to the lungs or liver and occasionally other organs where they encyst. The cycle is completed when a carnivore eats the internal organs of an intermediate host and thereby ingests the hydatid cyst — hydatid cysts rarely occur in muscle meat.

Depending on geography the worm is adapted to different primary and secondary hosts. In Australia and the United Kingdom dogs are usually the primary and sheep the secondary hosts. Other strains include a wolf/moose strain in North America, dingo/wallaby strain in Australia, coyote/deer in California and fox/hare in Argentina. Providing the worm stays in those hosts there are few problems. The situation changes radically if the worm eggs find their way into a human and develop into a hydatid cyst. Such cysts can grow to enormous size and if located in an important organ, such as the heart or brain, the consequences can be fatal.

The question then arises, how do the worm eggs get into a human? The answer is that they mostly come from an infected domestic dog. The eggs are slightly sticky and adhere to the coat of the dog. Transfer to a human, more commonly a child, occurs if the dog licks itself and then the person. Alternatively petting the dog and then handling food or sucking fingers achieves the same outcome.

How do domestic dogs become infected? Not by eating raw meaty bones purchased from the butcher — meat passed for human consumption poses little or no threat. They become infected by scavenging on sheep and wallaby carcasses found dead in the paddock. Some farmers slaughter sheep for home consumption without checking the offal for signs of hydatid cysts.[38] If infected offal is fed to farm dogs, or city dogs spending time on the farm, then they will become infected. Generally however hydatid problems are restricted to rural dogs living in well-known rural areas. Veterinarians living in those rural areas are the best source of advice, for farm dogs and visitors, regarding prevention and treatment of hydatid disease.

Bogus problems

Most problems involving natural food feeding have negligible impact and when measured against the benefits recede into insignificance. For the artificial pet food industry the reverse is true — natural food feeding poses a threat to the viability of the industry. As a tactical response the industry erect imaginary obstacles which they hope will deter pet owners from forsaking their artificial products. In 1993 a television program looked at the benefits of natural food feeding and sought comment from the pet food industry. A veterinary spokesperson raised a series of objections, which were then referred to me for response.[39] The following table briefly summarises the points made.

OBJECTIONS RAISED	VALIDITY	RESPONSE
1. Natural food feeding is impractical.	False	Modern distribution and refrigeration make natural feeding easy.
2. Dietary imbalance problems will occur.	False	Chemical imbalance occurs today as before — when owners resort to home-cooked diets. Better education will enable us to eliminate imbalances.
3. It costs more.	False	Depending on source it usually costs less.
4. Some processed foods assist with dental hygiene.	Dubious benefit	Raw bone diet far outstrips biscuits and raw hide chews for dogs. Dry food exacerbates cat dental problems.
5. Only a couple of bones need to be given weekly.	False	Consumption of bones is a powerful cleanser of teeth. Plaque and calculus are active between times.
6. Short-nosed breeds cannot handle bones.	False	Started from a young age they soon learn. Given their predisposition to dental disease their need for prevention is greater. Short-nosed breeds are in the minority — why hinge any argument on the minority case.
7. Physically impossible for some breeds.	False	The short-nosed breeds were genetically selected over hundreds of years of natural food feeding.
8. Little research has been done to justify natural feeding.	False	Evolution is an ongoing experiment.

OBJECTIONS RAISED	VALIDITY	RESPONSE
9. Dogs live longer and have higher pedigree and therefore cannot cope.	False	Old pedigree dogs surviving a lifetime without bones become addicted to the wrong food and usually suffer painful mouth conditions making chewing difficult. There may be breed dispositions to problems but none documented.
10. Bones get stuck in the teeth.	Seldom occurs	An animal practised in handling the correct style of bone has little difficulty.
11. Teeth get broken.	Seldom occurs	Any system in use can become damaged. All systems require suitable exercise. Inappropriate bone (e.g. ox marrow bone) most likely to inflict damage.
12. Constipation is a problem.	Seldom occurs	Dogs accustomed to bones have regular, firm stools of powdered bone. Bones fed infrequently in large quantity can give rise to excessively dry stools. It is cooked, sharp indigestible bones which are mostly associated with bowel problems.
13. 'Complete' diet is impossible (i.e. chemically complete).	False	Natural diets readily meet complete *physical* and *chemical* needs.
14. Nutritional disease will become common.	False	Removing animals' processed 'complete' diets and putting them on natural diets has always resulted in increased health.

OBJECTIONS RAISED	VALIDITY	RESPONSE
15. Deficiencies are bound to show up.	Unlikely	Processed foods have been implicated in most direct deficiency states, e.g. taurine, arachidonic acid. In the unlikely event that a deficiency is detected then appropriate action can be taken.
16. Excess nutrient disorders will occur.	Unlikely	Carnivores can process limitless quantities of bone. Many processed foods have excess salt and protein as judged by their own standards.
17. Table scraps are no better than canned or dried food.	False	Scraps are cheap (free to user) and less highly processed, even raw. It is true they do not massage teeth and gums.
18. Raw bones and scraps are not a viable alternative.	False	They are available, moderately priced and health giving.
19. Legal implications of advising raw bones may be a concern.	False	It's nonsensical to suppose that recommending a natural diet would carry legal penalties. Advising use of processed food giving rise to dental and systemic disease is much more likely to invite legal action. (And pet food companies themselves recommend raw bones.)

Securing the benefits

Since I cannot be with you at your pets' feeding time I offer this chapter (in particular) as guidance. Some of the best things in life — skiing, marriage and motor car transport — are best enjoyed by taking account of the risks as well as the benefits. The same pertains to the natural feeding of pets. When you progress beyond the novice stage you may not need assistance, but until then you may like to keep this book handy.

9

The bite on veterinary dentistry

In the bad old days dentists had a reputation for drilling, filling and billing. I know because as a British post-war baby growing up in the fifties and sixties I suffered the pain and taste of rotten teeth. In fact my sisters and I were well known to the dentist and we each have a mouth full of fillings to prove it. Never once do I remember him commenting on a suitable diet or the need for preventive brushing and flossing. Now forty years later children enjoy good dental health with fewer visits to the dentist. Reduced health care costs benefit the community and the dental profession has shrunk — in size but not in stature.

So what differs between then and now? Sugary diets are much the same and the dentist's drill still makes the familiar whine. At one level the answer would be fluoridation of the water supply, along with increased awareness of the benefits of brushing and flossing. With these changes dental caries has become a rarity and gum disease, though still prevalent, is lessened. But such an answer, while true, overlooks what I believe to be the essential difference, namely the *committed change in attitude* by the dental profession. Guided by their conscience dentists recognised that *prevention*, not treatment or their own financial interest, should govern their approach. In 1996 Patrick Dalton, President of the Australian Dental Association, looked back over the preceding few decades with justifiable pride:

> Our focus has always been prevention rather than treatment. In many instances treatment indicates failure of prevention. The dental profession is a very visible leader among the health professions in the philosophy and practice of prevention. While the major battles for fluoridation may not be remembered by

the younger members there are many who remember the long, and at times, bitter fights in the public forum and in local government to achieve this positive proven benefit.[1]

So ingrained is this preventive approach that Kevin Gillings writing in the *Australian Dental Association Bulletin* stated: 'The goal of all dentistry should be prevention.'[2] He reminded his readers that *time* should be added to the traditional factors of *tooth*, *bacteria* and *food* which regulate tooth decay and periodontal disease. He then described his sixteen point program for boosting patients' dental health.

> Guided by their conscience dentists recognised that *prevention,* not treatment or their own financial interest, should govern their approach.

Both chemical and physical aspects of food receive regular mention in dental health promotion literature. In 1995 the Australian Dental Association made 'Good Food, Great Teeth' their slogan for Dental Health Week.[3] Besides advocating the benefits of raw natural food, the campaign specifically targeted the adverse effects of junk food for schoolchildren and the hazards of sugary drinks for nursing infants. Progressively, such messages hit home, with resultant decrease in need for dental treatment. Dentists continue to accentuate prevention. They may supplement their income with the sale of toothbrushes and dental floss but never packaged junk food.

Veterinary preventive dentistry

The slogan 'Good Food, Great Teeth' is especially apt for our pet carnivores. Eating good food was the only avenue to dental health throughout the long evolutionary process. Now, despite the diversity of pet shapes and modern technological know-how, the physical form of the food is just as important as before. Dr Peter Higgins, veterinary adviser to Uncle Ben's, admits: 'It is ironic that preventative dentistry towards the end of the 20th century is based on what dogs and cats found in nature thousands of years ago.'[4]

Just as human dentists are concerned for the welfare of nursing infants we need to consider the needs of young kittens and puppies. Commencing at two to six weeks of age all of the deciduous teeth erupt through the gums. This physiological upheaval gives rise to pain and inflammation. In an attempt to gain relief kittens and puppies often resort to chewing old slippers, fabric or wooden furniture. Raw meaty bones provide a more effective teething aid.

Commencing at about three weeks of age large pieces of chicken or rabbit or similar should be offered. At first kittens and puppies mouth the food, but soon learn how to shear the tough meat off the hard bone. The fibrous tendons floss between the teeth which become anchored tight in their sockets. Gnawing on bone requires effort and the neck and jaw muscles strengthen accordingly. An important feature of this early education is that the young animal learns how to deal with natural food without choking.

By about six weeks of age kittens and puppies can crunch their way through meaty bones of appropriate size. This coincides with their increased need for calcium and provides vigorous cleaning of the oral cavity. Between four and six months of age the animal's immune system is still immature and the passive immunity gained from the mother's milk starts to wane. Simultaneously temporary teeth are shed as the permanent dentition erupt. Vigorous chewing on natural food helps dislodge deciduous teeth and heal damaged gums.

Once the permanent teeth are established and gums have healed there is an ongoing need for cleaning and massage. Providing that the daily food supply is fed in one large piece (smaller pieces require less chewing and predispose to choking) this should provide sufficient quality, quantity and frequency of cleaning for most pets.

There is one important exception. Domestic pets do not kill their food and as a consequence do not use their canine teeth. During the gnawing and chewing action pets actively shield their canine teeth from abrasive forces. Negligible cleaning occurs as a result of salivary flow and movement of lips and tongue, with the net result that plaque accumulates. Fortunately the canine teeth in dogs are the easiest to inspect and clean with a toothbrush or old wet rag. (Calculus deposits can be scraped with a teaspoon.) For these reasons I recommend that dog owners clean the outer surface of their pets' canine teeth regularly. Daily would be best, but once weekly is better than not at all. Attention should be directed at the gum margin where plaque does most damage and where small hairs can become trapped.

Cats seldom cooperate with toothbrushing, but providing they eat an adequate diet they do not suffer major problems with their canine teeth. Nevertheless occasional rubbing of the canines with a moist rag can be of benefit. (Try to avoid being bitten or scratched.)

Primary dental treatment

Just as diet is the best preventive it is also the best first line treatment for oral disease. Plaque build up, sore and bleeding gums and even calculus accumulation can be resolved with a few meals of raw meaty bones. Owners frequently remark how the breath and vitality of their pets improve in response to a change of diet. Human dentists employ the same reasoning when embarking on the early treatment of inflamed gums. The Dental Health Foundation of the University of Sydney recommends the use of toothbrushing and flossing to cure gingivitis:

> Gingivitis can be cured in about four or five days. The secret is to clean the bleeding gums more, not less. This tends to run counter to normal medical advice for other bleeding areas on the body… On the first day the gums will bleed and feel sore. The second day the gums will bleed more and feel even sorer. The same thing will happen on the third day, by which stage you may be saying that the whole treatment is madness and you may be thinking of giving up. Do not! By about the fourth or fifth day the gums will start to feel better and become firmer and healthier.[5]

Of course, not all dental disease is easily resolved. Pet dentistry is now a boom industry and a few comments are appropriate.

Secondary dental treatment

The need for dental treatment almost always implies a failure of prevention. Since the majority of pets fed processed food are in need of treatment we face a multifaceted problem.

Dogs and cats do not make good dental patients. Even when suffering from advanced oral disease there may be no outward signs. Such behaviour in wild carnivores has survival value — to display signs of weakness is to invite ostracism or worse. Occasionally pet owners report on their observations. Perhaps the pet has cried in pain, drooled saliva or appeared to suffer problems when eating. Such information can help, but there is no substitute for a thorough inspection.

With experience it becomes possible to assess the majority of conscious patients. The smell of the breath and sight of gums, teeth and tongue all tell a story. If there is obvious danger to patient and handlers, or lingering uncertainty, then a decision needs to be made regarding inspection under general anaesthesia. Apart from safety considerations a general anaesthetic provides opportunity for treatment once the inspection has been completed. Prior to commencement veterinarians need to estimate likely costs and gain owner approval for the removal of diseased teeth.

The need for dental treatment almost always implies a failure of prevention.

Human dentists employ a variety of subtle tests to detect advancing periodontal disease.[6] For people, preservation of a radiant smile is a high priority and accordingly efforts are expended in order to save teeth. For pets the situation differs. By the time the animal is presented for treatment, periodontal disease is often far advanced and seriously affecting the patient's general health. Restoration of function, not cosmetic effect, becomes the priority. Consequently those teeth which are likely to cause pain or continue to suffer from severe periodontal changes should be removed.

There are established criteria for diagnosing the severity of periodontal disease in dogs. Visual inspection and probing with a metal probe usually provide sufficient evidence; occasionally X-ray examination is necessary. Cats are more difficult to assess. Sometimes swollen gums obscure tooth root problems. At other times the gum grows over painful tooth neck lesions. Sometimes a cat's canine teeth appear to be growing longer, a condition known as super-eruption. In fact the combined effect of gum recession and ejection of the tooth gives the false impression of increased length.

When dealing with difficult cases it is best not to seek to achieve too much at once. It can be beneficial to remove the worst teeth, clean the others and then re-evaluate on a regular basis. Sometimes several bouts of surgery are required to fully resolve problems. And of course it is wise to bear in mind that pets do not complain when they have toothache, and continue to suffer in silence. Similarly they cannot be instructed to pay careful attention to the cleaning needs of a lone tooth. This puts the onus back on the veterinarian to do the best for the pet. Since the pet's overall health is more important than a single tooth my motto is: 'If in doubt — take it out'.

Ongoing dental care is paramount, especially in pets which have had teeth extracted. The main tools at our disposal are raw bones, lots of raw bones. Just as puppies and kittens gain relief for sore gums from gnawing on bones, so do dental patients. I recommend that chicken carcasses be fed to most dental patients the day following surgery. For some cats I make an exception: for instance if dental work is a secondary consideration with a change in diet being the priority. These animals may not accept bones straight away and need to be coaxed with minced whole fish or minced chicken necks. Sometimes all or nearly all of the teeth need to be removed from a cat. Lacking teeth a cat cannot gnaw bones so whole minced fish or chicken carcasses/necks/wings, including the bones, should be fed. No teeth means no need for cleaning, but the diet should provide the chemicals found in carcasses or raw meaty bones plus a few table scraps.

Dogs seem to do well even with few teeth with which to chew. Somehow they are able to employ toughened gums for crunching chicken bones. When teeth stand isolated in gums or lack an opposing tooth in the other jaw the scissor action of chewing is lost. I advise owners that these teeth may require to be cleaned by brushing. Commonly there is a steady deterioration in the gums around isolated teeth which necessitates periodic checkups and dental scaling under anaesthesia.

After successfully providing long-term treatment for hundreds of dental patients I can confidently recommend the two-phase salvage effort. First, calculus-encrusted teeth should be cleaned and any teeth that are diseased or cannot perform a useful function should be removed. Then start a more natural diet comprising carcasses, raw meaty bones and table scraps. Although this is the best available option for periodontal disease affected animals, I always remark to owners that it really represents failure. I emphasise the need for future generations of cats and dogs to be raised on natural food and thus avoid unnecessary suffering and expense — owners agree.

A word to vets and pet owners

Pet owners seldom consult veterinarians for dietary or dental advice — yet a sound natural diet and healthy teeth are priority issues for every patient. The secret, therefore, is for veterinarians to mention dietary and dental requirements at each consultation — which I can assure you is easier said than done.

In an environment of increasing malpractice litigation watched over by veterinary authorities the risks for veterinarians are many. Pet owners are justifiably wary regarding overservicing and on their guard against advice and treatments for which they see no purpose. Even if advice is provided at no cost, clients may feel uneasy. Why would someone spend slabs of professional time promoting concepts which are claimed to increase health and reduce business? Why indeed? As we shall see later, many veterinarians don't consider suggesting a natural diet as the pathway to dental health. Others, who are aware of the benefits, may be less than enthusiastic when promoting those benefits.

> **Pet owners are justifiably wary regarding overservicing and on their guard against advice and treatments for which they see no purpose.**

If, however, veterinarians are to honour the first rule of medicine, 'Do no harm', and give full weight to the dictum 'An ounce of prevention is worth a ton of cure' they are duty bound to provide full and honest advice. In the first instance this entails informing themselves of priorities and then making arrangements to deliver on those priorities. False or misleading advertisements — telephone 'on hold' messages, posters and product displays — must be culled. In their stead various teaching aids, books, posters and videos can assist veterinarians to communicate the prevention message. But since misunderstandings can occur, and in keeping with the prevention ethic, veterinarians need adequate malpractice insurance.

'Accessibility, accountability and transparency are expected of every self regulating profession' intones the Royal College of Veterinary Surgeons.[7] Thus it seems a good idea for vets to acknowledge, even apologise for, past misleading dietary and dental advice. In negotiating these awkward u-turns I have found such confessions help to clear the air and build trust between veterinarian and client. In a trusting environment each consultation provides a further opportunity to monitor a pet's overall health and promote a healthy diet.

Puppy and kitten, first vaccination

Pet owners have become accustomed to attending the veterinary hospital with their new pet for vaccinations and worming. Most owners have an expectation that a commercial diet will be mentioned, even promoted, during the consultation. Gums and teeth are invariably assumed to be healthy. The reality for many six-week-old puppies and kittens is that their breath already stinks and lifelong periodontal disease is under way. By inviting the owner to sniff the pet's breath the consulting veterinarian can introduce the vital aspects of a more natural diet and preventive dental care.

Puppy and kitten, second vaccination

Puppies and kittens, at twelve weeks of age, frequently have accretions of calculus on their premolar teeth. Young animals are easy to restrain while calculus is scraped away. I explain to owners that manual scraping is an imperfect means of removing calculus but that ongoing daily chewing of bones provides prevention.

Six months of age, neutering appointment

For many owners the first contact with a veterinary hospital occurs when their pet is neutered. By the time kittens and puppies have reached six months of age, and if they have been raised on processed food, their mouths reek. For the sake of the animal it is vital that this contact with the client be utilised to explain the significance of halitosis. If the client is receptive to good advice and a ready supply of natural food is available then those young animals can overcome their bad start in life.

Cats with moderate calculus presenting for any problem

The presenting problem should receive treatment and dietary changes should be initiated. Most cats permit tooth scaling while conscious, if restrained by an experienced assistant. Follow-up inspections allow the veterinarian to assess progress and make recommendations.

Dogs with moderate calculus presenting for any problem

I mention to clients that periodontal disease is a silent disease which frequently requires examination under anaesthesia. If the animal needs an anaesthetic for treatment of the presenting complaint then I offer dentistry at a further charge, but utilising the same anaesthetic.

If anaesthesia is not required, I treat the presenting complaint and recommend dietary changes and a return inspection in one to two months. If at the return inspection calculus persists I recommend full examination and treatment under anaesthetic.

Dogs and cats with moderate to severe periodontal disease presenting for another problem

I emphasise to owners the interrelationship of all disease processes. Pain relief and restoration of function should be our guiding principles and accordingly I establish a treatment protocol including dentistry and diet change. From the outset I advise that the patient has probably become addicted to harmful foods — comparable with a person's dependence on nicotine or alcohol. I advise that for cats the changing of dietary habits may prove difficult and may be better accomplished under supervision in the veterinary hospital.

The future of animals which have had teeth removed should not be left to chance. For some I recommend toothbrushing and for all I recommend regular six to twelve monthly rechecks.

Special groups — Persian cats, Pugs, Pekingese and Chihuahuas

'Flat-faced' breeds are predisposed to dental disease due to misshapen jaws, mouth breathing and the propensity of owners to treat them differently. I emphasise that cats and dogs with flat faces have carnivore physiology with an increased need for preventive dental hygiene. Regular checkups — and possibly toothbrushing — can help to maintain oral hygiene, but the mainstay remains a natural diet of carcasses or raw meaty bones.

Orthodontics, endodontics and false crowns

Elaborate dental treatments have little or no place in a preventive regime. The treatments are costly, time consuming and — except in rare instances — do not contribute to the health of the patient. Endodontic treatments in particular are highly suspect. They are usually performed on fractured teeth where plaque bacteria have already colonised the root canal and dentine tubules. The dentist reams out the root canal and plugs the cavity. Unfortunately bacteria still resident in the dentine tubules continue to pour toxins into the circulatory system.

In human endodontic surgery dentists estimate the failure rate at 5 to 10 percent of cases but they may be overly optimistic[8] — many patients suffer continued pain and abscess formation requiring repeated treatments. In veterinary dentistry the failure rate of endodontic treatment is higher, but often undetected. I recommend that dead, endodontically affected teeth should be removed. Jess, my own dog, had calculus accumulation on all teeth on one side. On close inspection I found a single broken tooth which inflicted pain, leading to failure to use that side of his mouth. I removed the tooth and all was well.

Periodically I have encountered dogs living a life of torture due to food-induced periodontal disease and multiple endodontic teeth. The connection between diet and periodontal disease is clear enough. The endodontic connection is indirect and involves the incisors and canines. As a result of the irritation of a dermatitis — most likely due to diet and periodontal disease — patients constantly nibble at their rump. The skin becomes thickened and the hair chewed away and in the process front teeth become worn to the pulp cavity. Multiple extractions and a change of diet are necessary to rescue these animals from their acute distress.

Boarding and grooming

Pets booked in for boarding or grooming are frequently assumed by their owners to be healthy. In my opinion it is a travesty if these animals spend time in a veterinary hospital and then leave without efforts being made to correct chronic dietary and dental problems — if veterinarians won't do something, who will?

Owners sometimes suspect my motives when I recommend extra services for their pet that's resident in the hospital. Similarly I am not at liberty to make diet changes and treat teeth without prior approval. Being denied the opportunity to help a pet while it resides under my direct care is one of the most distressing aspects of professional life.

Compound benefits: healthy pets and happy owners

There is something satisfying about a simple idea which spreads health and happiness. As a veterinarian it has been a privilege to communicate the natural feeding message and then watch that message proliferate throughout the community. For many people the experience of pet ownership assumes new meaning once they become attuned to the feeding of natural food. An enthusiast said in a letter:

Dear Tom   6 January 1996

I am writing to you and your associates on behalf of Cindy, who is a small terrier crossbreed. Since coming to see you, after finding your advertisement in the phone book, Cindy has been a very happy dog (although she may be a little too plump for her size).

At the time of our consultation, you advised me about the natural diet which you recommend to all dog owners. As soon as I brought Cindy home, I immediately gave all of her processed food away and bought a kilo of chicken wings. Cindy could hardly believe her nose, when she sniffed at her dinner. She lay down next to her bowl for a while and guarded her food from the birds (who always annoy her and try to steal pieces of her food); soon all I could hear was a crunching noise as she finished her wings in record time. Her usual 'My Dog' cat food size dinner was usually still in her bowl the following morning. Not so now; as soon as Cindy sees anyone opening the freezer, she expects that her wings will be forthcoming (a disappointment when the kids are getting the ice cream out).

I have also told my friends and family about the new ('old') way of feeding their dogs. It took a little convincing, but my sister-in-law was having so much trouble with her dog's waste practically filling their back yard, that she tried the bone diet and actually rang back to thank me for a happy dog and a much better back yard.

On behalf of   Cindy
                     Billy (Labrador)
                     Mitch (Spaniel)
                     Harry (Bull terrier)

(Who are now all happily munching on meaty bones and pleasing their owners by not making a huge mess in the back yard.)

THANK YOU.

Finding veterinary help in an artificial pet food world

Truth must out; eventually advocates of natural feeding and dental health will prevail. Meanwhile pet owners face a dilemma. How can they find good veterinary help in an artificial pet food world? Since I have no easy answers I would prefer to dodge the question. But reality dictates that pets need to visit the vet and I feel I should offer some guidance.

In our attempts to secure the future we should learn from past mistakes. And mistakes I have made aplenty. In the days when I advocated processed pet foods and was ignorant of pet dental needs the suffering of my patients would have been immense. At the same time my clients thought I did a good job, my patients didn't complain and I had a good opinion of my work. I now understand that appearances can be deceptive, and would like to pass on that awareness to owners. The suffering of Jane, a Labrador, provides a case study.

Jane's life spanned three careers. First she lived the life of a champion show dog — regular grooming, outings and ribbons. At three years she exchanged the parade ring for the halls of a retirement home. As canine companion to the old folks Jane was a firm favourite. But as she aged her popularity began to wane. Although only ten years of age Jane moved slowly and smelt bad, which the management reasoned must be signs of old age — they knew Jane received an approved diet and regular veterinary attention. Jane's future came under review. Of two options considered, euthanasia or finding Jane a new home, euthanasia seemed the more likely.

Mrs D heard of Jane's plight and offered to help. She guessed that Jane's infirmity was probably due to an artificial diet and poor dental health, not old age. Mrs D hoped that something could be done to halt Jane's decline, even restore her to health, and sought my advice. At our consultation Jane stood meekly, tail sagging under its own weight. Foul breath odours filled the air as I examined the patient and discussed alternatives. Mrs D, a trained nurse, and I speculated about the chances of irreversible organ damage due to the vile mouth and poor diet. To assist with our decisions we decided to obtain the previous medical record and commission some blood tests.

Within a couple of days the test results arrived. Although not a dependable guide, the results revealed a low white blood cell count, otherwise organ function appeared OK. Jane's medical record was comprehensive. As a Pets As Therapy dog she had been a regular patient at a well-known veterinary practice — sometimes for vomiting but mostly for routine checkups. According to the record Jane's diet had been canned and dry food. Over the years several veterinarians had added to the record but until the final entry never a mention of teeth. 'General health good other than some tartar developing on teeth' remarked a young veterinarian. Four months later Jane's life hung in the balance.

On the evidence Mrs D and I believed that Jane's ill health was primarily attributable to periodontal disease — there could have been other underlying and undetectable problems too. It seemed to us worth taking a gamble that dentistry would do the trick. We scheduled an

appointment and as a precaution against misunderstandings arranged
for the surgery to be filmed. At the final count I extracted twenty-one
teeth. One tooth had already fallen out, leaving Jane with twenty
remaining teeth. On her new diet of chicken carcasses and table scraps
Jane made good progress, her gums healed and white cell count
returned to normal. As a happy family pet her third career lasted a
further twenty months until pancreatic cancer claimed her life.

If Jane's story helps others then perhaps her suffering will not have
been in vain. But some things never change. Animals will always be
dependent on us and owners are vulnerable — without specialist
training they encounter difficulty assessing the validity of veterinary
pronouncements. Accordingly the onus remains on veterinarians.
When they say diet and dental health are good, the statement needs to
be true and their inaction justified. When choosing action it also needs
to be justified in keeping with the need to 'cure sometimes, relieve often,
and comfort always' — the fundamental purpose of medicine.[9] The
following case, I believe, illustrates how this purpose can go awry.

Lassie the TV series chronicled the adventures of a rough collie,
the attractive breed with the long sharp nose and wavy hair. Mr Y
found a stray Lassie dog wandering in his neighbourhood. A perfect
pet, he thought. But before taking the stray home he called at the
veterinary surgery for some advice. I was glad to oblige and began
examining the stray. A multitude of ailments can hide under a fur
coat; the thicker the fur the more elusive the clues. For this reason I
depend upon information gained from an open mouth. My left hand
saddled on the muzzle, I confidently reached for the lower jaw —
Lassie dogs are generally docile and seldom bite.

After several fumbled attempts I opened the mouth. A foul stench
wafted over the writhing tongue which seemed large and misshapen.
Eyes wide I tried to understand what I saw — perception depends on
expectations, which depend on prior experience. I had no experience
of this. One long mandible floated freely — the other had been
surgically removed, probably for treatment of cancer — all teeth were
calculus encrusted and covered with slime. A 'can do' surgeon had
followed recommendations contained in the textbooks, but his patient
was left with the aftermath. I released my hold as the jaw swung back

into position, teeth pressing into pits in the roof of the mouth.

I explained to Mr Y that one jaw floating freely could not function properly. Without the scissor cleaning action all teeth were affected by raging periodontal disease and the patient was condemned to perpetual torment. Euthanasia might be the kindest option, I suggested, but since the dog was a stray he should go to the pound. I regret not knowing subsequent events. But I do know that millions of pets, affected by diet and dental ill health, endure a lifelong series of interventions straight from the veterinary textbooks. Only in death do they find a merciful escape.

Holistic and alternative veterinary therapies

An army of practitioners now proclaim the benefits of holistic and alternative veterinary therapies, which on the evidence, often appear to work. But without going into the intricacies of Bach flower remedies and iris maps, the main reason for improvement appears to be a con-current change in diet. By advising against commercial foods, holistic and alternative therapists ensure removal of a range of toxins from their patients' diet. Unfortunately, many practitioners then peddle supplements to which they attribute all manner of magical powers. As a Colorado veterinary student lamented:

By advising against commercial foods, holistic and alternative therapists ensure removal of a range of toxins from their patients' diet.

> I am committed to feeding my dogs fresh foods, but I am not sure how or what. Most advocates of fresh food diets for dogs who I have read or spoken to recommend the feeding of homogenous, supplemented stews: raw meat mixed with grains and vegetables, and supplements.[10]

Some veterinarians advocate the mincing and cooking of food in the kitchen, others sell 'Premium (Natural) Pet Foods' manufactured in a factory. In either case the food is processed. The distortion is worsened when veterinarians identify natural pet foods as 'premium foods that do not contain artificial ingredients or preservatives'.[11] Manufacturers of the so-called natural pet foods make outlandish claims which, judging by the sales figures, many pet owners believe. These beliefs may give owners a sense of security but no comfort for their pets. When pets demonstrate signs of ill health, instead of advising dental care and a diet based on carcasses or raw meaty bones, many holistic practitioners prescribe oriental herbs.

Conventional veterinary dentistry

In the late 1980s conventional veterinary dentistry was touted as a money spinner with many practitioners rushing to capitalise on the epidemic of dental disease. Members of the Raw Meaty Bone Lobby took a different view and by the early 1990s were in open rebellion. Earning an income for legitimate services cannot be faulted. But to sell or recommend harmful substances which create dental ill health and then to sell what are, for the most part, ineffectual dental services offends against common decency. In December 1991 Breck Muir wrote in the *Australian Veterinary Association News*:

> The pet food situation has concerned me for some years, my feelings brought to this by the current competitive marketing of various dental work stations for veterinary use… Here we have the perfectly engineered commercial circle — a problem doesn't exist, so we create one, and then come up with all the remedial treatments.[12]

Many conventional veterinary dentists carried on regardless. Some holistic veterinarians expressed concerns. Dr Susan Wynn remarked: 'Since it is preferable to avoid anesthetic procedures wherever possible, preventive measures are particularly important.'[13] Dr Wynn recommended that pets be fed 'a treat of "chunk" meat once or twice weekly' — which seems a somewhat limited measure. Even pet food companies acknowledge the benefits of raw bones.

Dental prophys

Dental 'prophys' — deriving from prophylaxis, meaning preventive treatment of disease — form the corner stone of conventional veterinary dental treatments. According to Dr Ben Colmery:

> Professional dental prophylaxis involves four stages of equal importance. The first stage involves scaling the crowns and removing the chunks of calculus and plaque. In the second stage we clean subgingivally. Concurrently, in the third stage we curette [scrape] the soft tissue and root plane [the tooth roots] with the same instrument. Crown polishing is the final stage.[14]

In my view dental prophylaxis — unless a first stage treatment in combination with diet change — equals a mechanised abomination in modern veterinary practice. Some veterinarians perform prophys if and when they detect signs of dental disease — remember Jane the Labrador whose needs were never detected by a succession of vets. Others stage cut-price specials where owners are encouraged to drop their animals at the hospital for production line dentistry. Still others schedule their patients to attend the clinic on a recurring six-monthly basis on the assumption that dental treatment will be required. Oftentimes it is not a veterinarian but veterinary technician or nurse who performs the prophy.

Immediately after the prophy — if calculus and loose teeth have been removed — the patient may experience fleeting benefit. But sadly the prophy is often inadequately performed. Since owners generally disapprove of teeth being removed, many technicians take pride in preserving teeth in gums — regardless of the continuing adverse effects of those teeth. Patients enter the veterinary hospital with a putrid mouth full of loose, tartar-encrusted teeth. After enduring mechanised cleaning under general anaesthetic the patients are discharged with polished but still loose teeth. In recognition that plaque reforms within minutes of the prophy, conventional veterinarians place emphasis on 'homecare' — a euphemism for toothbrushing, mouthwashes and supposed tartar control diets.

Dental homecare

Some veterinarians are slow to acknowledge the benefits of nature's toothbrush — raw meaty bones. Instead their shelves are crowded with pet toothbrushes, dentifrice, breath deodorisers and other traps for the consumer dollar. Colin Harvey, a professor of veterinary dentistry, says:

> Each of the techniques ... is somewhat effective. By combining several of these approaches (periodic brushing, application of an anti-plaque agent, playing with the dog using a chew toy, feeding rawhides and biscuits as treats following the brushing sequence), individual effectiveness of each technique can be maximised while creating a non-stressful (even fun!) interaction between the animal and the owner.[15]

Brushing the outside of the canine teeth of dogs and cats may have merit. These teeth are reasonably accessible and can be brushed or rubbed with an old cloth. Otherwise toothbrushing (with rare exceptions) is generally impractical and doomed to failure. In fact it seems reckless to encourage people to undertake an activity which is potentially dangerous for themselves and their pet, yet with the prospect of little net gain. In order to experience the limitations may I suggest that you try brushing a friend's teeth. Then reciprocate and let your friend hold your nose and brush your teeth while you snarl, scratch and bite. Please don't overact, for the consequences could be severe. I doubt that either of you will want more than one session to convince you that brushing the teeth of dogs, cats or friends is not a worthwhile activity.

During the transition phase to more natural feeding of pets, owners will have to make difficult decisions.

Caveat emptor

During the transition phase to more natural feeding of pets, owners will have to make difficult decisions. Will they continue to patronise those vets who sell artificial food and promote six-monthly dental prophys or will they look elsewhere?

Much will depend on individual situations, including the willingness of veterinarians to reject the old failed methods. My hope is that veterinarians and owners will forge a new alliance in the interests of pets — and the sooner the better.

PART II

OF, BY AND FOR
THE INDUSTRY

10

————— ❧ —————

Misdirected science

Communication across the revolutionary divide is inevitably partial.

THOMAS KUHN [1]

You may be wondering at the incongruity that science can put a man on the moon but cannot resolve the question of how to feed pets. Is it science itself or the usage made of science that creates the problem? My short answer would be that science is often lopsided and performed badly. For veterinary science matters are made worse by the ties, both subtle and not so subtle, that bind it to the artificial pet food industry.

Others have voiced criticism. J E Lovelock FRS, author of the Gaia Hypothesis, says: 'Science has taken over from religion and it has become a rather corrupt church. It's in its mediaeval theological phase.'[2] At a rather different level veterinarian Dr Jon Lumley suggested: 'You do not need a postgraduate degree in nutrition to evaluate the effects of raw bones on a dog's dentition — in fact, it appears that the qualification would be a serious disadvantage!'[3] If some science is fundamentally flawed then in part this may be due to uncertainties surrounding scientific methodology. Nobel prizewinner Sir Peter Medawar commented:

> Ask a scientist what he conceives the scientific method to be and he will adopt an expression that is at once solemn and shifty-eyed, solemn because he feels he ought to declare an opinion, shifty-eyed because he is wondering how to conceal the fact that he has no opinion to declare. If taunted he would probably

mumble something about 'induction' and 'establishing the laws of nature', but if anyone working in a laboratory professed to be trying to establish the laws of nature by induction we should begin to think he was overdue for leave.[4]

> '**Science has taken over from religion and it has become a rather corrupt church. It's in its mediaeval theological phase.**' *J E Lovelock FRS*

And this statement points up yet another problem. Scientists themselves will need to bring about changes. But if they remain uncertain of their methods and objectives they remain hampered in their ability to evaluate and improve their performance. Philosophers of science have had more success analysing scientific method. Thomas Kuhn, author of *The Structure of Scientific Revolutions,* showed that:

> Science is not the steady, cumulative acquisition of knowledge that is portrayed in the textbooks. Rather, it is a series of peaceful interludes punctuated by intellectually violent revolutions ... in each of which one conceptual world view is replaced by another...[5]

During peaceful interludes scientists perform tasks within a framework which Kuhn described as a paradigm; which taken literally means pattern. However he had in mind a more elaborate meaning, encompassing specific achievements of a given science and the problems and range of solutions available to that scientific discipline.[6] Those inducted into the discipline come to accept and defend the world view held by the discipline despite the arbitrariness of personal and historical accidents which inform that view.

At the inception of a new paradigm new findings fit relatively easily into the framework but, as the paradigm reaches the limits of its potential, difficulties arise. Scientists at first tend to ignore inconsistencies and continue in dogged support of their world view. Alternatively they declare that information at variance with their paradigm belongs in another field of study.

In a curious way a paradigm's flaws enable scientists to make progress through increased ingenuity and determination — they try harder. Eventually, however, trying harder is not enough. Unexplained inconsistencies come to overwhelm the paradigm and it has to give way to a replacement. At this difficult time, equating to a revolution, the new paradigm provides for a reinterpretation of existing 'facts' plus additional explanatory powers. New paradigms come with new language and new uses for existing language such that many incoherent battles ensue. In veterinary science three dominant paradigms guide research and practice and each is under threat.

Germ theory paradigm

The evolution of the germ theory of disease provides an example of the pattern of events typical of a scientific paradigm. There can be no doubting that this theory, developed in the last years of the 19th century, has been of immense benefit to us all. In the beginning Frenchman Louis Pasteur and German physician Robert Koch encountered opposition to their opinion that microbes were responsible for the epidemic and contagious diseases of their time. By means of technically simple but intellectually brilliant experiments they were able to persuade a doubting public of the veracity of their claims. Previously held views that disease developed spontaneously or was dependent on the weather or on other aspects of environmental change fell by the wayside.

Soon laboratories throughout the world were working full time on the subtleties of infectious disease. Joseph Lister's work on antiseptics was validated by demonstration of bacteria in infected wounds. The benefits of good hygiene and sterilisation of instruments became accepted, and quarantine laws requiring isolation of the sick could be acted upon with an improved understanding. In almost every application the new science of microbiology seemed to hold sway. Vaccination against infectious disease became part of the new biotechnology and in 1928 penicillin was discovered by Alexander Fleming.

This new weapon against the microbial enemy heralded the development of more antibiotics. Early success was impressive and soon the medical and veterinary professions and their public came to depend upon the pharmaceutical industry's 'magic bullets'. In recent times the bullets have lost some of their shine. Newspaper reports speak about the emergence of resistance as the microbes evolve chemical defences to the antibiotics. And while the antibiotics fail to kill harmful bacteria they continue to harm the body's beneficial microbial populations. In the absence of helpful bacteria, yeasts, fungi and super-resistant bacteria come to predominate.

While these problems seem to be of the modern age it is more a case that the problems are only now being recognised. Where the germ theory accentuated the importance of microbes, a new realisation now emerges. The patient's physiology, age, sex, nutrition and previous exposure — aspects of the environment — are of equal significance. Ironically Louis Pasteur, the originator of the germ theory, while on his deathbed, reportedly said: 'The terrain is more important than the germ'.[7] Considering the breadth of the terrain that influences bacterial disease, it is remarkable that the germ theory has enjoyed such success. But this again serves to illustrate the power of paradigms, for even though the theory is flawed its exponents believed it with a passion and within its rigid confines were able to force the discovery of remarkable new information.

In the germ theory a disease is said to be of bacterial origin if it 'fulfils Koch's postulates' — by which is meant:

- The micro-organism must be present in every case of the disease.
- The micro-organism must be isolated and cultivated in pure culture.
- Inoculation of such culture must produce the disease in susceptible animals.
- The micro-organism must be observed in and recovered from the experimentally infected animals.[8]

However, in most cases, fulfilment of the postulates requires a good deal of licence — scientists have been known to fudge the evidence and make approximations to support their case — and even with highly contagious diseases not all susceptible individuals succumb to infection. Koch's postulates, which used to be accepted with certainty, are now surrounded with doubt.

Abandoning or tempering the germ theory seems like heresy in light of past achievements but that is exactly what should now occur — an eclectic theory of disease can then arise. With the benefits of knowledge generated by the germ theory and with the aid of computer technology it is now possible to handle large volumes of information in a flexible format. Patterns of disease, health and suboptimal health can be obtained instead of the old rigid bipolar division — sickness and health.

Disease treatment paradigm

Conventional doctor/patient relationships have changed little over thousands of years. In all societies the medical man enjoys special status and patients are generally appreciative of the service provided. The framework of the relationship can be said to fulfil three conditions of a paradigm. First, there is a long history of achievements; some bordering on the miraculous where the sick have been healed. Second, the innumerable departures from health provide the particular medical profession with plenty of problems. Third, the profession has access to a number of solutions.

Although not exclusive, the main focus of the relationship is to treat existing ill health — usually end-stage disease. People consult a doctor, dentist or veterinarian when they perceive they have a problem. Theirs is a subjective assessment, but they expect that the medical person will employ objective means to arrive at a diagnosis and recommendation for treatment. Caught in this cycle of expectations the medical professions and patients have subscribed to the view that solutions are always available; it is just a matter of doing more tests with ever more sophisticated equipment. Similarly technology and the pharmaceutical industry can be relied upon to deliver increasingly sophisticated surgical and drug treatments.

Now, I don't wish to appear a Luddite and I am the first to consult a doctor when I am sick. However, I am concerned that this paradigm of techno-medicine so often fails to deliver the goods or indeed actively does harm. And I am far from alone in this view. In 1972 Archie Cochrane, a British medical researcher, published his book *Effectiveness and Efficiency* in which he drew attention to the lack of systematic reviews of current medical treatments (and preventive methods).

Cochrane Groups have since become established throughout the world, their systematic reviews often demonstrating that existing treatments are neither objective nor helpful.

Providing treatment, sometimes of questionable worth, but at the same time omitting preventive advice, characterises much of modern medicine. Some exceptions occur, for instance treatment of a cough coupled with advice on how to stop smoking. Direct, detailed advice on the promotion of good health is seldom provided. Occasionally doctors promote breast feeding for infants and healthy diets and exercise for adults. More commonly such advice is seen as part of another paradigm — a function of health education in schools and media rather than a matter for medical practitioners.

> **Providing treatment, sometimes of questionable worth, but at the same time omitting preventive advice, characterises much of modern medicine.**

As discussed in Chapter 9 the dental profession used to be locked into the same doctor/patient contract of providing treatment when the patient presented with a problem. Old-time dentists could point to their success in alleviating pain and obliterating cavities. They simply pulled those teeth which could not be filled — and the patients did not complain. Fortunately some dentists realised that passively responding to demands was not the best way to serve the interests of their patients. The concept that the need for treatment implies a failure of prevention enables dentists to shift focus and hence the greater preventive orientation of modern dentistry.

In the veterinary sphere there is no Cochrane Collaboration for the review of treatments. And we have no reason to believe that veterinary outcomes are better than those obtained by the medical profession. In response to requests from clients veterinarians employ ever more sophisticated diagnostic techniques leading to ever more expensive medical and surgical interventions. Students are taught at veterinary school to be resolute in pursuit of the most esoteric diagnoses. At the Sydney University Veterinary School a machine, for the diagnosis of rare heart disease affecting a handful of old animals, and costing half a million dollars, was installed. Meanwhile the students graduate with either wrong or misleading ideas regarding diet and dentistry affecting not some but all of their patients.

Pet owners caught in the treatment paradigm recount their veterinarian's heroic achievements. The story might involve mention of a four figure veterinary fee and a series of nasty afflictions of the skin, bowel and other organs. If you ask the owners about their pet's diet the answer may well involve a 'super premium' line of food sold by the veterinarian. On the subject of dentistry owners often recite veterinary advice to use a toothbrush. But the real needs of pets are not met by expensive treatments in the absence of effective preventatives. A new paradigm, emphasising prevention, would be a better option.

The accompanying box contrasts interpretations made by a veterinarian who subscribes to the existing treatment-based paradigm with interpretations made by a vet whose approach focuses on disease prevention and health promotion.

Question/Test	Observation	Orthodox Vet Attitude	Enlightened Vet Attitude
Presenting Signs and Owner Observations			
Tell me your problems	Sleeps a lot	Older dogs frequently do	Animals with chronic periodontal disease frequently do
	Restless sleeper — howls a lot	Ditto	Ditto
	Seems a bit stiff	Ditto	Ditto
	Seems bad tempered	Many cats are bad tempered	Cats with periodontal disease and 'neck' lesions suffer much pain
History Taking			
What diet do you feed?	Commercial 'complete and balanced' food	Excellent	That's a worry
Do you offer bones?	Large ox bones once a week	Good	That's a worry
Is your animal listless and slow?	Yes	Usual	That's a worry

Question/Test	Observation	Orthodox Vet Attitude	Enlightened Vet Attitude
Clinical Examination			
Cursory examination of mouth	Nothing noticed due to poor patient cooperation	All is probably OK	Visual observation yields partial information only
Sniff the breath	Rancid	This test not performed	That's usual, highly significant and likely to respond to dietary change
Skin/coat condition	Poor	That's usual	That's usual and likely to respond to dietary change
Abdomen shape	Flabby	Ditto	Ditto
Clinical Aids			
Thermometer	Temperature normal	That's OK	Thermometer seldom yields useful information in chronic disease
Stethoscope	Unremarkable	That's OK	Cardiac and pulmonary signs undetectable until too late to reverse
Clinical Pathology			
Haematology	Within reference range	That's OK	Reference range misleading
Biochemistry	Within reference range	That's OK	Frequently within the range until too late to effect change
Examination under Anaesthetic			
Oral	Apparently normal	That's OK	Periodontal disease is insidious and hard to detect— probing, tooth movements and gum shape are unreliable signs
Other	Apparently normal	That's OK	Conscious animals do not relate how they feel, anaesthetised animals reveal even less

Question/Test	Observation	Orthodox Vet Attitude	Enlightened Vet Attitude
X-rays			
Oral	Unremarkable	That's OK	Highly unreliable
Whole body	Unremarkable	That's OK	Collagen and other periodontal-induced diseases do not show up
Whole body	Heart, liver, kidney abnormalities detected	Needs treatment	Probable over-diagnosis of the problems — constant toxaemia from mouth likely chief problem
Diagnosis			
	None made	Leave as is	Change diet +? scale teeth
	Suspect bacterial disease	Antibiotic treatment trial	Antibiotic treatment trial + change of diet +? scale teeth
	Suspect immune problems	Steroid treatment trial	Steroid treatment + change diet +? scale teeth
Prognosis			
	Standard for age of animal	Will have recurrent problems	Will likely not see the patient for several years

Reductionist paradigm

Perhaps the most powerful and successful paradigm of science is reductionism — reducing complex problems to component parts. This approach is already over 300 years old and dates from the days of Descartes, who wrote:

> I consider the human body as a machine. My thought compares a sick man and an ill-made clock with my ideas of a healthy man and a well-made clock. I say that you consider these functions occur naturally in this machine solely by the disposition of its organs not less than the movement of a clock.[9]

In order to better understand the workings of this mechanistic world

Descartes resolved to:

> Divide each of the difficulties which I examined into as many
> parts as possible, and as might be necessary in order best to
> resolve them.[10]

Nowadays we fall into reductionist analysis to such a degree that it
seems not only the best but the only way of grappling with complex
issues. The other paradigms of scientific enquiry are built on this
foundation. For example, the germ theory, the disease treatment
paradigm and the information in this book can all be managed if
divided into bite-sized chunks. Early scientists reduced food to its
component parts, which they named proteins, fats and carbohydrates.
Further subdivision led to the discovery of amino acids (the sub-units
of proteins), fatty acids of fats and the sugar molecules which make up
carbohydrates.

But we need to take care with our reasoning as, like the other
paradigms, this one is also flawed. While the divisions may seem
logical to us they are in fact arbitrary. In nature there are no clearly
defined units. Protein exists in cells in close and intricate association
with water and a host of other chemicals. Cells exist in complex
interaction with their neighbours and with other cells at remote
locations via the nervous and circulatory system connections. By
imposing our labelling system on the disembodied parts we rob those
parts of their vital interconnectivity.

We saw an aspect of that in Chapter 4 where we examined the
folly of trying to reassemble a whole raw rabbit from what are
believed to be its component parts. In that case we saw that the whole
raw rabbit is more than the sum of its named chemical constituents.

Linear relationships

Other oft unstated assumptions bedevil the reductionist model of
scientific enquiry. One such assumption is that elements of complex
systems vary in direct proportion to one another in what is described
as a linear relationship. When plotted on a graph linear relationships
produce a straight line. In the laboratory where conditions can be

standardised it is possible to progressively add a known carcinogen, for example a food colourant, to rats' diets and then check the rate of increase in cancers during a six week period. But in the real world relationships are non-linear; things are not strictly proportional and continue much longer than six weeks. The same food colourant when fed to dogs will be consumed in widely varying proportions by old and young, sick and healthy, pregnant and non-pregnant animals over a lifetime. Not surprisingly, and should the investigation be carried out, there is no neat, straight line graph which captures the relationship of the chemical intake with the state of health of the animals — in the real world statistics are brought into play, but as we shall see they have major shortcomings too.

Belief in linearity infests all corners of scientific endeavour, and life in general as well. We often assume a big stimulus will give rise to a big outcome. For instance a billiard ball struck with great force travels further and faster than one just nudged by the cue. However, even in the mechanical world small events can lead to disproportionate outcomes — for instance lightly squeezing the trigger of a gun serves to propel a bullet at great speed. Greater force applied to the trigger does not increase the speed of the bullet. Medical researchers have studied the nexus between severe periodontal disease (a big stimulus) and heart disease and stroke — both 'big' outcomes. But perhaps mild or persistent periodontal disease has the same effect. Maybe it acts as a trigger which, combined with other factors, for instance stress and cholesterol, can give rise to severe systemic disease. To find the answer researchers will have to shelve assumptions and design complex experiments — not an easy task.

A particularly worrying aspect of the reductionist paradigm is the belief that life's intricacies are due to unidirectional causes which produce predictable effects.

Unidirectional causes

A particularly worrying aspect of the reductionist paradigm is the belief that life's intricacies are due to unidirectional causes which produce predictable effects. In the first instance we can say that influences are not unidirectional. As the quantum physicists showed, the electrons in an atom are each dependent upon the others for their precise location and movement. Similarly there are multiple feedback mechanisms regulating the internal environment of the mammalian cell, organ, body, family group and ecosystem. Instead of causality we should be speaking about connectedness of the constituent parts.

Of course if the word 'cause' is used to mean the most recent event in a series, or the trigger for a cascade of events, then the word can have some utility. Generally its use depends on the perspective of the observer. Commenting on an outbreak of food poisoning in an HIV AIDS community, an immunologist might implicate reduced white cell counts as being the cause of the problem. A bacteriologist might say the cause was a strain of salmonella bacteria, while a religious fundamentalist might say that the patients had sinned and thus caused their own downfall.

But gradually, as the utility of the reductionist paradigm is called into question, so is the concept of causality. The following quote from the World Cancer Research Fund sounds more like an apology than a statement of conviction:

> The concept of causation is used as a tool to understand the world and the way it works, without necessarily thinking about what 'cause' means. Causation is an *interpretation* placed on an *observed association of events.* The causal process can never be directly observed; it is always *inferred.* Scientists in any discipline, physical, chemical or biological, whether doing an active experiment or observing a natural system, *cannot absolutely prove causation,* and it is always possible that further research will produce evidence that changes conclusions. Nonetheless, *scientists can be more or less confident* of the causal interpretations that they place on associations observed as a result of research, *depending on its type and quality* [emphasis added].[11]

If you look at this quote — concentrating on the words in italics — you will see that the entire enterprise is a subjective venture surrounded by semantic constructs designed to preserve the world view of the scientists who populate the dominant field of endeavour.

The disclaimer at the end, *'depending on its type and quality'*, confirms that it is someone's arbitrary view that qualifies the suitability of the research and whether the so-called causes have any validity.

Niels Bohr, father of quantum theory, said in Chicago in 1933:

> We have been forced to recognise that we must modify not only all our concepts of classical physics but even the ideas we use in every day life... We have to renounce a description of phenomena based on the concept of cause and effect.[12]

Professor Alan Watts of the University of California echoed those sentiments when discussing the case of a cat passing a hole in a fence through which someone was looking. He posed the rhetorical question: Would it be fair to say ... since the cat's tail appeared after the head, that the head somehow caused the tail? Or alternatively, should the cat walk backwards past the hole, could the tail then be said to cause the head?[13]

Fortunately others are beginning to call into question the linear, reductionist, unidirectional, cause and effect model of scientific enquiry. *Saunders Veterinary Dictionary* defines cause in disease as:

> an agent, event, condition or characteristic which plays an essential role in producing an occurrence of the disease. Because there is nowadays much less certainty about what actually establishes a disease state it is becoming more common to use terms such as disease determinants, causal association, causal relationship. Koch's postulates are no longer the sole criterion used in establishing causality.[14]

Slowly, ever so slowly, the reductionist paradigm of causal connections is surely on the wane. Meanwhile I recommend that you listen carefully as scientists speak. Be reassured if you hear them employ a holistic outlook in which the reductionist approach is used as a tool. If their utterances are littered with the word 'cause' then please be wary — it suggests an overemphasis on reductionism.

Measurement

Reductionist science puts great faith in the creation and interpretation of data. As is frequently quipped: 'What gets measured gets done; what is important gets ignored.' Dr Rick Atwell, a veterinarian at the University of Queensland, puts the point gently when he says:

> Subjective assessment can be just as important and by its nature is accepted with less stigma and finality than is a hard figure, which is often given more authenticity and authority than is deserved.[15]

In practice the use of figures is taken to extremes. One example involves the American Association of Feed Control Officials (AAFCO). This United States body, made up of government, university and company representatives, oversees the contents and labelling claims of a vast range of animal foodstuffs. Various subcommittees report on the constituents of artificial pet foods and, where once the National Research Council (NRC) was considered the primary authority on pet foods, that role is now fulfilled by AAFCO and its subcommittees.[16]

If you look at the side of a packet of artificial pet food, you will often see a claim that the contents meet AAFCO guidelines. This is the gold standard by which the consumer is supposed to be assured of the adequacy of the product. AAFCO lists its test protocols for 'proving' that an artificial dog food is 'complete and balanced' and suitable for feeding to a dog for life (see the accompanying box[17]). No reference to how closely a foodstuff compares to the chemical and physical form of a natural diet but a surfeit of measurements instead.

Consider that any artificial foodstuff is manufactured according to reductionist calculations for quantities of carbohydrates, fats, proteins etc which bear scant relationship to the actual diets of wild carnivores. AAFCO then sets out to validate those calculations using another set of arbitrary figures. Figures relating to the number of dogs (8), weeks spent in a cage (26), some physiological measurements and the dogs' weights. But, says AAFCO: 'No dog shall lose more than 15% of its initial body weight.'

AAFCO FEEDING PROTOCOLS FOR DOG AND CAT FOODS MINIMUM TESTING PROTOCOLS FOR PROVING AN ADULT MAINTENANCE CLAIM FOR A DOG FOOD.

DOGS
A minimum of eight healthy adult dogs at least one year of age and of optimal body weight is required to start the test. All animals starting the test must pass an initial examination by a veterinarian. Bitches in gestation or lactation shall be excluded.

DIET
The same formulation shall be used throughout the test although different production batches may be used. If a concurrent control group is used, the diet fed the control group must have been demonstrated to meet the maintenance requirements of the dog as determined by AAFCO feeding protocols.

DURATION OF TEST
The test shall run for a minimum of 26 weeks.

FEEDING PARAMETERS
The test diet shall be the sole source of nutrients except for water. Dogs shall be fed ad libitum or based on energy needs. Fresh water shall be provided ad libitum. Any interruption in feeding protocol must be disclosed and may invalidate the test.

CLINICAL OBSERVATIONS AND MEASUREMENTS
1. Daily food consumption may be measured and recorded.
2. Individual body weights shall be measured at the beginning, weekly and at the end of the 26th week of the test.
3. RBC number, hemoglobin, packed cell volume, and serum alkaline phosphatase and albumin shall be measured and recorded at the beginning and at the 26th week of the test.
4. All dogs shall be given a complete physical examination by a veterinarian at the beginning and at the end of the test. Each dog shall be evaluated as to general health, body and hair coat condition, and comments shall be recorded.
5. Any medication and the reason for its use must be recorded.
6. A number of dogs, not to exceed 25% of those starting the test, may be removed for non-nutritional reasons. The reasons for their removal must be recorded. Dogs may be removed for non-nutritional poor food intake only during the first two weeks of the test. Data already collected from dogs removed from the test shall be retained although it does not have to be included in the final results.
7. A necropsy shall be conducted on any dog which dies during the test and the findings recorded.

INTERPRETATION
A. The diet shall fail if any dog shows clinical or pathological signs of nutritional deficiency or excess.
B. All dogs not removed for non-nutritional reasons must successfully finish the test.
C. The average percent body weight change (final compared to initial) of the group shall not be less than either: ... [certain criteria are laid down including: 'No dog shall lose more than 15% of its initial body weight.']
D. The average final RBC number, hemoglobin, packed cell volume and serum albumin values shall not be less than either: ... [certain criteria are laid down]

In almost every sentence of the protocols there is a statement sufficient to destroy credibility of the test. For instance the requirement: 'All animals starting the test must pass an initial physical examination by a veterinarian.' From our knowledge of periodontal disease we should expect to find processed food fed dogs entering the test already suffering from the disease and thus failing the test. If perchance they happened to be free of the disease then a 26 week period eating a canned or dry diet would ensure the development of a foul mouth.

Much of the protocol seems to be a public relations exercise rather than a genuine attempt to screen unsuitable products. Item 5 requires the use of medication to be recorded, item 6 requires the reasons for removal of dogs to be recorded, and item 7 requires necropsy results to be recorded. But once sick, removed or dead dogs are recorded there appears to be no obligation on anyone to do anything. Perhaps the most damning aspect is that the test is done in-house by the manufacturer. An affidavit of accuracy needs to be filed — seemingly impossible unless definitions are distorted — and from that point on millions of tons of product can be sold carrying the claim that it has passed the AAFCO test.

Dr R L Wysong fulminated against the 'confusion, even blindness' of high-ranking veterinary authorities who support the extraordinary AAFCO procedures. As an example of this blindness Wysong quoted a statement from the October 1992 *Veterinary Forum,* in which the authors refer to AAFCO studies when they say:

> These protocols were designed to assure that pet foods would not be harmful to the animal and would support the proposed life stage. These protocols were not designed to examine nutritional relationships to long-term health or disease prevention.[18]

Wysong sums up the issue:

> In other words a food could cause disease and destroy long-term health yet at the same time 'not be harmful' and be '100 percent complete'! So after a pet has been fed the 'proven' food for a period of time equal to the duration of an AAFCO study (26 weeks), all bets are off. The '100 percent complete and

balanced' food may then be literally poisoning the animal with the blessings of the entire academic, professional, scientific, governmental and industrial pet food establishment.

Since the artificial pet food manufacturers shelter behind the AAFCO badge of approval I decided to investigate further. In 1993 I wrote to the committee concerned noting that two of the eight dogs starting the test could be removed and asking:

> 'The '100 percent complete and balanced' food may then be literally poisoning the animal with the blessings of the entire academic, professional, scientific, governmental and industrial pet food establishment.'
>
> Dr R L Wysong

- Should animals undergoing tests develop gastric dilatation volvulus [distension and twisting of stomach] or intussusception [telescoping of the bowel], would this be an appropriate reason for withdrawal?
- Would the condition be listed as a nutritional or non-nutritional reason for withdrawal?
- Should animals be removed from the test due to gastric dilatation volvulus or intussusception, then how would this affect the test result for the food being trialed?

In less than a month I was astonished by the reply. The lengthy statement, on a Federal Drug Administration letterhead, was signed by Dr David Dzanis of the Center for Veterinary Medicine. As chairman of the AAFCO committee which revised the protocols, Dr Dzanis declared that dogs could indeed be removed due to gastric dilatation volvulus or intussusception and the food could still pass the test (see Chapter 6 regarding GDV and intussusception). In Dr Dzanis's view the conditions would be deemed non-nutritional. In further correspondence with Dr Dzanis regarding the test subjects suffering from periodontal disease I received the reply:

> Regardless, although periodontal disease may be a food-related problem, it is not a nutritional problem per se. Thus, the AAFCO feeding trials do not address this aspect.

Deductive reasoning

Perhaps it should not come as a surprise that the officials making up the AAFCO committees are locked into a mindset that deems numbers to be important but overt fatal disease to be of little or no concern. Some committee members work for artificial pet food companies and others work in close association. While this provides a possible reason for faulty decisions, it does not explain or excuse the use of flawed logic. Logic is a system of thinking that we use to make reasoned judgments on things affecting our lives. We are not able to observe directly the reasoning processes of scientists, but from their utterances, either verbal or in written form, we can make judgments. That scientists can be careless about following the rules of logic to the point of damaging their own credibility has always, for me, been perplexing.

There are two main types of logic, inductive and deductive. Inductive logic allows us to derive a general principle by observing particular events. We tend to say: 'This crow is black so all crows must be black.' For practical purposes that assumption usually holds — until we encounter an albino crow.

Because there is scope for debate regarding the uses of inductive logic we need not dwell on it here; although scientists, like all people, are adept at manipulating the strengths and weaknesses of inductive arguments for their own purposes. The other type, deductive logic, imposes rigorous requirements ensuring that conclusions follow from the initial premises (statements of fact or assumption). Such arguments are said to be valid. When the premises are true, and providing the rules of deductive logic are followed, then the argument is said to be sound and the conclusion will also be true.[19]

Logical content

But we need to be wary. An argument can be logically valid and seem plausible even though the content, the initial premises, may be false. As the saying goes, 'garbage in; garbage out'. One pet food company spokesperson is rumoured to have told a newspaper reporter: 'Give me a tyre, an old leather shoe and a quart of oil and I can meet the specifications for the NRC diet.'[20] I suspect that he was only half joking because the actual contents of the packet comprise soy bean and maize and a host of bizarre chemicals — ingredients which, the companies tell us, are either beneficial or necessary for the wellbeing of our pets.

False premises are so deeply embedded in the artificial pet food mythology that the National Research Council publications on the nutrient requirements of dogs and cats make the statement: 'Dogs/cats require specific nutrients not specific feed stuffs.'[21] This implies that animals do not require natural foodstuffs such as whole raw rabbit but that chemicals — for instance those found in tyres, old shoes, engine oil and other garbage — will suffice.

Logical form

For an argument to be considered logically valid the conclusion must follow from the premises. In the next two examples the premises (1 and 2) are both true, but the conclusion (3) is false, as a result of faulty logic.

1. This commercial pet food is 100 percent complete and balanced as defined by the NRC guidelines.
2. Eight adult dogs, undergoing an AAFCO trial, can live for six months on this diet.

3. Therefore the diet is proven suitable as an adult maintenance diet for dogs everywhere.

1. We are respected manufacturers/professionals/bureaucrats.
2. There are laws governing our industry/profession/bureaucracy.

3. Therefore what we say is true and our product/service/administration is wholesome/good/effective.

Bureaucrats and regulators are renowned for their ability to use false premises and invalid logic in their resolve to serve the status quo. Dr Gerald Guest, Director of the US Federal Drug Administration (FDA) Center for Veterinary Medicine, had this to say:

As the United States federal regulatory body charged with

ensuring the safety of animal foods and drugs, the Center for
Veterinary Medicine is also concerned about the effects of pet
food products on oral health.

In fulfilling this mandate, the Center must rely on scientifically sound data generated from well-controlled studies as the
basis for its regulatory decisions. Any information of this nature
you may offer, particularly scientific studies published in peer-
reviewed journals, would be of substantial benefit.[22]

Unfortunately the information I sent to Dr Guest seems to have been
either ignored or dismissed. But in any case the regulatory function of
the US FDA should not depend on my searches of the scientific
literature — they have staff employed for the purpose. One such staff
member, Dr David Dzanis, Veterinary Nutritionist at the Food and
Drug Administration, also chaired the AAFCO pet food committee. As
we saw, AAFCO protocols cannot be considered 'scientifically sound' or
dependent on 'well-controlled studies'. That the FDA believes it can
fulfil its mandate to make 'regulatory decisions' while being closely allied
with AAFCO is, in my opinion, a matter warranting investigation.

Statistics

Statistics and nuclear power share features in common — they can be
of immense public service or immense public threat. And the threat is
not always intentional, as mistakes do happen. The power of statistical
analysis can turn incomprehensible mountains of raw data into
coherent information. Similarly those with a good grasp of statistical
method can tease out subtle relations between factors under
investigation. The trouble is that those with the good grasp of statistical
method are usually not the people who perform the scientific research.

Ian McCance reviewed, for their statistical content, 279 papers in
23 consecutive issues of the *Australian Veterinary Journal*.[23] He said
that only 29 percent of the papers would have been acceptable to a
statistical referee without revision; revisions would have been needed
in 66 percent; and the remaining 5 percent had major flaws. In
passing comment on the review John Ludbrook told readers that

'statistical flaws revealed by McCance's review are no different in quality or quantity from those that can be found in other life science journals'.[24] Some of the conduct, Ludbrook argued, did not originate from ignorance and was on the borderline of scientific fraud.

Of course, those researching and 'proving' the alleged benefits of artificial pet foods make extensive use of statistics. The validity of those statistics, and the way they are reported, are beyond the ken of the majority. In 1995 the *British Medical Journal* published a paper indicating that, when it comes to the use of statistics, trained health care professionals often get the answer wrong. When asked to evaluate four 'different programs' only three out of 140 professionals spotted that the different results referred to were in fact the same set of statistics expressed in four different ways. If trained people experience such difficulties with data the dangers for you and me are likely to be considerable.[25]

Statistical traps abound. Sometimes research scientists set a trap to catch the unwary and sometimes they unwittingly fall victim to the trap themselves. The 'correlation does not imply causation' trap represents a good example. In an AAFCO feeding trial 100 percent of the dogs consume the test diet 100 percent of the time. If all pass the final veterinary examination some observers might conclude that the statistics prove the diet correlates with and therefore *causes* a successful outcome. But the water the dogs drink and the air they breathe have the same 100 percent correlation. Clearly food, water and air *permit* the dogs to survive until the final veterinary test, but they do not *cause* the outcome of that test.

Altman and Bland drew attention to an important aspect of statistics in their paper entitled 'Absence of evidence is not evidence of absence'.[26] A dramatic illustration of this principle involves not just lack of correlation but total lack of evidence — artificial pet food advocates make much use of this trick. Whenever they fail to use naturally fed control (comparison) groups of animals they avoid providing evidence on the success of a natural diet. And when evidence adverse to the pet food industry is generated, whether in a company laboratory or elsewhere, it is easy to withhold that evidence.

Random and uncertain findings result from poorly conceived

and badly conducted experiments. While this may suit artificial pet food makers, we should bear in mind that some of the research performed in the absence of natural controls involves studies relating to human health. When I pointed out to the veterinary director of a medical research facility that their colony of dogs, fed a commercial dry food, was likely to be adversely affected by the chemical and physical form of the food, I was met with a shrug. The director said there was no evidence their experimental results were compromised, nor did it matter that dogs seek to disguise evidence of ill health.

A particularly distressing example that 'absence of evidence is not evidence of absence' involved a research project at the University of Sydney. A group of veterinarians operating as the Australasian Veterinary Oncology Group set out to test the effects of chemotherapy on cats affected with malignant cancer of the lymph nodes. I wrote to the University Ethics Committee suggesting that it would be wise to assume that animals in the trial would be likely to suffer the combined adverse consequences of:

- an unnatural diet
- a foul mouth
- a clinically diagnosed lymphosarcoma
- administration of Doxorubicin, a cytotoxic agent.

I went on:

All, except the lymphosarcoma, will be under the control of the researchers and as such must be seen as a cruel infliction of suffering. Any experimental results arising out of such trials must at best be applicable to a set of diet and periodontal disease affected animals only.

The Ethics Committee fobbed me off, as did Professor Margaret Rose, Chair of the NSW Animal Research Review Panel, when she told me: 'we all have to accept that we are not always going to get the outcomes that we might want to achieve'.[27]

When the Australian National Health and Medical Research Council (NHMRC) revised its code for the care and use of experimental animals they reviewed submissions and inserted the statement:

'Consideration should be given to providing variety in the composition and presentation of food.' Evidence demonstrating carnivore dietary imperatives appears to have been discounted.[28] As recently as 1995 the US Food and Drug Administration wrote saying that they had not received any 'scientifically sound data' from me 'or any other source' regarding the 'effects of pet food products on pet health'. Perhaps publication of this book may prompt discovery of the evidence?

Controversy over human health and pet ownership

When the international science magazine *New Scientist* ran a cover story entitled 'Secret power of pets', the Pet Care Information and Advisory Service (PIAS), a division of the Mars Corporation, claimed that two pieces of research 'demonstrated irrefutably a correlation between human health and pet ownership'. PIAS sent glossy copies of the article to health care professionals in order that 'all interested parties have accurate and reliable information on the human–companion animal bond'. They urged all

> who are in some way involved in the health field — be it direct involvement as a doctor or other health care worker, or indirect involvement as a formulator of broad social policy — to use this article to help familiarise themselves with the key issues. Regardless of whether or not one is a professed 'animal lover', it is becoming increasingly clear that when considering the overall health of our society, the role of companion animals must be taken into consideration.[29]

PIAS did not mention that the Mars Corporation pays for much of the so-called research which generates the purported 'accurate and reliable information'. Tania Ewing, journalist on *The Age* newspaper, explains it this way:

> Australia's pet ownership is declining and the $1.5 billion [estimated annual sales] pet food industry is worried.
> As families get smaller, and inner-city living becomes more

popular, fewer people are adopting a moggie or mutt.

But at least one pet food company is fighting back, determined to keep Australia one of the highest pet-per-person countries in the world.

The pet food giant Uncle Ben's Australia is 'promoting socially responsible pet ownership' by sponsoring medical research, conducting widespread programs on pets in primary schools and running TV commercials.[30]

Prominent in the enterprise was Professor Warwick Anderson, Chair of the Medical Research Committee (the committee which oversees grants to research projects) within the National Health and Medical Research Council. Together with PIAS veterinarian Jonica Newby he starred in a TV 'community service announcement' promoting pet ownership and undertook research on the benefits of pet keeping. In his article 'The benefits of pet ownership', published in the *Medical Journal of Australia,* Professor Anderson told readers:

> The place of animals in Australian society is under scrutiny, and owning pets can no longer be taken for granted. Newspapers trumpet about how dog faeces pollute city streams and rivers as well as footpaths; cats get bad press because their predatory nature leads them to kill native birds and mammals. We are understandably upset when a rottweiler or pit bull terrier that has been trained to attack people does just that, with tragic human consequences... It's no wonder that pet ownership is falling... Should any of us (other than veterinarians and pet food manufacturers) be concerned about this? The answer is 'yes'. For while the main benefit that pets confer is probably companionship, it is very likely that better health is another benefit.[31]

Professor Anderson went on to say:

> From the findings of less frequent visits to a doctor in the National People and Pets Survey and estimation of lower use of medication for cardiovascular disease, we calculated these savings to be in the order of $800–$1500 million.

The National People and Pets Survey was a telephone poll of 1011 people conducted by a market research company for the Urban Animal Management Coalition. Major pet food companies and pet industry organisations contributed to the survey.

Dr Jonica Newby, who assisted with Professor Anderson's research,[32] promoted his findings in a book published by the Australian Broadcasting Corporation:

> With more and more people living in cities and alone, studies have shown that keeping pets may be essential for our health. Research suggests the savings to health care could be in the billions. Yet our city councils legislate against pets and our town planners ignore them.[33]

'Better than a dose of medicine', said a family health magazine endorsing pet ownership.[34] Mars Corporation executives surely echoed those sentiments. It must have seemed that they had found the $1.5 billion antidote to the bad press arising from dog poo, stray animals, devastated wild life, dog bites, cat scratches, pet-induced traffic accidents, escalating veterinary fees and noise nuisance.

Others were skeptical. Dr Anthony Jorm, researcher at the Australian National University, noticed that Professor Anderson's claims in the *Medical Journal of Australia* had not been subjected to the usual peer review process and the methodology employed seemed doubtful. Within a year Dr Jorm had designed an objective study — 'To determine whether pet ownership by elderly people is associated with lower use of health services' — and done the research and published a peer-reviewed paper.[35] His results showed that: 'Elderly pet owners did not differ from non-owners on any of the physical or mental health measures or in use of health services.' The implications were clear: instead of health care savings 'in the order of $800–$1500 million', the savings were quite possibly zero.

Professor Anderson was unavailable when journalists sought comment.[36] Jonica Newby accepted an invitation to comment in *Vic Vet*, newsletter of the Victorian Division of the Australian Veterinary Association. Two years later *Vic Vet* revisited the controversy. Readers were reminded of Jonica Newby's allegations of 'spurious concerns and misleading statements by Jorm et al.' and her opinion that 'one negative result doth not bring the whole edifice crumbling!'.[37] *Vic Vet* then provided details from a second article which echoed the Jorm findings and cast further doubt on Professor Anderson's calculations.[38]

11

Collaboration at every level

Peer review

Ostensibly the peer review system ensures information entering the mainstream of scientific thought has integrity and validity, thus advancing the interests of the community. But in relation to diet and diet-related diseases peer review has tended to result in conformity of views — views consistent with the commercial interests of the artificial pet food industry. What has gone wrong, and how much is the system to blame?

The mechanics are straightforward and commence with submission of a scientific paper, usually in triplicate, to a journal known to publish material in that particular field of enquiry. The editor, whose name is published in the journal, assesses the document and decides upon suitable reviewers, also called referees. In general referees are two or three in number and their identity is not disclosed. As peers of the author they are expected to advise the editor to accept, conditionally accept or reject the paper for publication. The final decision rests with the editor who then communicates with the author.

Editors and peer reviewers praise the system. In his book *How to Write and Publish a Scientific Paper* Robert Day quotes the opinion: 'all editors, and most authors, will affirm that there is hardly a paper published that has not been improved, often substantially, by the revisions suggested by referees.' Day agrees with the scientist who asserted: 'editors encounter very few instances of unfairness and blatant bias expressed by referees; perhaps for 0.1 per cent or less of the manuscripts handled, an editor is obliged to discount the referees' comments.'[1]

Authors are the other major group participating in and reinforcing the peer review process. Successful authors seldom have reason to complain and the majority of unsuccessful authors simply increase their efforts to comply with the system. A small minority of failed authors harbour dissenting views but their views suffer the same fate as their manuscripts — they are neither seen nor heard. Members of the public are outside the loop and gain no knowledge of this secretive process.

Editors and peer reviewers should ensure papers published honour the need for control groups of naturally fed animals free from the effects of periodontal disease

Affirming that the peer review system is not widely challenged is not the same as saying it provides benefit to our science-dependent society. Barber in his paper 'Resistance by scientists to scientific discovery' provides psychological, cultural and social explanations for why vital information is frequently suppressed or rejected. He explains:

> cultural blinders are one of the constant sources of resistance to innovations of all kinds. And scientists, for all the methods they have invented to strip away their distorting idols, or cultural blinders, and for all the training they receive in evading the negative effects of such blinders, are still as other men, though surely in considerably lesser measure because of these methods and their special training. Scientists suffer, along with the rest of us, from the ironies that evil sometimes comes from good, that one noble vision may exclude another, and that good scientific ideas occasionally obstruct the introduction of better ones.[2]

If this is a fair description of scientists then it is true of editors and referees in similar measure. David Horrobin takes up the subject in his paper, 'The philosophical basis of peer review and suppression of innovation'.[3] His thesis is that peer review is not merely a matter of quality control. While he recognises the necessity for this rather mechanistic aspect, he believes that the fundamental purpose in the biomedical sciences must be consistent with that of medicine itself: 'to cure sometimes, to relieve often, to comfort always'. Horrobin believes that the peer review process should deliver by actively discriminating in favour of innovation.

While peer review often serves to suppress good new information, the corollary is that it can also tend to perpetuate old outmoded dogma. In the 1995 *Annual Review of Microbiology* J W Costerton states:

> As disciples of Koch and Pasteur, we have been taught to extrapolate from single-species laboratory cultures to predict bacterial behaviour in actual environments. With modern tools we can now make direct observations of structure and of chemical function in living biofilms growing in specific ecosystems. This perception of functional biofilm communities, reinforced by novel methods for direct observation, will usher in a new golden age of understanding in virtually all fields of microbiology.[4]

This sounds like a reconsideration of the germ theory which, for 100 years, has been uncritically supported by the peer review system.

In Australia, the peer review process has continued to support artificial pet food dogma, even though the Australian Veterinary Association recommended: 'those investigating small animal health problems should also take diet and diet consistency into account when researching systemic diseases — possible confounding effects of diet and poor oral health must be considered in such studies'.[5] This injunction is clear enough. Editors and peer reviewers should ensure papers published honour the need for control groups of naturally fed animals free from the effects of periodontal disease — reductionist scientific methodology also requires the use of naturally fed control groups. However the veterinary peer review system seems to honour the rules more in the breach than the observance.

What if anything can be done about a system which self-evidently fails? Not much, I fear. In 1998 the *British Medical Journal* (*BMJ*) attempted to tighten standards regarding author and peer reviewer conflict of interest because 'transparency and accountability are increasingly expected in all aspects of society'. Richard Smith, editor of the *BMJ*, defined conflict of interest as 'a set of conditions in which professional judgment concerning a primary interest (such as patients' welfare or the validity of research) tends to be unduly influenced by a secondary interest (such as financial gain)'. To limit the problem the *BMJ* requires authors and reviewers to complete a declaration regarding financial conflict of interest, but it confesses: 'Our impression … is that many authors are willing to sign that they don't have a conflict of interest when by our definition they do.'[6] If that be the case for authors whose names are published alongside their articles, then for anonymous peer reviewers the prospects for full and accurate declaration seem remote.

Scientific fraud

Does scientific fraud occur in veterinary and pet food research at a level similar to that occurring in other scientific disciplines? Why would researchers engage in scientific fraud when the current paradigms and peer review system favour maintaining the status quo? Robert Bell, writing about scientific fraud in general, suggests: 'the fraud cases that come to light are but a small fraction of the whole. A study at a major university showed that of the 32% of researchers who suspected that a colleague had falsified data, 54% did not report it or try to verify their suspicions.'[7]

In the world of the scientist only other scientists can interpret scientific output. When inconsistencies are detected they can often be said to be inadvertent or accidental, and thereby escape censure.[8] But manipulated data and false conclusions however they occur, once committed to print, have the potential to circulate forever. Theodore Rockwell, in his paper 'Scientific integrity and mainstream science', said:

> *there are cases where mainstream scientific opinion is bad science* —
> where scientific positions are maintained long after their invalidity becomes clear to any who will unblinkingly examine the refutory evidence. When reputations and incomes have been made and maintained by the 'established wisdom' and the interests of funding agencies, there are strong personal and institutional incentives to hold off any changes as long as possible, pleading that we still do not know enough for sure, and a little more research money may make the situation clearer.[9]

Suppression in the scientific arena

*Science presented us first with normative ethics, then with
relativistic ethics, and at last with no ethics at all.*

GEORGE FALUDY[10]

Brian Martin is well qualified to comment on conduct in the scientific research arena. He has a doctorate in theoretical physics, teaches
social science at the University of Wollongong and was President of
Whistleblowers Australia. In his book, *Suppression Stories*, Martin
reveals how parts of the scientific community — especially the scientific elite — tend to cooperate with dominant political and economic
groups. Martin quoted the opinion of the celebrated US sociologist,
C Wright Mills, that: 'the deepest problem of freedom for teachers is
not the occasional ousting of a professor but a vague general fear —
sometimes politely known as "discretion", "good taste" or "balanced
judgment". It is fear which leads to self-intimidation and finally
becomes so habitual that the scholar is unaware of it.'[11]

'Systems can maintain incompetence' said the psychologist Ashley
Conway in his review of medical research conduct. He complained that
where commercial interest lobbies are involved — and the profit motive
foremost — beneficial research may not be sponsored, information
detrimental to a company, may be suppressed.[12] According to Conway,
publicly funded research may not be open to the same commercial
influences, but may be adversely affected in another way. He used 'game
theory' to help understand what he called the Research Game, a game
which enables experts 'to avoid taking risks, and therefore to avoid being
wrong'. Conway's rules for the Game are:

1. *The player's first obligation is to maintain the status quo of
   the Game. Within the Game the object is to rise above the
   other players.*
2. *Do not research an entirely new field...*
3. *It does not matter if the ground explored is old or obvious. The
   way the Game is played is much more important than the
   practical significance of the research results...*

4. *Doing something that is useful outside the Game is not only irrelevant, but seriously discouraged.* One player finding a solution for a real-life problem seriously disrupts the Game. Other players' 'expertise' is lost, and such a result may give rise to embarrassing questions about why other researchers are not doing something useful too.

5. *Objectivity must be maintained at all times.* Players should not be too concerned for the health or well-being of their subjects. This could become a contaminant to objective observation, but more importantly may bring emotion into the Game, one of the very problems that it has developed to avoid.

6. *Players must at all times show detached coolness towards their research.* Enthusiasm over a research goal is discouraged; it promotes the expectation of useful results, and again introduces feelings into the Game.

7. *Research should always be seen to be good science.* If only it were as straightforward as Newtonian physics! Still, one of the advantages of the Game is that it enables those playing to pretend that it is...

8. *Players must at all times use correct language.* The creation of Game language is an important way of maintaining the feelings of being elite. The language rules, together with complicated statistical analysis of data, ensure that the illusion of real expertise is maintained.

9. *The rules of all psychological games are unspoken. Never make the rules of the Game explicit, even to oneself.* This is one way of spoiling a psychological game, which is my [Conway's] intention here.

The preceding discussion refers to the conservatism of scientists in general. For the majority of veterinary researchers who work with domestic pets, there are many reasons for supporting the status quo. Some work for the pet food industry or institutes and universities funded by the industry. A small minority carry out research as part of their private practice, which usually means working with processed food-fed pets. Topics which may reflect adversely on processed pet food may remain unresearched.

Royal College of Veterinary Surgeons and British Veterinary Association

The Selborne Committee

In September 1996 the Royal College of Veterinary Surgeons (RCVS), governing body of the British veterinary profession, announced the formation of a committee of enquiry into the future of British veterinary science and research. Under the chairmanship of the Earl of Selborne, seven professors, one doctor and Miss Kirsten Rausing, the owner of a horse stud, called for submissions to assist with their enquiry. Drawing on my well of naive optimism I resolved to make a contribution. In a submission titled 'The whiff of dogs' breath, money and veterinary research' I set out reasons for rejection of pet food company funds and reform of veterinary science.

Leaving nothing to chance I sent each Committee member a copy of the submission, accompanying documentation and a videotape of TV programs illustrating the points I wished to make. (As a further safeguard against tipping good information into a dark uninhabited space, I placed the information on my web site where it can still be found).[13] Intent on encouraging the Committee to contemplate flaws in the system, I resorted to a dictionary definition and went on from there.

> Poison, according to *The Concise Oxford Dictionary*, is: 'Substance that when introduced into or absorbed by a living organism destroys life or injures health.' I believe that artificial pet foods fall into this category of substances when they form the basis of a diet for small domestic carnivores. The effects of the 'poison' and the effects of the manufacturers of the 'poison' are to be found throughout all levels of the small animal veterinary science.

The Committee received the information, because my name appears in the list of contributors in the final report. Dr Neil Gorman's name also features, as the provider of both written and oral submissions.[14] It was not specified whether he provided information in his capacity as President of the Royal College of Veterinary Surgeons or as head of

Waltham, the Mars pet food research institute. The Committee did mention — and appeared to endorse — that a number of those giving evidence recommended increased funding by pet food manufacturers.[15]

> By funding research the pet food industry pays the piper and calls the tune

By funding research the pet food industry pays the piper and calls the tune, a point perhaps not appreciated by the Committee. Perhaps they felt threatened by the problem and chose to deny its existence — a strategy common to organisations, as reported in the *Sydney Morning Herald*:

> According to Chris Argyris [Harvard professor of education and organisational behaviour], all organisations are prone to this because it flows from a natural human response that we practise from the time we leave the cradle. This is the response we have to particular problems, problems that we see as personally threatening. What we do, with increasing skill as we mature, is develop ways of by-passing the problem, then of covering up the by-pass and then covering up the cover-up... As a result, instead of being cleared up, the original flaw not only goes on festering, but its very existence becomes taboo — undiscussible, and so irremediable.[16]

Covering up cover-ups

As a member of the RCVS, despite residing in Australia, I am able to contest elections to the London-based Council of the College — and in a limited way to stimulate discussion of the undiscussible. The College circulates candidates' manifesto statements to its 18,000 members and *The Veterinary Record*, journal of the British Veterinary Association, also publishes the information. Encouraged by the votes gained at the 1999 election I asked the College to take action on the pet food issue. On receiving a brush-off I submitted a letter for publication in *The Veterinary Record*.

——— *Letter for publication* ———

Dear Sir,

ARTIFICIAL PET FOODS AND THE RCVS

If you are not part of the answer, you are part of the problem.

— JOHN F KENNEDY

Following the 395 member vote [11% of vote] in support of the proposition that artificial pet foods and the veterinary promotion of such products may be harming animals under the care of veterinarians ... I asked the College ... 'to adopt a responsible course of action' and 'to enter into open discussions in order to establish the composition and terms of reference of an independent committee of enquiry'. The RCVS replied:

> Officers have ... taken the view that the issues which you raise in your manifesto do not fall within the remit given to the College by its Charter and Statute. The College exists primarily to regulate the education and professional conduct of veterinary surgeons, and to maintain a Register of veterinary surgeons who are qualified to practise in the United Kingdom. Whilst it exists to act in the public interest, rather than in the interests of the profession, it does not engage in lobbying on, for example, animal welfare issues, even though these might be construed to be generally in the public interest. The marketing of pet foods, if misleading (or worse, as you suggest) would be a matter for other regulatory bodies and possibly even the courts.

Dietary recommendations are fundamental to 'the education and profes-sional conduct of veterinary surgeons'. Many veterinary surgeons, including Council Members of the RCVS, promote artificial products. If these activities are 'misleading or worse' we can expect 'other regulatory bodies and possibly even the courts' to take an interest.

The RCVS appears to have dealt itself out of this ethics debate without first informing itself of the dangers. Does the RCVS decision benefit pet animals, the community, the profession or the RCVS? What role will be available to the RCVS when regulatory and judicial bodies rake over the evidence?

Signed, (Tom Lonsdale)

Thus ensued a protracted struggle with *The Veterinary Record*. I tried invoking the need for free speech and the need to warn British Veterinary Association members 'of legal opinions which hold far-reaching implications' and finally I asked to pay to have the letter published in the advertising section. Mr Alder, the editor, remained steadfast, stating: 'I must again tell you that we will not be publishing it [the letter] in *The Veterinary Record*. I am afraid I must also tell you that, like other journals, we do not publish letters in our advertising pages.'

At last I took the hint that the British veterinary authorities were unwilling to permit open discussion. Besides, it was better to conserve energy for the year 2000 RCVS elections which were fast approaching. At elections candidates have an opportunity, even a duty, to air significant issues — the authorities have a duty to facilitate discussion. Mindful of defamation laws, I penned a manifesto and sent it off to the College for circulation to the members.

2000 RCVS Election Manifesto

Hans Christian Andersen's fairy tales for children sometimes feature less endearing aspects of human behaviour told in an enchanting way. In 1837 he published 'The Emperor's New Clothes' depicting how nonsensical situations can persist in face of the evidence. In the story two swindlers traded on the Emperor's vanity. They persuaded him that their cloth was of the highest quality with magical properties. Fools, they said, could not see the cloth. Whilst the rogues busied themselves feigning to make cloth — and pocketing the silk and golden threads — courtiers and citizens pretended that the nonexistent cloth was magnificent.

No one wished to be thought foolish and, for their own reasons, connived at the deception. The hoax became more elaborate when the nonexistent, and therefore invisible cloth, was tailored into nonexistent clothes. 'Dressed' in his new clothes the Emperor strutted at the state procession. But the charade could not withstand an innocent's gaze. When a child exclaimed that the Emperor had nothing on the truth gained momentum. Soon the citizens were saying 'The Emperor has nothing on', but not the Emperor nor his courtiers. Those with the greatest responsibility to guard against stupid error marched on more proudly than before.

In the 1860s the fairy tales of another man created an impact on the commercial world. Jack Spratt travelled from Cincinnati to London to sell lightning conductors but on seeing the stray dogs on the London docks turned to manufacturing dog biscuits instead. He touted his wheat, beetroot, vegetable and beef blood product as superior fare. Spratt declared fresh beef could 'overheat the dog's blood' and table scraps 'break down his digestive powers'. Sadly for the pets of the world, veterinarians did not adequately speak out against Spratt's fanciful notions — **from the beginning some veterinarians were paid to endorse artificial products**.

Now in 2000 the majority of domestic carnivores are fed from the can and packet with, I believe, serious consequences for pet health, the global economy and natural environment (see www.rawmeatybones.com). Last year, on the strength of an eleven percent vote, I asked the RCVS 'to enter into open discussions in order to establish the composition and terms of reference of an independent committee of enquiry'. The RCVS declined, stating that: 'The marketing of pet foods, if misleading (or worse, as you suggest) would be a matter for other regulatory bodies and possibly even the courts.'

In my opinion the RCVS, governing body of a self-regulating profession, should review its decision. Already there has been trial by television and children point out the obvious. **Perception of bias — some RCVS Councillors either sell or promote artificial pet foods — must also be avoided.** Accordingly I seek your vote in favour of the establishment of an independent committee of enquiry into the health, economic and environmental effects of artificial pet foods. If as a by-product I gain election to Council I undertake to promote transparency of administration, proper attire at RCVS processions and the interests of animals under our care.

You can guess the authorities were displeased, but what might they do to counter the satirical message? Turning the election into a petition to establish a committee of enquiry would also offend against their wishes. When the anticipated letter arrived from the College, detailing proposed amendments to my manifesto, I was surprised to see that two passages (highlighted in bold) were to be deleted on 'legal advice'.

If for many years the College has been turning a blind eye to veterinary promotions of pet foods and if such activity is illegal, it should be discussed and resolved at the earliest. But, in keeping with Chris Argyris's predictions, the College opted to cover up the cover-up. Eventually, after legal representations, the Registrar 'decided to take the risk and publish [the] statement — complete with the contentious phrases'.

At the election Professor Bob Michell, incumbent President, topped the poll with 54 percent support. For the fourth successive year I trailed the poll; although 359 veterinarians (9 percent) voted for an enquiry. Encouraged by this level of support, I sent an e-mail message to the Registrar of the College. 'Hitherto the RCVS has either ignored or attempted to suppress the allegations. Will the RCVS now act?' I asked — a question requiring legal advice and consideration by all forty members of the College Council; or so I thought. But in less than two hours a reply arrived, not from the Registrar but from the President, stating: 'RCVS Council Elections are not designed for single issue politics... I have no plans for any such enquiry... 91 per cent of the voters appear to be uninterested in this issue.'

Regulatory action

When scientists refuse to play by the rules of the Game — by replacing self-censorship with independent thought — the scientific establishment has been known to engage in active suppression. For the heretic the effects can be distressing and onlookers are encouraged not to contemplate similar acts of indiscretion. On 1 April 1993 Doug Hyslop, the External Relations Manager of the Mars company Uncle Ben's, complained to the Australian Veterinary Association:

We are also concerned that strong inference [sic] has been made in letters and statements by Dr Lonsdale that large sections of the veterinary profession are somehow in collusion with Uncle Ben's of Australia and other pet food companies to the detriment of pets. These comments could hardly have escaped the notice of the AVA and we are surprised there appears to have been no official response from the AVA on a matter that surely strikes at the heart of the integrity of the veterinary profession...

Uncle Ben's of Australia will always welcome suggestions as to how it may improve its products and its service and is quite happy to see vigorous debate on anything that will ultimately benefit pet owners and their pets. We will not accept, however ill informed, unproven, unsubstantiated claims that run counter to the opinions, experience and proven knowledge of world leaders in the fields of pet nutrition and pet dentistry and will strenuously defend our good name and the reputation of our products by all means open to us.

Where disputes occur in the public domain, televised debates ought to provide an opportunity for Uncle Ben's, or any other pet food company, to muster facts and defend their name. However, the companies seem to avoid public debate and prefer to conduct their campaigns behind the scenes.

Veterinary Board stance

'When I use a word', Humpty Dumpty said in rather a scornful tone, 'it means just what I choose it to mean — neither more nor less'.

LEWIS CARROLL[17]

Veterinarians need to be licensed in order to practise their profession. Licence-issuing bodies can thereby exercise power for the good of the community — for instance where untrained people are barred from practice and those with training encouraged to maintain standards. But when licensing authorities resemble Humpty Dumpty, outcomes become uncertain or worse. Such was the case when the Board of Veterinary Surgeons of New South Wales chose to ignore matters of great concern and instead called me, the whistleblower, to account. In their letter of 9 May 1994 they informed me:

The Board has received a complaint concerning statements allegedly made by you in the media.

While the Board does not wish to enter into the scientific controversy surrounding the matter, the Board is concerned that the statements, if made as presented in the media, could place you in breach of Clause 10.1 under the Code of Professional Conduct.

This Clause states that — 'Veterinary Surgeons have an obligation to their colleagues, individually and collectively, and to the public, to conduct themselves at all times in an acceptable manner.'

Such claims as —

'A Sydney veterinarian, Dr Tom Lonsdale, said 75 percent of the income vets earned from treating cats and dogs was derived from ailments caused by inadequate diet'

'dog and cat food should be banned because it causes shocking tooth and gum disease in 85% of pets' may imply that the veterinary profession as a whole is negligent in not advising against the use of proprietary foods, or performing adequate dental and other health checks.

It is the Board's opinion that before claims or statements can be publicly made, there should exist sound scientific evidence supporting them. Otherwise such claims could be detrimental to the veterinary profession and misleading to the public.

My legal adviser provides scrutiny of most of my articles and media releases before they are published. He knew the quotes attributed to me complied with the requirements of law, and yet here was a Board operating without regard to fundamental principles — in particular refusing to disclose the identity of the complainant. He wrote to the Board:

We advise as follows:

1. Your letter does not require a response and therefore raises a question as to why it was written. Perhaps you would be good enough to enlighten us.
2. It is cowardly and unprofessional of the complainant not to release a copy of his letter and thus prevent a professional colleague from defending both his actions and reputation.
3. It would be most improper of the Board to take action which might, and very probably would, adversely affect our client's professional standing and thus his livelihood and at the same time refuse even to provide a copy of the complainant's letter so as to give at least some semblance of foundation for the Board's stance.

Any action taken by the Board prejudicial to our client in the present circumstances would constitute a complete denial of natural justice and would be treated accordingly.

It is or should be a basic tenet of the approach of every professional regulatory body in Australia in these circumstances that no action will be taken based on anonymous complaints and that every member of a profession has a fundamental right to be able adequately to defend charges levied against him especially if those charges are wilfully, mischievously, falsely or stupidly based.

Accordingly you are requested within seven (7) days to provide a precise statement of the Board's stance on this matter together with a photocopy of the complete letter of complaint.

Thankfully my lawyer managed to fend off the Board and a stalemate ensued. But why did they refuse to disclose the identity of the accuser? Three years later I made use of the provisions of the NSW *Freedom of Information Act* which provides for release of government documents, especially those relating to personal records. Only then did I obtain the letter of complaint and the identity of the complainant. Dr Barbara Fougere, veterinary adviser to Uncle Ben's, had written the two page letter, asking for 'prevention of further publicity of Dr Lonsdale unless authorised by the Veterinary Surgeons Board'.

'The scandal that is the Veterinary Surgeons Investigating Committee'

In America, where democracy and free speech are highly valued, aggressive organisations may use SLAPPs to circumvent the system. The acronym stands for Strategic Lawsuits Against Public Participation which 'are filed by one side of a public, political dispute to punish or prevent opposing points of view'.[18]

The judge in one such action pointed out:

> The conceptual thread that binds [SLAPPs] is that they are suits without substantial merit that are brought by private interests to 'stop citizens from exercising their political rights or to punish them for having done so'... The longer the litigation can be stretched out, the more litigation that can be churned, the greater the expense that is inflicted and the closer the SLAPP filer moves to success. The purpose of such gamesmanship ranges from simple retribution for past activism to discouraging future activism.[19]

At least SLAPPs are heard by independent judges sitting in open courts. Actions brought before the NSW Veterinary Surgeons Investigating Committee (VSIC) — a committee of three veterinarians, one psychologist and a lawyer — are conducted in private with rules preventing publication of the deliberations. Breaching the no-publication rules invites punishment, including a fine of up to $2000 and/or imprisonment for up to one year.

For these reasons I cannot provide details of the four separate VSIC actions against me. Nor can I name individuals whose complaints and 'evidence' formed the basis of those actions. But I can reveal that the costs — money, time and energy — became unsupportable. The physical and mental pressures mounted to the point where, rather than be crushed or surrender, I was forced to sell the practice.

Two activist colleagues, citing personal or family pressures, withdrew from the fray. But others continue with the struggle and there are signs things may be changing. The VSIC is itself the subject of an investigation by the NSW Ombudsman and there have been comments in State Parliament about 'the scandal that is the Veterinary Surgeons Investigating Committee'.[20]

12

There's a cuckoo in the nest: a deceptive bird

In human societies man is his own parasite, a circumstance which seems to ensure that all civilised societies shall be fully infested.

SIR RONALD FISHER[1]

Product advertising owes much to the patent medicine salesmen around the time of the American Civil War (1861–65). Promoters of elixirs such as Coca-Cola — first produced in Atlanta in 1886 — promised instant gratification and an eager population accepted the promise. A few remote tribes have not yet experienced the barrage of Coca-Cola advertising, but for the rest of us Coca-colonisation is well established. Even our jolly Santa Claus, dressed in red and white, is a creation of a Coca-Cola artist. Images, labels and brands define our cultural reality and advertisers tell us what to think (but not to think too much).

Artificial pet food producers were quick to mimic the tone and style of the patent medicine men. Stopping short of breaching advertising codes, but at the same time making unsubstantiated health claims, the companies found a sure way to extract cash from wallets. 'Trust us, we are the experts', the ads seem to say.

And from an early stage some experts willingly participated in the promotions — for a fee. American veterinarian Dr A C Daniels, around 1910, endorsed 'Medicated Dog Bread' which he proclaimed did not contain 'cheapening ingredients such as talc powder and mill sweepings' but was made with only 'the best winter wheat, rice meal and fresh meat'. Rival products, Daniels warned, might result in 'constipation, indigestion and skin ills'.[2] By 1943, the smiling veterinarian in the picture advertising Pard canned dog food was advising the owner of a listless sporting dog: 'He'll be ready to hunt anything in a few days — all he needs is a good balanced diet ... one proven high in nutritional value. Dogs need food rich in meat proteins and minerals to maintain top health and plenty of "go" energy.' And the manufacturers assured owners:

> Dog owners, breeders and veterinarians acclaim Pard the 'one-dish-dinner' that's got everything! That's because Pard's nutritionally correct formula is based on feeding studies scientifically conducted by experts in Swift's own great research laboratories — *no additional meat is ever needed*. Get Pard now.[3]

Fast-forward fifty years to 1993 when veterinarian Ian Griggs appeared in a TV commercial promoting canned cat food. He cautioned viewers that cats: 'Like fish but, on its own, it's not a complete meal. Therefore it's not completely healthy for your cat. So you need to add essential fatty acids for a shiny coat, thiamine for its nervous system and folic acid for healthy growth — now that's a complete meal.' 'And so is this', said Griggs as he displayed a can of Whiskas. 'Everything a cat loves, everything a cat needs, everyday.' A voiceover assured viewers: 'Because Whiskas knows cats best.'[4]

But eventually advertisements, whether designed to boost product claims or denigrate rival products, become stale. At such times manufacturers often reinvent their product as 'NEW, IMPROVED'. This tacit admission that their product was neither 100 percent complete nor balanced as previously claimed, does not appear to matter. PAL canned dog food is relaunched on a regular basis and always enjoys a boost in sales.[5] If you take time to study the advertisements you will soon become familiar with the methods of the advertisers.

In the 1960s the industry fought its 'beef wars', with companies seeking to outbid each other regarding the meat content of cans. Lorne Green, star of the TV show *Bonanza* (a story about the adventures of a family of rich cattle ranchers), held up a juicy steak before the camera in support of the virtues of pure beef dinners. 'More beef means better appetite appeal', said the makers of Ideal, who also advised consumers:

'All dogs and cats need some Ideal regularly as health insurance.' By the 1980s the belief that dogs are carnivores was overturned with the certain pronouncement that dogs are in fact omnivores.[6] The 'complete and balanced diet' claim by this time rested squarely on the alleged need for grains. 'Let's get the facts straight!' proclaimed an advertisement directed at Australian veterinarians:

Fact ... Golden maize from Australia's grain belt provides essential carbohydrates. No wheat gluten means there is less likelihood of irritating skin conditions.

Fact ... Golden Sunflower and Linseed Oils help maintain a shiny, lustrous and healthy coat.

Fact ... Rice is the staple food for more than half the world's people. Gluten free and highly digestible.[7]

One pet food company backflip provided minor amusement. In the mid-1960s Ralston Purina tested its Bonanza Dog Meal in Wichita and Kansas City. They claimed the product was 'preferred in taste tests six-to-one over the largest selling dog meal'. Unfortunately for the company the biggest seller in the test area was their own product, Purina Dog Chow.[8]

The consistent losers are of course consumers and their pets — that does not amuse.

As a society we have become inured to the advertisers' puffery. The government regulators stand idly by and now we have several generations of pet owners who know no alternative to the commercial offerings. If I were to chance a one word explanation for all of this I would say, 'Money'. The transnational corporations coin the big bucks and other groups queue up for their share. If an advertising company secures a contract it has the potential to create advertisements across categories and across continents. Similarly television stations transmit commercials for pasta sauce, candy bars and artificial pet food all for the same giant company. It clearly pays to speak politely when dealing with such influential giants. In a single year Mars are said to spend $400 million advertising their products across America.[9]

When industries generate super-profits at the expense of consumers — and then reapply those profits to advertising which further disadvantage those consumers — I consider there has been a breakdown in the workings of the market. Two oft cited examples are the tobacco and alcohol industries which manage to get away with consumer exploitation despite active lobby group opposition. In the case of artificial pet foods, while not directly affecting the health of the human customer, the financial exploitation is comparable. After a century of anti-freshmeat and anti-tablescraps advertising, the cheaper, healthier pet food industry alternative has been killed off.

Occasionally small time entrepreneurs attempt to resurrect the market for healthy pet foods. In the unlikely event that a large natural pet food company were to use advertising to challenge the artificial pet food industry the company would encounter serious financial obstacles.

- Artificial pet foods are sold as branded products and thus define and create control of their niche of the market. While there are many candy bars there is only one Snickers. Why do companies fight fiercely to create brand recognition and then fight fiercely to defend that brand against imitation? The reason is simple — access to super-profits. In contrast, raw food must always remain a generic product. The producers will always find their market crowded with other producers. No brand name cushion for them.
- Giant companies with numerous brands control the artificial pet food market. Mars and Nestlé are the main operators and can be said to have semi-monopolist status. But even a 5 percent share in a huge market such as the US provides a pet food company with extraordinary purchasing power. And such firms never give their smaller competitors an even break.
- Giant artificial pet food companies gain a third and major advantage by virtue of their multinational status. Their cross-border structure enables them to arrange their reported revenues

in such a way that the tax paid in a given country is minimised or even zero. In Australia in 1996 it was reported that 60 percent of all multinational corporations paid no tax and that most of the remaining 40 percent claimed to be only marginally profitable and therefore paid only a small amount of tax.[10]

Finally, and despite the odds, if our intrepid natural pet food company were to enter into an advertising battle with the current market leader it would find itself pitted against the marketing machine of Mars, Inc. As a privately owned company Mars don't have to submit to stockmarket analysts, the whims of pesky shareholders or the general interference of busybodies. In fact they can pay who they like for what they like and nobody ever gets to find out. All large corporations engage in marketing, of course, but few compare with Mars, Inc. Let's take a look.

Persuasive ways

A lie can travel half way around the world while the truth is putting on its shoes.

MARK TWAIN[11]

When Jack Spratt, the original pet food entrepreneur, launched his Patent Dog Cakes on the London market in the 1860s, the marketing industry was already under way. What we now know as market research firms, publicity agencies and opinion pollsters assisted the advertising agencies to create the most persuasive advertisements. Persuasion works better if people believe that they themselves have thought of an idea, not that the idea has been implanted by someone else. Better still, from the marketer's point of view, is the situation where consumers act unconsciously without any thought at all. Everywhere I look I see examples of this, but I was shocked when a veterinary colleague of mine asked his eleven-year-old daughter what food for dogs and cats was. She promptly listed several commercial brands despite her father both using and recommending more natural foods for pets.

Had Jack Spratt kept faith with nature, and alerted consumers to the fact that carnivore food is predominantly raw meat on the bone, our society and the veterinary profession would now be very different. Instead, the notion of food as something wholesome, nutritious and necessary was usurped in favour of brand name products. The act of giving something a proper name and repeatedly portraying that name in writing has a powerful effect on the psyche. The Lexicon Company says about its approach:

> Our mission is to create great names and everything we do is devoted to that result. Since 1982 we have completed over 1300 assignments.
>
> By combining personal creativity with structural linguistics, we create new brands like Pentium processors, PowerBook computers, Vibrance shampoo, Zima clearmalt beverage, Embassy Suites hotels and Slates dress slacks.
>
> Our philosophy is that a great name is a 'vessel' that allows you to tell a story, deliver an idea, or make a promise. A great name uses semantics, sound symbolics, and phonetics to deliver a message and a personality — in less than a second.[12]

Nothing is left to chance by the companies which secure trademark rights over our words: Science diet, Advance, Dine, Chum, Lucky dog, and Pedigree. They hire the best advertising and marketing people — who probably know little about the biological needs of carnivores or the dangers of an unnatural diet. They do however know what colour packaging attracts consumers, the optimum position in the supermarket rack, and at which end of the aisle products sell best. They know that brightly coloured shapes of fishes and imitation bones appeal to the child in all of us, but make absolutely no difference to the pets forced to eat these creations. Children, of course, control a large part of family spending. Just watch young children helping mother do the shopping.

Children grow up and become parents. As unpaid sales staff for the corporations parents play a valuable part in the battle for the child's mind. This image of a 'battle for the mind' was used by William Sargant to describe the processes of thought control and brain washing.[13] Writing just after the Second World War, Sargant was able to draw on the imagery of war, as that is where so much of modern propaganda was refined. I think we can extend the analogy further and say that *armies* of *professionals* now act as *mercenaries* in *targeted* marketing *campaigns*.

> **brightly coloured shapes of fishes and imitation bones appeal to the child in all of us, but make absolutely no difference to the pets forced to eat these creations.**

Single-minded determination

Never underestimate the pet food giants: they are bigger and stronger than us and besides they work to a different schedule. Old age and retirement never feature in *their* planning schedule and no mountain of money is ever enough. Instead they strive for efficiency, constantly building on past successes. They are fastidious to a fault and Mars's pet food plants are said to be cleaner than most factories that process human food. Describing Forrest Mars Senior's zeal for quality control, Brenner wrote in *The Emperors of Chocolate*:

> On visits to his pet food companies in Europe — and after he purchased Kal Kan in the United States in 1966 — Forrest would hold court in the 'cutting room' or testing center, where he would taste every variety of Mars's pet food and compare it with the competition, a practice that continues today.
>
> 'It tastes just like cold stew,' John Murray explained during a tasting session at the Kal Kan plant in Vernon, California. 'It's very meaty, moist and succulent.'
>
> The point of these trials was not the flavor of the product — after all, a dog's palate and a human's are considerably different — but the overall quality of the pet food.[14]

The colonisation of the Australian pet food market demonstrates Mars's approach. With a one way ticket young John Mars, on his first assignment for the company, was sent to Australia to establish Uncle Ben's. By 1966 the company had created the largest meat canning operation in the southern hemisphere. PAL and Whiskas were the first products to roll off the production line. At that time Australian canned dog food sales amounted to $2 million annually. By 1990 Australian dogs slurped an annual 70,000 tonnes of the product worth $106 million. Still more is shipped to Japan where, as Pedigree Chum, the brand tops the market. In New Zealand two years after the launch, PAL accounted for 30 percent of canned dog food sales.[15]

Mars executives suggest product quality and consistent marketing are the key reasons for the product's success. Competing manufacturers are not convinced and cite the massive marketing budget and ruthless attitude to rivals as major factors. Retailers meanwhile are forced to accept an 8 percent profit margin compared with other products which provide them with a 15 percent margin. The *Business Review Weekly* provided this assessment:

> Uncle Ben's annual television advertising budget for PAL is an estimated $4 million, the biggest budget in the pet-food market for one brand. The company has used the British-developed "Top breeders recommend PAL" theme since 1974 and Sammons [marketing and sales director] says it keeps the campaign fresh by changing the presenters, and the dogs, each year. George Patterson has been PAL's advertising agency since 1966.
>
> In addition to TV advertising, Uncle Ben's runs a host of marketing programs designed to encourage dog ownership and the use of prepared pet-food, and educate Australians about how to care for their dogs. It has been involved with the Royal Guide Dogs for the Blind Association since 1967 and has staged PAL dog shows since 1968.
>
> In 1966 Uncle Ben's set up Petcare, an information and advisory service that runs pet shows and educational programs with schools and local councils. Petcare is funded by Uncle Ben's at an estimated cost of $300,000 a year and managed by

International Public Relations. But none of the Petcare programs refers to Uncle Ben's brands. "Petcare is designed to promote responsible pet ownership," Sammons says. "It would be inappropriate to use it to push our brands."[16]

Nothing more than a front

Despite such assurances about 'responsible pet ownership', some commentators appear to remain skeptical. In 1997, Stuart Littlemore said, 'it seems fair to say [Petcare] is nothing more than a front for the multinational pet food manufacturer Mars, through its Australian subsidiary Uncle Ben's'.[17] Leaflets distributed by Petcare depict cats and dogs eating out of bowls marked Whiskas and PAL. A scheme called Selectapet — designed to encourage children to supply their particulars to the Petcare database in exchange for advice on how to select a pet — carries the statement 'Proudly sponsored by Whiskas/PAL'. How, I ask, can a company sponsor itself? Sammons is right when he says it is inappropriate to 'push our brands'. However, this statement becomes irrelevant when we consider that pushing pet ownership is intended to grow the total processed pet food market. Since Uncle Ben's already controls 65 percent of the market the chances are that each additional pet will also consume Uncle Ben's products.

Petcare creates conditions favourable to the sale of Mars products by promoting the benefits of keeping pets and at the same time blunting anti-pet sentiment in the community. Wherever possible it works through 'experts'. These people become wedded to Petcare, if only on a friendly social basis, and the ultimate targets of the Petcare propaganda remain grateful for their indoctrination. A Council dog control officer spoke enthusiastically about the nice Petcare representative and revealed a cupboard full of Petcare leaflets intended for distribution to schoolchildren. The flip chart in the 'School talk kit' made no mention of schoolchildren becoming lifetime purchasers of Mars products. But since feeding pets is one of the joys associated with pet ownership, children would likely pay attention to the advice that:

- **The best diet for dogs and
  cats consists of high quality
  canned or dry pet food, or a
  mixture of both**

- **Specially formulated,
  commercial puppy and kitten
  food is the safest way to
  ensure your new pet has the
  correct nutritional balance.**

The thoughts I expressed on the Petcare methods were poorly received. I questioned the wisdom of schoolteachers uniting with an officer from the local Council in the careful programming of our children with Mars propaganda — propaganda not readily identifiable with Mars but with its vehicle, the Petcare Information and Advisory Service. I raised the matter of food related ill health and the use of taxpayers' funds to the detriment of the community. The Council officer stared blankly but did not wish to contemplate such notions.

The trouble is that Petcare has over many long years insinuated itself into the mindset of community people in a number of fields. It appears to be a power behind the annual Urban Animal Management Conference where Council employees gather at taxpayers' expense for a week in a luxury hotel. Delegates hear praise from a government minister for the top job they are all doing. Experts are flown in to tell of the alleged health-promoting and other benefits of pets while other experts downplay the downside. As for children mauled and adults savaged by dogs, experts are on hand to advise.

In 1998 the New Children's Hospital staged an injury prevention symposium, entitled 'Dogs'n'kids'.[18] The published line-up of speakers included the Petcare spokesperson and Delta Society director, Sue Chaseling. Delta Society, whose two speakers talked about bite prevention, is sponsored by pet food companies. Dr Kirsti Seksel spoke on animal behaviour. Her views on dog bites, published in conjunction with Petcare vet Dr Jonica Newby, include:

High profile dog attacks during the last two years have raised community awareness and a demand for solutions. Without veterinary input, some of the 'solutions' currently being advocated are extreme. For example, several child health professionals state that no family with a child under the age of four should have a dog.[19]

Paediatric surgeons and other child health professionals need support, not disparagement, as they contend with the disfiguring injuries and occasional death of toddlers. What price canned dog food?, I ask.

Petcare mostly escapes notice as a Mars funded organisation and consequently remains unchallenged. Occasionally events permit disclosure and allow us a rare chance for celebration. On 4 February 1993, quite by chance, I heard program announcements on the Australian Broadcasting Corporation (ABC) radio station 2BL. A Petcare segment on pet feeding was scheduled for the next day. As the appointed time drew near work stopped at the veterinary practice and we crowded around the radio, tape recorder at the ready.

The edited transcript of the program (Appendix D) shows how the ABC relayed information favourable to the Mars Company, Uncle Ben's. Brand names were not mentioned but listeners were steered towards artificial milk and canned kitten food. Competitors' canned fish received condemnation and the issue of dental disease — publicised by the Raw Meaty Bone Lobby not long before — was trivialised.

When I spoke with Julie Steiner, the interviewer, she seemed genuinely concerned that she had inadvertently aired a Mars Corporation advertorial. She offered, and I accepted, the opportunity to respond on her program providing that I avoided criticism of Mars.

Inside run at the ABC

'Thank you for your cassette and letter on [Pet foods'] Insidious Consequences, it looks fun but unfortunately I'm about to go overseas … I'll try to deal with it when I get back,' wrote Robyn Williams after receiving my tape-recording of three radio interviews dealing with the pet food story.[20] Robyn Williams first presented the 'Science Show' on

ABC radio in 1975. Publicity blurb states: 'Scientific issues, debates, events, personalities, exposing scientific fraud, discoveries and broadcasting pranks have been the hallmarks of the Science Show over the past 20 years.'[21] I was confident the pet food story met the program's criteria, and having gained the attention of the great man a good result could be expected.

But events turned out differently. An ominous silence ensued and further correspondence went unanswered. Something worried me over this about-face. Had I in some way offended and was never to know? It was not long before I gained an inkling as to the reasons for the silent rejection of the story. I tuned into one of Robyn Williams's programs and was surprised to hear Dr Jonica Newby, the Petcare Information and Advisory Service vet, reporting. No mention was made of her pet food promotion job; instead she was described as a veterinarian from Melbourne.

Jonica Newby does have a veterinary degree and was based in Melbourne — at the Petcare offices.[22] She has appeared in Petcare 'community service announcements on commercial TV' and written magazine articles. Without declaring her employment details these articles, flanked by ads for PAL and Whiskas, extolled the benefits of pet ownership.[23]

Imagine my further surprise when I came across a newspaper article written by Robyn Williams and entitled 'Cruel to muzzle age-old love'.[24] The article, at first sight about why we should keep dogs, on closer inspection, seemed like a coded proclamation of *old-age* love. And yes, it appears that the object of the then 52-year-old Robyn's adulation was 'Dr Jonica Newby, a Melbourne veterinarian'. After 1996, when the article appeared, a few more details have emerged, including Robyn and Jonica's setting up house together.

I asked ABC management for an explanation of the fate of my proposed story, and was informed: 'Robyn Williams' recollection of that matter from seven years ago is that he considered Mr Lonsdale's research was based on a small sample size and that it was not appropriate for The Science Show.'[25] Few people knew that Robyn Williams declined to broadcast the pet food story — acts of omission frequently go undetected. But acts of commission more readily gain attention, as occurred when Robyn and Jonica staged 'Animal Friends: a four part [ABC radio] series about pets'.

To gather material Jonica Newby travelled abroad and interviewed 'some of the world's leading experts'. A number of those interviewed had carried out work for Mars. Besides the general audience, the material was crafted to reach administrators and professionals responsible for such things as building design and urban spaces. Jonica insisted that we should plan buildings and public parks for pets because 'being a multi-cultural society means being multi-species as well'. Mars are concerned that with increasing urbanisation fewer people are keeping pets.[26]

Journalists and lawyers vented their anger at the disregard for ABC rules designed to protect the 'independence and integrity' of the taxpayer-funded ABC. Lawyer Stuart Littlemore, on his watchdog program 'Media Watch', told viewers that Robyn Williams had 'just completed a presentation of a four part series on why people should keep dogs and cats. Oh, they didn't admit that was the subject, but it was. Written and narrated by a publicist for something called the Petcare Information and Advisory Service which, it seems fair to say, is nothing more than a front for the multinational pet food manufacturer Mars, through its Australian subsidiary Uncle Ben's.'[27]

The Science Show's producer admitted knowing that Jonica Newby worked for Mars, but nevertheless Robyn Williams introduced the program by saying: 'Today is the start of a four part Science Show series, written and presented by Dr Jonica Newby, who's a vet from Melbourne.' Stuart Littlemore told Media Watch viewers: 'What he should have said is that she works in the pet food promotion business. No, I'm wrong. She shouldn't have been on the ABC at all. It's a crudely subtle pitch. Jonica Newby didn't tell us to buy PAL in so many words, but to keep pets — well, we have to buy food for them, don't we?'

Despite the publicity over what Littlemore labelled 'arrant tosh, highly insulting to her audience's intelligence', ABC management responded by circling the wagons with Robyn and Jonica safe inside. In a media release, the ABC defended the programs against what it said were 'false and misleading allegations'.[28] When the furore finally died down, I thought that there might be a change of policy, but I was mistaken. The ABC commissioned Jonica Newby to broadcast a five part TV series called 'The animal attraction'. Her book, which mirrored the radio programs, was renamed and reissued to coincide with the TV series.

Media Watch ran two more exposés on 'Jonica the vet' who they said was 'the public face of the pet food caper' and still ABC management refused to act.[29]

A fundraising arrangement

Among the great and the good that lend their name in support of the pet food industry are Guide Dogs for the Blind, World Wide Fund for Nature and the RSPCA. These are not shampoo commercial film stars or breakfast cereal sports stars whose glory days are short-lived. Instead they are internationally recognised organisations which constantly work on and promote their image through networks of paid and unpaid supporters.

Make no mistake, this is about global markets. Increasingly the image of Mars, or more tellingly Pedigree, the trademark name of Mars, becomes connected with respected charities. Mars has instituted a policy of global branding in order to exploit the TV advertising potential of global events such as the Soccer World Cup. Participating charities gain exposure in association with a successful corporation — but the main motivation is money. The bigger and more favourably regarded the charity the bigger the fees it can negotiate.

No one believes that film stars have a deep understanding of the brand name benefits of shampoo. For animal charities things are different. They cultivate the impression that they are authorities whose objectivity and insight are beyond question. They are used to getting their own way and resent criticism. Whenever I have challenged animal charities regarding their support for the artificial pet food company expropriation of billions of dollars from the masses I have met with hostility and denial.

The World Wide Fund for Nature campaigns to save endangered elephants, tigers, cheetahs and other charismatic species. Less well known are its efforts to preserve forests and wetlands. All of these activities are costly, difficult and deserve the highest commendation. WWF's association with artificial pet foods, though, deserves condemnation. In October 1992 I wrote to the Director of WWF regarding the organisation's participation in Uncle Ben's of Australia marketing campaigns. I encouraged him to consider that

> the dreadful consequences arising out of the unrestricted promotion and, in turn, consumption of processed pet foods involve effects on animal health, human economy and the global environment.

After ten months of close combat I gave up the unequal struggle when the WWF Corporate Relations Manager wrote in a letter:

> I would like to add that a corporate relationship with WWF is not an endorsement of their product. It is a fundraising arrangement that allows us to raise much needed funds for conservation. We are happy to be associated with a professional and well run organisation such as UBA. We have reviewed their environmental policies and visited their factory and found nothing in either to change our view of the organisation.

Cheetahs at the zoo

Cheetahs capture the imagination. As the fastest four-footed animal with striking good looks we want them to be winners. Alas, their plight in the wild, as a result of human population pressure, places the species on the endangered list. The unfairness touches us all but especially children who see the world in stark terms and are prone to feelings of guilt. They want the best for cheetahs and are delighted with any efforts to improve their fate. My sons tell me these things, especially Tom whose favourite animal is the cheetah.

It was thus in a spirit of high expectation that we set off for the Western Plains Zoo near Dubbo, NSW, where a cheetah captive breeding program is under way.

Tourist promotions by the government bring thousands of visitors to the zoo each year. Our visit coincided with the school holidays when other families were enjoying the outing. Or so I perceived from the excited chatter and smiles on the young faces. We were enjoying ourselves too; until we arrived at the cheetah enclosure where we encountered a huge disappointment. At the entrance a prominent A-frame sign announced:

> The cheetahs
> are regularly
> fed
> WHISKAS
> MILK PLUS
> courtesy of
> UNCLE BEN'S
> of Australia.
> This essential
> vitamin supplement
> is also enjoyed by Chester,
> the white tiger, sponsored
> by WHISKAS at
> Taronga Zoo

The boys and I were concerned at the implied disregard for cheetah biology. What could possibly be *essential* about a liquid food for adult wild carnivores? More information was soon made available and simply reinforced the commercial message.

At 11.30 am an attentive throng gathered to hear a Keeper's Talk. Pressed against the safety rail we gazed across the moat at the pair of cheetahs. Speaking into his microphone the keeper told us of elaborate surgical techniques employed in an attempt to breed from the pair. He went on to discuss feeding, which he said consisted of beef or horse meat three days a week, two days with no food and two days with whole chickens. His effusive comments on Whiskas Milk Plus left the clear impression that it *is* an essential part of the diet fed two or three days each week. Just as you buy in the supermarket for your cat, he said.

During question time I asked if he was under instructions to speak favourably of Whiskas Milk. He appeared surprised at the question and mentioned that heightened promotional activity commenced when Mr

John Mars paid a visit to the zoo. Uncle Ben's, he said, provided the Whiskas Milk in 500 ml containers. At this point I indicated my disapproval of the information so far delivered. The keeper, detecting trouble, telephoned the zoo office to organise a meeting with the zoo director. Rejoining the crowd my sons and I headed back down the path — past the sign which on the outgoing side repeated Uncle Ben's message.

The director, Dr Ian Denney, was in a jocular mood when he introduced me to his assistant, Dr David Blyde. But both were dismissive of my concerns. They would continue to promote the feeding practices which had been in place for five years. Dr Denney admitted that he would stop short of feeding Jelly Meat Whiskas, but in his opinion the milk version of the product was OK. And besides, it was impossible to ignore the sponsorship agreement with Uncle Ben's. I came away from the meeting dismayed at my inability to persuade the zoo's directors by reference to the facts. The zoo did have alternatives. Rabbits and free-ranging kangaroos were readily available — why were they not fed to the carnivores?

In total I collated twenty points of complaint which formed the basis of a five page letter. My solicitor approved the wording and I included several supporting documents, in particular a paper detailing the gangrenous liquefaction of the roof of the mouth of cheetahs fed an artificial diet in San Diego Zoo, California.[30] In some of the animals studied, discharges ran out of the nose, but for others it was impossible to tell until the animal was examined at autopsy. Such is the problem with wild animals: they can disguise the presence of severe disease. Unnatural solid foods are harmful to cheetahs; liquid foods must be considered worse.

I sent the letter and waited for a reply. None came and after three months I tried raising the matter with Members of Parliament. But this approach came to an end when the Minister for the Environment wrote: 'Finally, I wish to state the issues raised by Dr Lonsdale should not be pursued any further.' Three years later I revisited the zoo during school term time. A few tourists pedalled their bikes between the enclosures and in the distance I could see the cheetahs. The Whiskas Milk sign was still on display.

RSPCA deals

TV advertising works. The pet food companies know that the average American watches 30 hours of television each week and sees over 100 ads per day.[31] (They have the figures for other nations' TV watching habits too.) They know which programs attract the whole family and tailor their sales pitch accordingly. But of course the message is not just to buy 'Good-dog chow' or 'Happy-cat treats' but to purchase the entire fantasy that pets are an enhancement of everyone's life. In a Petcare TV commercial, broadcast as a community service announcement, Jonica Newby told her audience that:

> All [dogs] have one thing in common, they make great companions.
>
> No matter what type of person you are — or what type of lifestyle you have — there's a dog that's perfect for you.
>
> And remember, a dog is a friend for life.

The dogs in the ad gambol playfully and birds sing in the trees. The multiple realities of pet ownership for most people are very different. Pet ownership requires know-how, money, time and suitable surroundings. Puppies piddle on an expensive carpet in just the same way they piddle on a cheap one. Cats sharpen their claws on trees in the garden but the leather armchair provides a perfect substitute — as far as Pussy is concerned.

Of course, not everyone believes the ads. Most people accept that owning a 'friend for life' entails costs as well as benefits. Others remain confused or believe that pets, like consumer goods, can be discarded when circumstances dictate. The net result is millions of unwanted pets filling the welfare shelters and pounds to overflowing. Some pets suffer inhumane and cruel outcomes. But I believe that this is often due to ignorance on the part of the owner, not a conscious wish to injure the animal.

Integral to and benefiting from this commercially inspired mess are the humane societies. While protesting to the contrary, they have a stake in the continued flow of unwanted pets. This after all is how they justify their existence and their constant appeals for money. In

Australia the Royal Society for the Prevention of Cruelty to Animals
(RSPCA) are the biggest animal charity. In addition to providing
shelter for unwanted pets they wield the equivalent of police powers
where cruelty to animals is concerned. Acting on complaints, mostly
from neighbours, they investigate and prosecute hundreds of people
for neglect or cruelty to their animals.

In my view this often involves further victimisation of the victims.
How, I ask, are disempowered people supposed to know what is right
and what is best to do? However, the morality of the situation seems
to make little difference. The RSPCA prosecutes offenders and little
old ladies show their approval by bequeathing their life's savings to the
cause. Nowadays the RSPCA has the money and power, and I suggest
the responsibility, to challenge the commercial interests in their
wholesale exploitation of animals and the community.

Trading on its position of trust the RSPCA did for a time
produce its own brand of pet food. I bought some packets to learn
more about this commercial venture. Consumers were assured:

RSPCA PLEDGE
The RSPCA monitors the processing
of this pet food to ensure
your pet's vitamin and mineral
requirements are considered.
Proceeds from sales are devoted
to upgrading and expanding RSPCA
shelters for dogs and cats.
We pledge to help all creatures
great and small — especially yours.
Thank you for your support.

Something needed to be done about this marketing ploy, but what? Past
encounters with the RSPCA — trying to persuade them that feeding
processed food to carnivores involves the cruel infliction of suffering —
was like trying to nail jelly to a tree. I envisaged spending the rest of my
life in futile correspondence with this insular organisation. Initially I
wrote to the President, veterinarian Dr Hugh Wirth. I did not receive a

reply. The governments of Victoria, Queensland and Tasmania, the States where RSPCA pet food was marketed, were evasive or unhelpful. Eventually, more in desperation than in hope, I bundled up copies of all the correspondence plus supporting literature and sent it to the Patron of the RSPCA, Justice Michael Kirby.

Justice Kirby sits on the High Court of Australia along with six fellow judges. Additional to a comprehensive understanding of the law he is credited with a strong social conscience. I was delighted when he replied to my letter, stating that he had called for a report into my allegations, and ending on a personal note:

> I should say that with my two Abyssinian cats, I only rarely feed them tinned or packeted food. Like every living creature, they need a variety and it is not much more expensive to buy fresh products and to vary their diets.

Just one month later the Judge wrote again: 'I gather that RSPCA Australia is re-thinking its role in the production of pet food. I support that reconsideration for various reasons.' Within a few months production of the RSPCA brand stopped. Victory at last, or so I thought. Did this mean that the RSPCA had accepted that processed pet food is detrimental to the health of pets?

Any illusions were soon dispelled. Clients started to complain about their experiences at the Sydney RSPCA shelter. Owners collecting new puppies from the shelter were provided with 'Science Diet' leaflets and samples of the product. From those early beginnings in 1996 the cross-promotional activities of the RSPCA and the Science Diet people have grown to major prominence. Together they stage publicity gatherings at which politicians mingle with the throng. Science Diet advertisements trumpet:

- **Pet nutrition used in all RSPCA shelters.**

- **Pet nutrition trusted by Veterinarians.**

So what is special about Science Diet besides its cost — several times that of supermarket brands? In November 1997 the *Wall Street Journal* provided the answer under the heading: [32]

For You, My Pet

Why the Veterinarian Really Recommends That 'Designer' Chow

Colgate Gives Doctors Treats For Plugging Its Brand, And Sees Sales Surge

Colgate-Palmolive chairman Reuben Mark was struck by the success of Colgate toothpaste endorsed by dentists. He set out to replicate this success for Science Diet using veterinary endorsement as a marketing tool. In order to induce veterinarians to support the brand, Colgate spends

> hundreds of thousands of dollars a year funding university research and nutrition courses at every one of the 27 US veterinary colleges. Once in practice, vets who sell Science Diet and other premium foods directly pocket profits of as much as 40%.

Tons of free Science Diet are made available to impoverished veterinary students and the favour is returned many thousand fold. In 1996 Colgate-Palmolive paid just $1.9 million to advertise its pet food in the US as compared with competitors who spent between $40 and $90 million each.[33]

In Australia various sales gimmicks are employed, mostly through the veterinary profession.

Justice Kirby explained the RSPCA's conduct in terms of the high cost of feeding animals in its shelters. He said that the RSPCA had approached two companies for sponsorship funds and that Colgate-Palmolive had offered the better deal.

To the RSPCA the earlier pledge 'to help all creatures great and small' no longer seemed to matter.

In one final attempt at persuading the Judge to look again at what we believed to be a regrettable arrangement, Breck Muir and I sent him evidence for our views of RSPCA/Science Diet marketing campaigns. Justice Kirby declined to make a judgment because, he said, the matter related to expert opinion and he had to be guided by the duly elected Council of the RSPCA.

Pets and vets in the classroom

Free cat … free canned cat food for life … free veterinary checkups. These or similar promises are made by the nice lady from the pet food company as she introduces the new classroom cat. Children are grateful for the gifts, for even primary school children know that a lifetime's supply of cat food and veterinary services cost a lot. The nice lady from the pet food company, though, knows the costs are trivial when compared with the anticipated returns.

If one classroom cat converts 25 students into lifelong owners of cats who each spend a dollar a day on the company's products then that equates to half a million dollars. Maybe not all the students become cat owners but it matters little — each year another batch of students pass through the classroom. In a magazine photograph of children with a classroom cat posters on the wall proclaim 'A cat turns a house into a home' and 'A solitary cat is like Laurel without Hardy'.[34] (No prizes for guessing the angle. Start with one cat then add another — two cats eat twice as much as one.)

Strategic front or back door entry into the world's primary schools is the name of the marketing game. My first encounter with the phenomenon occurred in 1981. As the new vet in town I was pleased to officiate at the primary school pet show. The children and parents wanted to assess the new vet, and I was keen to give a good impression. Happily I can say that all went well, and even those that didn't finish first, second or third still received a prize … the 'Pet Show Kit', which the organisers had obtained, contained heaps of prizes bearing a Mars company label. 'Good-O's, a semi-moist processed food, was available by the bucket load, sufficient for a speed eating competition for all the dogs.

At the time it felt so natural, but looking back I am appalled at my unwitting involvement in the pet food marketing exercise. Twenty years on, those children at the show are now adults who will have seen thousands of pet food ads and fed tons of processed food to their unfortunate pets. Their children, besides being targeted at pet shows, are the focus of the Australian Veterinary Association PetPEP Program. Ostensibly designed to educate school children on the responsibilities of pet ownership, the Program contains subtle and not so subtle marketing messages to buy artificial pet food and make use of the veterinarian.

The early version of the Program contained naked promotional messages. Under the heading 'Nutrition Guide' the teacher was advised to recommend to the pupils:

- A mixture of dry and canned food is good for dogs and cats. Dogs can live on dry food only but it is probably best not to feed cats dry food only.
- Ask your vet about feeding your pet as he or she is very knowledgeable in this area.[35]

For ten and eleven year olds the lesson plan in the 1995 edition included a trip to a supermarket to price items, collect pet food labels and compare 'nutritional' information. In another section the teacher was advised to photocopy the Selectapet chart on pet selection for each of the children — completed Selectapet questionnaires to be mailed to Petcare. The resources section told how to obtain a Pet Show Kit from Petcare and how to obtain a classroom cat. A wallet at the back of the book contained Petcare promotional leaflets.[36]

The Australian Veterinary Association says that around $500,000 has been spent on PetPEP.[37] It has been rewritten several times and now travels under the guise of a 'Community Relations Program'. (Earlier editions, I believe, are still in circulation.) As a propaganda Trojan Horse the venture has direct access to the child's mind, endorsed by class teachers and most State Governments in Australia.

New South Wales, the State where I live, was the last State scheduled to receive the PetPEP Program. Before the launch of the Program I managed to obtain an interview with Dr Terry Burke, the Education Department officer responsible for the State's primary schools. Dr Douglas Bryden accompanied me on the visit, which produced excellent results. In a letter to the Australian Veterinary Association Dr Burke wrote: 'they would campaign against the use of such materials in schools in whatever ways might bring about a stop to the use of the materials; ... I have decided to put the project on "hold" until there is some resolution of this controversy.' (Did he imagine us wearing placards, chained to school railings?)

Unfortunately Dr Burke's ruling did not last. A change of government produced a new minister who seemed reluctant to confront commercial pet food and veterinary interests. Although he allowed PetPEP into schools the Minister required the AVA to avoid creating the impression that the Program had official approval. As my local Member of Parliament, the Minister permitted me a couple of interviews at which he showed me correspondence between the AVA and his department.[38] One letter indicated that the AVA had undertaken to remove from the Program any references to commercial food.

However the teachers' manual contained direct and indirect references to commercial food. This same manual, bedecked in red ribbon, was presented by TV vet Stephen Van Mil to a headmaster at a PetPEP publicity launch. TV cameras rolled and the children appeared delighted. Film footage showed Dr Joanne Sillince among the onlookers. Dr Sillince chaired the AVA Ethics and Complaints Committee and was a fierce supporter of the PetPEP Program. Subsequently, writing in AVA News, she made allegations against me.[39]

Modern society remains in the grip of the artificial pet food cult. Parents willingly permit their children to participate in the PetPEP Program, so strong is their trust in the veterinary profession. Even the President of the NSW Federation of Parents and Citizens Associations praised PetPEP, and said that it enjoyed the full support of the Federation.[40] Mars, Inc. and the AVA are no doubt pleased at such expressions of faith.

13

⟹⟾⟸⟸

Righting the wrongs:
charting a new course

*There is one thing stronger than all the armies in the
world: and that is an idea whose time has come.*

VICTOR HUGO[1]

What's to be done? The answer is lots, and it depends on many
factors, not least our imagination. First off we could ask John Mars
to reconsider the role of Mars, Inc. We could suggest to him that he
dismantle the company's artificial pet food empire and direct the
profits of its other ventures to the establishment of a natural pet food
industry. But I suspect that that idea, for a number of reasons, will
not receive early acceptance. Better, then, that we prepare the ground
for a lengthy campaign.

The environmentalists' catchcry 'think globally, act locally'
inspired millions, such that Margaret Thatcher was moved to say: We
are all environmentalists now. Not long ago, before 1962, that could
not be said. In that year Rachel Carson published *Silent Spring*, her
account of the poisoning of waterways and forests by agricultural
chemicals. The chapter headings bored into the global consciousness.
'Elixirs of Death', 'And No Birds Sing', 'Needless Havoc' and 'The
Human Price' were effective because they were true. Carson lamented:

> We allow the chemical death rain to fall as though there were no
> alternative, whereas in fact there are many, and our ingenuity
> could soon discover more if given the opportunity. Have we
> fallen into a mesmerised state that makes us accept as inevitable

that which is inferior or detrimental, as though having lost the will or the vision to demand that which is good?[2]

The definition underlying Carson's message is crucial. Rachel Carson heaped derision on the situation, and thus redefined what others considered to be innocuous, commonplace and normal. She complained about state and federal agencies and the ruthless power of the regulatory entomologists who 'function as prosecutor, judge and jury, tax assessor and collector and sheriff to enforce their own orders'. She could have been referring to the pet diet issue when she said:

> There is still very limited awareness of the nature of the threat. This is an era of specialists, each of whom sees his own problems and is unaware of or intolerant of the larger frame into which it fits. It is also an era dominated by industry, in which the right to make a dollar at whatever cost is seldom challenged. When the public protests, confronted by some obvious evidence of damaging results of pesticide applications, it is fed little tranquillising pills of half truth. We urgently need an end to these false assurances, to the sugar coating of unpalatable facts. It is the public that is being asked to assume the risks that the insect controllers calculate. The public must decide whether it wishes to continue on the present road, and it can do so only when in full possession of the facts. In the words of Jean Rostand, 'The obligation to endure gives us the right to know'.[3]

How does the public become informed? With difficulty, it would seem. Sir Richard Doll, the scientist credited with discovering the adverse effects of smoking — although Nazi scientists preceded him by eight years — was convinced of the health risks by 1949. By the 1950s the medical profession shared his opinion, but the public's smoking habits only began to change in the 1970s. According to Doll 'the crucial factor was the media beginning to report the dangers as proved rather than controversial'.[4]

There are 43 known carcinogens in tobacco smoke, there have been 57,000 reports on the health hazards of smoking, and still tobacco company executives deny that their product kills, despite their own research which confirms the dangers. For us, dealing with the pet food scourge, we shall encounter much the same humbug or worse. Most veterinarians, unlike medical doctors, champion artificial foods and the authorities smile benignly. However we should not be deterred; each of us can unleash 'the power of one'. The results should be amazing.

Start with your pet — and your vet

I cannot know your circumstances, but if you are like me you appreciate rewards. And since 'what gets rewarded gets done', I encourage you to build in a system of rewards for joining the fight against the pet food monster. By reading this book you have already acquired much new knowledge. This can empower you in your further dealings with pet health issues — practical engagement is the next step.

If you own a pet, then start by feeding it a more natural diet (the particulars are located in Appendix C). As a pioneer you may feel lonely and insecure, so try to liaise with others engaged in the same project. Once you overcome the initial obstacles the sight and sound of happy pets drooling over their natural diet will be its own reward. But beware, many pet owners become overtaken by missionary zeal once they experience the rewards of happy healthy pets. I applaud any effort to spread the word, but I don't wish you to become a social bore!

Sooner or later you will need to broach the junk food issue with your veterinarian. From my experience as a candidate for veterinary elections I believe that about 10 percent of all veterinarians are in agreement with the principles outlined in this book. What do you do if your veterinarian is a determined member of the 90 percent majority? You can try to convince him or her otherwise, find another veterinarian or accept the need for pragmatism. Situations differ and some people take a while to see the obvious. Max Planck, the pioneer quantum physicist, remarked: 'A new scientific truth does not triumph by convincing opponents and making them see the light, but rather because its opponents eventually die, and a new generation grows up that is familiar with it.'[5] It may be a while before the last vestiges of the current generation die out. Meanwhile, we need a strategy.

The best strategy I know is to ask questions, lots of questions. When confronted with a veterinarian's waiting room full of artificial pet foods, ask for an explanation. Enquire why your veterinarian recommends six monthly dental prophylaxis. Ask if the skin complaint, joint disease or any other disease he or she diagnoses could be associated with an artificial diet and a diseased mouth. If the veterinarian bluffs, fails to provide an answer or says something patently absurd, respond with another question. Eventually, in the privacy of his or her own thoughts, your veterinarian may retreat from a position of received certainty.

At the next meeting you can start again where you left off the time before. Try to build on agreements reached. If your veterinarian accepts that a natural diet and a healthy mouth are best for pets, ask why she or he continues to sell junk food. Common decency and veterinary rules require that veterinarians cannot lie to their clients. Keep on asking questions and you will begin to tease out the commercially inspired dogma from wherever it resides. No one will be able to accuse you of being argumentative; you will have simply asked questions.

Whistleblowing matters

All that is needed for evil to prosper is for people of good will to do nothing.

EDMUND BURKE[6]

> Every pet owner has a right, even an obligation, to question the suitability and safety of the veterinary advice they receive.

Every pet owner has a right, even an obligation, to question the suitability and safety of the veterinary advice they receive. Individual veterinarians may not like having their authority challenged but they are unlikely to retaliate. The dynamics change dramatically when a person calls into question the suitability and safety of the products of an organisation. By raising such issues a person may well encounter difficulties and consequences akin to the vicissitudes of a 'whistleblower'.

'Whistleblowing: a health issue' is how psychiatrist Dr Jean Lennane described the problem in the *British Medical Journal.*[7] Of 35 whistle-blowers, 29 experienced immediate victimisation upon blowing the whistle. 'Long term relationships broke up in seven cases, and 60 of 77 children of 30 subjects were adversely affected.' Stress and financial loss were other consequences, with 17 of the 35 people contemplating suicide. Lennane says: 'Whistleblowers received little or no help from statutory authorities and only a modest amount of help from workmates.'

Brian Martin in *The Whistleblower's Handbook* explains that those people in positions of authority, who in theory can respond to a whistleblower's concerns, in practice often can't. Martin says: 'The trouble is that the powerholders [company managers, politicians, bureaucrats] are most strongly affected by each other and by the need to maintain their power. Furthermore, from their point of view they have only a limited scope for action because of all the obstacles they face… They might actually feel powerless themselves. They are high-level cogs in a system of power.'[8]

If, despite the risks, you consider becoming a whistleblower, please check out the information in Appendix E — you need to be prepared for when the goal posts shift and the playing field tilts against you.

Home study

Assuming you plan to become an anti-artificial-pet-food-activist you will need to do some study. The best place to start is in front of the TV. Keep a diary handy, a cassette in the videorecorder, a TV guide at the ready and your finger on the remote control button. This may be your first experience of kicking off the consumer shackles and turning the tables on the propa-gandists. If so, take your time. Savour your new-found strength as you record the evidence.

Advertisers can be relied upon to pipe a steady stream of often false or misleading information directly into your lounge room.

Advertisers can be relied upon to pipe a steady stream of often false or misleading information directly into your lounge room. They are used to a system that operates in their favour and will not be pleased that you are recording their activities.

Just your lingering presence creates a dilemma for them. Do they modify their claims in order to satisfy critics or do they continue to manipulate the majority? Here in Australia they have tried both tactics. On the one hand they allow that raw bones are a desirable, even necessary part of the diet. On the other hand they make ever more outlandish claims for the alleged health benefits of their products.

Sandwiched between the ads, the pets-n'-vets programs are a standard feature of early evening viewing. Celebrity veterinary presenters enjoy a wide following and considerable influence, especially among the young. Until now the imbalance in power has been considerable, but videorecording can change all that. You can store and review the information presented. Is it of genuine and widespread benefit? Is it designed for some ulterior commercial motive? Are harmful products openly promoted or is there a welter of pseudoscience designed to distract the audience from important issues?

You may find damning pet food advertisements in newspapers and magazines. Check out the pet-oriented articles too. By maintaining a clippings file you start to lay the foundations for victory.

Supermarket action

For me the sight of artificial pet food stacked high at the supermarket conjures thoughts of sick, degraded animals. These days I avoid such stomach-churning experiences, but in past times I conducted research in the pet food aisle. Never once did I find a label which I considered to be true. Most products carry the 'complete and balanced' claim about providing every nutritional requirement. Purely in the line of duty I purchased samples to use as evidence. I also have examples of raw hide chews and milk-and-rice artificial bones which are claimed to be of benefit for oral hygiene — notwithstanding the companies' other products which are said to be 'complete and balanced' and requiring no supplementation.

Labels on canned products carry the least information and those on dry products carry the most. You can choose whether the errors of omission on the cans are more incriminating than the errors of commission on the packets, or vice versa. You can also learn the contact details of the manufacturer. In most instances the company will be a division of one of the conglomerates that make a range of packaged goods. In the supermarket I act on the information gathered. I simply boycott all products which carry a Mars, Nestlé, Heinz, Colgate-Palmolive, Ralston Purina or similar label.

Boycotts are an old and effective idea. Consumers boycotted Shell products due to that company's involvement in the Nigerian civil war. Nestlé were a target of a global boycott arising from their baby milk formula marketing practices in the Third World. If you consider organising a boycott make sure you first obtain legal advice. It may be that your State or national laws prohibit community action. Even if the laws encourage free expression it may well be that the target company will initiate a Strategic Lawsuit Against Public Participation or SLAPP (see Chapter 11) which as we know can mean an expensive exercise.

Eventually consumer protection and truth in labelling laws will be enforced against the pet food producers. When that happens, either the products will disappear from the supermarket shelves or they will bear warning labels similar to those on cigarettes. WARNING: RESEARCH CONFIRMS THAT THIS PRODUCT CAN HARM YOUR DOG. WARNING: THIS PRODUCT WILL PREDISPOSE YOUR PET TO PERIODONTAL AND OTHER SERIOUS DISEASES. In the meantime, you may consider chatting with fellow shoppers as you push your trolley down the aisles.

Don't expect expressions of gratitude if you proffer advice about the pet food dangers. Until the information appears in written form shoppers are likely to view you and your message with skepticism. Nevertheless things will not change until people do share information of public benefit. And let's be confident about this. Saving pet owners money and sparing pets the agony of diet-induced disease are a socially responsible activity.

On that basis it becomes perfectly reasonable to question the activities of the retailers of artificial pet food. On your next trip to the supermarket try taking cans and packets of pet food to the checkout in order to illustrate a complaint. Mention that you are concerned that the products were in full view and accessible to children and if fed to their animals over a long period could lead to severe ill health.

You may possess the courage to take the matter further. If so, ask to speak with the manager about the business policies of the company. He may appear to humour you as a weird eccentric. However, if you are the tenth person making the same point in the space of two days then at least you can feel part of a team. Try asking a few questions. If the manager's attitude softens ask him to liaise with head office regarding your concerns. As a sweetener mention the 'P' word. P is for profit and guaranteed to create a positive attitude in the most defensive supermarket manager. Tell him that frozen natural pet food returns a much higher profit margin than the standard grocery lines. Mention that you and your friends are looking for a dependable supply of natural food for your pets and ask if he will assist.

Regulating the regulators

Your safest assumption as a whistleblower dealing with regulatory agencies is that you will encounter resistance if not outright opposition. Keep in mind that the artificial pet food industry worldwide is worth more than $25 billion annually and yet no one in authority appears to be the least concerned. The reason is simple. The multinational pet food industry makes and polices its own rules. It likes things the way they are; the corollary is that it doesn't like whistleblowers.

- In the US the Federal Drug Administration (FDA) is responsible for ensuring that pet foods are safe for consumers. The FDA chairs the American Association of Feed Control Officials committee which sets the guidelines for the composition of artificial pet foods. Several pet food company representatives sit on the committee.
- The Royal College of Veterinary Surgeons regulates the veterinary profession in Britain. Some members of its governing council have links with or work for pet food companies.
- In Australia the RSPCA, responsible for policing animal cruelty laws, used to market pet food and now actively promotes pet food products of the Colgate-Palmolive Corporation.

Against this background of pet food industry influence, a range of regulators responsible for consumer protection in respect of advertising and labelling laws continue to provide endorsement of the status quo.

If you challenge the various pet food related bureaucracies you will encounter obstacles, but persistence pays. Wherever possible document responses, or lack of responses, and keep things simple. When writing to an agency, ask a couple of key questions and keep these anchored to the fundamental charter or purpose of the agency. For example:

- Anti-cruelty laws, overseen by the RSPCA, require animals to be fed appropriate foodstuffs in appropriate quantity.
- The American Association of Feed Control Officials boldly proclaims: 'The most important aspect of feed regulation is to provide protection for the consumer as well as the regulated industry.'[9]
- The Royal College of Veterinary Surgeons' Code of Conduct requires that each of its 18,000 members undertake to: 'pursue the work of my profession with uprightness of conduct and that my constant endeavour will be to ensure the welfare of animals committed to my care.'[10]

By holding regulators to their promises we might get enforcement of existing rules — no need for new rules — the global pet food machine would grind to a halt.

Politicians, the media

When you communicate with a regulatory agency you may well receive very little in the way of satisfaction and so resolve to take the matter to your political representative. Be prepared for more frustration.

My files are brimful with letters from politicians thanking me for communicating my concerns and expressing regret that they can do nothing to help. When a couple did try to be of assistance they soon faded after running into the inertia of the system. On one occasion I was invited to Parliament House to explain my concerns. My host turned to another MP and asked: 'Do you fancy taking on the multinationals?' Their guffaws of dread resounded throughout the corridor.

Pressure for change must come from the community. Until then we can expect the politicians to be either indifferent to or in league with the perpetrators of the current exploitation. Journalists, by contrast, are generally sympathetic to the anti-pet food cause. But they operate under constraints. In Australia, and elsewhere, defamation laws are notoriously restrictive such that journalists often prefer to avoid controversial issues. Commercial publishers and broadcasters need to keep half an eye on their advertisers.

In most newspaper articles I have seen on the dangers of artificial pet foods, a manufacturers' spokesperson had been asked to provide comment. Tobacco companies, baby milk formula makers and even brewers, however, no longer command the same attention when their products are criticised in the media. Community attitudes define those products as harmful — journalists can take a partisan line. Just as the media influences community attitudes, so changed community attitudes affect the media.

Newspapers try to meet the expectations of their readership with new and interesting stories. Importantly, a story should not turn out to have been a hoax. For this reason a story as big and complex as the pet health issue — and which contradicts established belief — may be neglected. If journalists are unable to evaluate the truth, for them the safest strategy is to avoid the story. This principle was well illustrated when I sent out 1200 individually addressed letters to journalists and politicians inviting them to investigate alleged maladministration. TV reporter Christopher Zinn was one of the few people who replied.

Christopher ignored warnings from his colleagues because, he said, he liked a challenge. By taking time to study the issues he was able to make a useful contribution to the Saturday morning viewing of a national audience. My opponents on the program maintained their line. Dr Jill Maddison, consultant to the Nestlé company Friskies, denied pets suffered an AIDS-like condition as a result of severe periodontal disease. Dr Robert Zammit was shown doling out dry pellets for his dogs. When Christopher Zinn asked 'What's wrong with feeding raw meaty bones?', Zammit replied: 'It's not natural.'[11] After the show viewers telephoned me to offer support and to condemn the company sympathisers.

Veterinary associations

Each of us is a product of our times and, even when motivated by the best of intentions, prone to human error. In chronicling the 'evolution of the veterinary art', Professor Smithcors adopts a sympathetic attitude to past foibles when he says: 'The true practitioner of the veterinary art [is] one whose practice is as rational as the knowledge of the times permits.'[12] Modern practitioners — juggling the needs of work and family — rely on professional associations to set standards of practice.

Veterinary associations prescribe guidelines for their members. Unfortunately no one sets guidelines for the associations who are therefore free to steer a course and trim their sails according to the breeze. Supposedly providing leadership, those gathering at the helm tend to be followers or opportunists looking for the main chance. Businessmen, detecting weakness, persuade the associations to hoist flags of convenience. 'There, framing our Association's officers, were two banners of pet food products. And there was no dissenting voice', complained two senior Australian veterinarians.[13] In America the Veterinary Medical Association nurtures a close relationship with Colgate-Palmolive; and the British Veterinary Dental Association helped promote a Mars Company milk-and-rice artificial bone.

On matters of diet and disease the knowledge of the times ought to be clear cut and fundamental to the practice of veterinary medicine. Associations, allied with pet food producers, manage to muddy the issues either by refusing to take pivotal decisions or by taking the wrong ones. When, in 1993, the Australian Veterinary Association were shamed into researching the diet and disease connection a Mars Corporation adviser assisted with the research.[14] Nevertheless, the research committee made the rational observation that 'if periodontal disease could be prevented then any secondary complications from this problem would be reduced'. Communicating this information to a dependent public would seem to be an urgent priority.

> On matters of diet and disease the knowledge of the times ought to be clear cut and fundamental to the practice of veterinary medicine.

Will veterinary associations be made to pay for their role in the promotion of harmful products to an unsuspecting public? Perhaps the experiences of the American Dental Association (ADA) may set a precedent. The ADA allows some toothbrush manufacturers to display its Seal of Acceptance on toothbrush packets. The manufacturers gain endorsement, the ADA receives a fee and consumers are led to believe that toothbrushes are useful and without harmful effect. Illinois resident Mark Trimarco disagrees, claiming that he sustained toothbrush abrasion requiring medical and dental treatment for pain and suffering. His legal suit cited the ADA for allowing its Seal of Acceptance to be used without requiring, as a condition of the arrangement, any warning or information about the harm that can be caused by tooth brushing.[15]

Win or lose, Mr Trimarco's case should send a shudder through those associations that trade integrity for a quick dollar. In May 1999 America's Veterinary Oral Health Council (VOHC) announced 'the awarding of the VOHC Seal to Friskies® Dental Diet, the first non-prescription dry cat food that helps maintain dental health in cats'. Dr Colin Harvey, director of the VOHC, stated: 'Just as consumers look for the American Dental Association (ADA) Seal of Acceptance on human dental products, pet owners should look for the VOHC Seal when choosing products to maintain their cat's dental health.'[16]

In due course pet owners, tired of being duped into feeding harmful products to their pets, may follow Mr Trimarco's lead. The resultant court hearings should prove most entertaining. Will Dr Harvey — who has published information on the benefits of natural foodstuffs — be required to show that his endorsement of artificial products 'is as rational as the knowledge of the times permits'?

Veterinary schools

Pet food company largesse percolates throughout veterinary schools without a sound — lecturers act as consultants and departments take research funds. But we have reasons for optimism. The more unsustainable the charade the sooner the crash will come. Or alternatively academics will realise their peril and effect changes.

Around twenty-five years ago dentists made a shift in emphasis — away from ineffectual treatments towards a widespread preventive approach. Sydney University Dental School used to have an annual intake of 120 students but now has 55. Australia-wide the number of new dental graduates has dropped from over 250 to 150 each year —

200 immigrant dentists once arrived each year too. Where previously one dentist could barely cope with the dental needs of 2000 people, a ratio of one dentist to 3000–5000 is now sufficient.[17] Dental school staff numbers have been slashed accordingly.

If, as seems likely, the need for veterinarians drops once most pets are fed natural food, various outcomes are possible. Consider the scenario where a veterinary school, sponsored by pet food companies, continues to promote artificial feeding of pets and continues to boost student numbers. Students enrol in the belief that the school provides full and accurate information and that a good job awaits them at the end of the course. But if, on graduation, students face unemployment, questions may be asked. While hypothetical, it is possible to imagine students, disadvantaged in such a way, seeking redress.

The pet food companies

The principle of opposition to exploitation is easy. Simply do the opposite of what the exploiters intend you to do. Look for the hidden message as well as the obvious one in pet food advertisements and resolve to do the reverse. When you see a shelf full of pet food cans ignore it and turn away. When the advertisers encourage you to support the RSPCA, Guide Dogs for the Blind or World Wide Fund for Nature, refuse on principle — but send the charity a letter of explanation. If just 10 percent of consumers disobey the pet food companies then each year $2.5 billion worth of products will remain on the shelf.

But you may wish to take a more active role. Simply discussing the issues with friends and family helps create a climate for change. If you discover a source of natural food or a veterinarian who believes in natural feeding then you can pass on the knowledge with good effect.

Direct action

Letter writing from the comfort of your own home represents the easiest way to begin a campaign of direct action. Letters to the press, your local council and primary schools can all have a beneficial effect. If you are tempted to contact the pet food makers it's best to write letters rather than telephone their free helplines. Helplines serve as early warning systems to help the manufacturers head off trouble. But regardless of how you contact them, once they have your name and address, they can keep track of your protests.

However, there are some useful procedures worth employing which can turn the encounters to your advantage.

- At all times keep meticulous records.
- Ask questions and avoid accusations and you will be more likely to get a response.
- Write to the customer enquiry department *and* to the head of the company.
- Try sending the same enquiry to several companies simultaneously.
- Ask for inconsistencies to be explained.

As more people join the campaign several things will start to happen. Individuals will become better informed and have first-hand knowledge of the companies' methods. Small informal protest groups will pool information and resources. It may be that organised groups will emerge to take up the fight.

Class action

In earlier times, no matter the strength of your case, courts were best avoided. Two developments have, in many jurisdictions, changed that. First, lawyers are able to fight cases on a contingency basis — the client pays only for a successful outcome. Second, the arrangement called a Class Action allows a number of litigants — sometimes a great many — to bring a joint action against a company. These procedures give lawyers an incentive to gather together a group of litigants and then to coordinate the subsequent court action. In the US, and increasingly in other countries including Australia, Class Action specialists advertise for business.

The first Class Action against a pet food company will be a dramatic affair. The owners of periodontal disease affected pets would seem to be an obvious first choice to launch an action, but will they be dog or cat owners? Many factors will govern the lawyers' choice, not least the past statements of the companies and their veterinary supporters. Evidence which demonstrates that the companies knew about the problem and did nothing, or alternatively instigated a cover-up, will be in demand. (See the accompanying box.)

SELECTION OF MARS CORPORATION STATEMENTS REGARDING THE ADEQUACY OF COMMERCIAL FOODS AND THE NEED FOR RAW BONES IN THE DIET OF PET CATS AND DOGS

It is imperative that in addition to this basic [commercial] diet bones, preferably, or rawhide chews or super hard baked biscuits be added to it so that periodontal disease can be prevented.

—1987: Dr P C Higgins (Uncle Ben's of Australia), Preventative Dentistry, Proceedings, No. 100 Post Graduate Committee in Veterinary Science, University of Sydney.

Offer large raw bones or rawhide chew toys.

—1993: 'Keeping your dog fit and healthy', Pedigree PAL brochure.

Thank you for your concerns regarding animal dental hygiene, but we feel satisfied with the Uncle Ben's policy that Pal and Whiskas are good pet foods which should be supplemented with chew bones to form a complete diet.

—28 January 1993: Scott Lyall, Corporate Relations Manager, WWF Australia (letter to the author).

For many dogs and cats, providing appropriate chews — such as raw bones or rawhide chews — can reduce the amount of plaque on the teeth... Give your pet only raw bones. For dogs, large marrow bones are best... Cats tend to cope well with raw chicken wings.

—April 1993: Dr Kathy McQuillan (Uncle Ben's) in the *Australian Women's Weekly*.

We have received at Uncle Ben's a number of enquiries from the general public ... who switched their dogs onto the [raw meaty bone] diet ... and they've raised concerns in that they've experienced problems with that recommendation. Animals have suffered intestinal obstructions and become constipated and they've rung Uncle Ben's asking us what are we going to do about Dr Lonsdale.

—16 June 1993: Dr Greg Mahon, Senior Veterinary Adviser to Uncle Ben's of Australia, speaking at Sydney University.

Uncooked bones can damage teeth and there is no evidence that they clean them. They also carry a number of diseases such as salmonella, and are smelly and unpleasant to have about the house.

— 12 May 1996: David Watson, Professional Communications Manager, Pedigree Pet Foods, quoted in the *Sunday Telegraph*.

CONTINUED...

As a corporation, our business unit in a country supports the views of the official body of veterinary experts in that country on this issue. As you will be aware, the recommendations of the Australian Veterinary Dental Association and the Australian Small Animal Veterinary Association is that dental health should be maintained by one or more of the following methods: supplementation of the diet with raw bones (2-3 times weekly) or large hard biscuits; provision of rawhide chew toys; home dental care such as daily rubbing or brushing of teeth and gums; and/or regular oral examination and oral procedures as necessary.
　　—10 July 1996: Dr N T Gorman, Head of Research, Waltham Centre
　　for Pet Nutrition (letter to the author).

The feeding of raw, meaty bones is not recommended due to the risk of digestive disorders and dental damage.
　　—Winter 1998: *Veterinary Practice Nurse* (quarterly publication of
　　Pedigree Petfoods).

Back in 1986 the Mars research unit, then called The Animal Studies Centre, asked Dr R Borthwick to report on periodontal disease in dogs and cats. He advised:

There does not seem to be any method, at present, to simulate in dogs and cats the protocols of oral hygiene undertaken in man. The marketing of a canine dentifrice some decades ago was a failure, the patients did not permit having their teeth brushed regularly and owners could not or would not attempt to do so for very long.[18]

Despite the absurdity of tooth brushing for dogs there are plenty of veterinarians who, I suspect, would be prepared to enter the witness box to defend the practice.

Despite the absurdity of tooth brushing for dogs there are plenty of veterinarians who, I suspect, would be prepared to enter the witness box to defend the practice. A judge might believe these apologists and conclude that the combination of junk food and tooth brushing is an acceptable health risk. But when it comes to cats few, if any, veterinarians recommend tooth brushing. Perhaps for this simple reason owners of cats affected by diet-induced periodontal disease may be the first to launch an action.

Defamation woes

Regardless of the uncertainties we should take courage in the future and be guided by the past. In particular I like the messages arising out of the Nestlé baby milk debacle and the McDonald's libel trial. Both events involved organised groups who challenged the companies head on. In both cases the companies took ill-advised legal action in an attempt to muzzle the groups. Let's look briefly at each of them.

In 1974 the British charity War on Want, in a 28 page pamphlet entitled 'The Baby Killer', targeted baby milk formula companies' activities in the Third World. Soon afterwards the article was reprinted in German under the heading 'Nestlé Kills Babies'. Nestlé struck back with a defamation action lasting more than two years. Although Nestlé won the legal battle they lost the propaganda war, as world attention became focused on the company and its activities.[19] In addition to a global consumer boycott of Nestlé products, the World Health Organisation/UNICEF established a code on the marketing of breast milk substitutes. The Code (see the box below) could, with slight modification, serve as a marketing code for artificial pet food formulas.[20]

WHO/UNICEF CODE FOR THE MARKETING OF
BREAST MILK SUBSTITUTES

---

1. No advertising of breast milk substitutes.

2. No free samples to mothers.

3. No promotion of products through health care facilities.

4. No company mothercraft nurses to advise mothers.

5. No gifts or personal samples to health workers.

6. No words or pictures idealizing artificial feeding, including pictures of infants, on the labels of the products.

7. Information to health workers should be scientific and factual.

8. All information on artificial feeding, including the labels, should explain the benefits of breast-feeding and the costs and hazards associated with artificial feeding.

9. Unsuitable products, such as sweetened condensed milk, should not be promoted for babies.

McDonald's, the fast food giant, discovered some unpalatable truths in its defamation action against two London Greenpeace activists. The longest trial in English history provided McDonald's with a paltry technical victory, but their costs were huge. They spent an estimated £10 million on the trial which became the focus of media interest for almost three years. 'What's Wrong With McDonald's?', the leaflet at the heart of the conflict, continued in even wider circulation and the two defendants became international heroes. Two aspects of the judgment hold particular significance for the junk pet food conflict. It was ruled that McDonald's 'exploit children by using them as more susceptible subjects of advertising' and that various advertisements 'have pretended to a positive nutritional benefit which McDonald's food ... did not match'.[21]

With Members of Parliament, senior lawyers and community groups rallying to the cause we can expect further developments. One commentator observed: 'If a high-cholesterol, fat-laden diet with no redeeming nutritional value is an express ticket to the grave, McDonald's may one day find itself explaining its marketing strategy to the courts and an increasingly hostile public.'[22] By way of mitigation McDonald's points out that few people consume its products at every meal. Junk pet food manufacturers do not have the same excuse to shelter behind.

Education and research

> *Therefore the rich are not necessarily secure, the poor are not necessarily insecure, the majority do not necessarily prevail, minorities do not necessarily fail. That which determines who will win and who will lose, who is secure and who is in peril, is their science, their Way.*
>
> SUN TZU II[23]

The plot of this book unfolded in 1991 when a Mars touring party of British scientists addressed a meeting of the Australian Veterinary Association. Avoiding adverse references to their paymasters, the

scientists talked around the subject of pet foods' insidious consequences but never *about* it. Periodontal disease and immune compromise of the majority of the world's domestic pets was not on the
agenda of the meeting either. This book seeks to redress the balance
somewhat, with the science of periodontal disease and immune
dysfunction occupying the early chapters. Veterinary teachers,
researchers, politicians and others play a role in subsequent chapters
— mostly in collaboration with the pet food industry.

Several passages in the book refer to denial and suppression by
the veterinary authorities. But despite their efforts some sense has
emerged from the diet and disease debate. Perhaps the single most
telling statement appeared in the February 1994 *AVA News*:

> Further research is required to better define the relationship
> between particular diet types and oral health in dogs and cats.
> Those investigating small animal health problems should also
> take diet and diet consistency into account when researching
> systemic disease — possible confounding effects of diet and
> poor oral health must be considered in such studies.[24]

When writing the final chapters of this book I was keen to include
up-to-date information. By coincidence, Sydney University hosted
a course, delivered by experts from Britain and America, entitled
'Immunity and Disease'.[25] In a spirit of optimism I enrolled. I wanted
to hear good news; how veterinary researchers are taking account of
diet and diet consistency. Instead I gained the impression that from
1991 to 1999 the artificial pet food industry had tightened its grip on
the veterinary mind.

During the five day course Drs Michael Day and Rance Sellon
piled immunological fact upon immunological fact but never once did
they raise the issue of periodontal disease, despite this being the most
widespread disease of pets and, by their own criteria, mediated by the
immune system. Similarly junk pet foods, which place an undue direct
and indirect burden on the immune system, were not mentioned.
Instead Rance Sellon spoke about the chemical components of diet
which affect the immune system, without considering the source of

those components. Following Rance Sellon's comments Michael Day enthused that the pet food industry is taking an interest in, and spending large sums on, researching diet and immunity — a range of new products should soon be available.

I raised my hand and asked Michael Day if he could tell us more. No, he could not because, as he explained, he did consultancy work for one of the companies and was sworn to secrecy. Tense silence gripped the room. I pressed on, asking if he was prepared to blind us with science, in a snowstorm of information, while leaving out important facts. Artificial diets appear to be the main reason for immunological disorders in pets, I said: surely veterinarians should be researching and informing pet owners — not assisting the manufacturers? Michael Day paused, muttered 'No comment', and gestured to Rance Sellon for help. Sellon's attempted reply lacked conviction — it seemed that he had never thought about things in this way before.

What can be done to encourage researchers to adjust their focus? Redefining aspects of pet food research as a potentially harmful activity may play a part. Thus stigmatised, researchers may find it less attractive. Of course, much depends on improved information regarding research activities. Questions will need to be asked and answers clearly given. Until Michael Day, during proceedings, mentioned his involvement with the artificial pet food industry neither the course organisers nor his audience knew of his connection.

When the research culture changes, instead of assisting the claims made for artificial pet foods, new work will expressly investigate the harmful effects. Subtle biochemical pathways will be charted, providing benefits for man and animals. Freed from the influence of the pet food giants a surge of new findings should fill the communication channels. Overnight textbooks will appear dated and need to be rewritten from the perspective of the new enlightenment. Some diseases will become preventable and others will be easier to cure with new drugs and techniques.

Practical knowledge, practical benefits

Pet owners may well be interested in the theory of carnivore feeding, but *practical* knowledge is essential. Owners need to know the location of natural pet food outlets and the price of goods — not knowing creates frustration. In my local area we are lucky to have butchers and pet shops that stock rabbits, kangaroo tails, chicken carcasses and other meaty bones. It was a simple matter to collate the information and produce a list for my clients. Most areas are not so well served and pet owners may need to search out available outlets or, for those with entrepreneurial flair, start their own.

Until we try the new way we cannot know the full range of benefits. Some owners, who believe that 'nature knows best' and wish to 'do no harm', may want to provide whole carcasses for their pets. The existing small industry that supplies rodents for snake owners and zoos can be expanded. Whole fresh fish are currently available, as are day-old male chickens surplus to the egg industry. Pests such as rabbits, currently targeted in wasteful and ineffective eradication campaigns, can be harvested instead.

As the natural pet food industry increases, so the artificial industry, together with its harmful effects, should go into decline. Farmland that is used to grow grains for processed pet foods can be released for other crops. Meat industry by-products, instead of undergoing needless processing, packaging and transportation, can be fed raw. Table scraps, previously consigned to the garbage tip, can be fed to pets with resultant economic and environmental benefits. With these and other changes rural communities should gain new job opportunities and urban communities should obtain cheaper pet foods — with everyone benefiting from healthier, longer lived pets. No more slurping of canned stew, no more rattle of dry pellets; instead, the sounds of nature, the crunching of raw meaty bones.

PART III

LIFE AND DEATH IN THE WILD

14

A cybernetic hypothesis
of periodontal disease

'In conclusion, I want,' he said
'ten thousand mixed chains of predation —
none of your simple rabbit and coyote stuff!
This ocean shall have many mouths, many palates.
    I want,
say, a hundred ways of death, and three thousand
    of regeneration —
all in technicolor naturally.'

MARK O'CONNOR[1]

In this final chapter I'd like to take you on a short journey into a realm of ideas that may seem strange or unfamiliar, and which may appear to have little or no connection with the rest of the book. But there is a connection — and there's an important difference.

Periodontal disease, as we shall see, has a place in the natural order of things: it is part of the cycle of life and death that ensures the balance of nature. Omnivores such as humans and herbivores such as sheep are affected by periodontal disease. In the 'wild' this can be expected to affect individual life expectancy and thus the composition of omnivore and herbivore populations. But it is the effect of periodontal disease on wild carnivores which will concern us here — how periodontal disease may influence carnivore numbers.

However, while nature is 'concerned' with balancing the needs of the majority, pet owners are concerned with the needs of their individual dog or cat, and want it to enjoy good health throughout its time on earth. And that, either directly or indirectly, is what this book is about. But by seeing things in a wider context, by gaining a better understanding of nature's ways, we should be able to improve the lot of individual dogs and cats.

> by seeing things in a wider context, by gaining a better understanding of nature's ways, we should be able to improve the lot of individual dogs and cats.

Coming to a commitment

In August 1992 a fair proportion of the Sydney veterinary community attended a lecture I gave entitled 'Pandemic of periodontal disease: a malodorous condition' (see Chapter 2). Having drawn the vets to a contemplation of the issues, I hoped I could persuade them to assume responsibility for further research — instead they scoffed. By implication they considered the issues trivial and me absurd for thinking otherwise. While their opinions of me were bearable the thing that rankled was the imputation that periodontal disease was trivial. I was sure they were wrong, but I was unsure how to go about proving it. Gradually over the following days the outline of a plan crystallised. Instead of working on periodontal issues part time I would make a bigger commitment.

The decision made, things fell into place. Alan and Jason, my veterinary associates, undertook more of the daily work of the practice, thereby freeing me for the research effort. My lack of office skills and dread of computers posed an obstacle. Luckily Charlie Garrison and Susan Rutter, long-time clients, came to the rescue. Together we bought a second-hand computer and established an office. Soon Susan and I were hard at work gathering and sorting references. With each new clue we gained encouragement that we were on the right track — and it was far from trivial.

Periodontal disease and its consequences are extremely important. For me the main breakthrough occurred with the recognition that the disease appears to be a necessary and desirable feature of carnivore biology. At first sight it was a counter-intuitive notion — until I separated the domestic scene from the wild. In domesticity periodontal disease runs out of control — the only desirable feature being that people debate why this should be so. In healthy wild carnivores periodontal disease is absent, but when they are sick or dying the disease appears.

Things which commonly occur in nature can be said to be necessary or desirable. This applies to diseases too; without them populations of animals would run out of control, displace other species and overtake food supplies. Some diseases are sporadic and acute in their effect, suddenly killing large numbers. Others, particularly the parasitic diseases, are slower to act and only affect a few individuals.

The question arises, what is the effect of periodontal disease on wild carnivores? Does it have sporadic devastating consequences or does it act by low level retardation of populations? Or does it serve a different purpose? In the quest for meaning it appeared that periodontal disease is not a typical disease, more a potential disease. When suitable conditions arise it makes an appearance — as though it can be switched on (or more rarely switched off) according to need. Chance discovery of the following passage from an old edition of *The Children's Encyclopedia* assisted me in the quest:

> Day and night the Carnivora are playing their appointed part in keeping down numbers. They themselves are without visible foes, yet have a mysterious check on over-multiplication. All the flesh-eaters are more numerous at birth than the herb-eaters. But an unseen agency takes off cubs from every nursery, or the flesh-eaters would be too numerous, and would destroy all herb-eaters. Check and countercheck are constantly at work to maintain the balance...[2]

Could periodontal disease be the means for the 'mysterious check on over-multiplication'? Was this disease the 'unseen agency' which 'takes off cubs from every nursery'?

Formulating the cybernetic hypothesis of periodontal disease

The Children's Encyclopedia reflects a willingness to pose big questions regarding life's patterns. Adults often shy away from such lines of enquiry, but these days there is one giant theory which tackles the interconnectedness of life head on. The theory, named after the Greek earth goddess, Gaia, was first put forward by James Lovelock FRS at a 1969 scientific meeting on the origins of life on Earth. Writing in 1987, Lovelock said:

> We have since defined Gaia as a complex entity involving the Earth's biosphere, atmosphere, oceans and soil; the totality constituting a feedback or cybernetic system which seeks an optimal physical and chemical environment for life on this planet. The maintenance of relatively constant conditions by active control may be conveniently described by the term 'homoeostasis'.[3]

At first the theory was derided by leading biologists. Gradually, over a 30 year period, this opposition has changed to widespread acceptance of the predictive and explanatory powers of the theory.[4] In speaking of Gaia and food chains, James Lovelock said:

> The theory of Gaia has developed to the stage where it can now be demonstrated, with the aid of numerical models and computers, that a diverse chain of predators and prey is a stable and stronger ecosystem than a single self-contained species, or a small group of very limited mix.[5]

The similarity between James Lovelock's 'diverse chain of predators' and *The Children's Encyclopedia's* 'check and countercheck [which] are constantly at work' was unmistakable. At the same time I was steeped in periodontal disease research and puzzling over each new finding. With these ideas swirling around in my head I began to ponder how periodontal disease fitted into nature's grand design. Three concepts seemed to be important:

- First — clinical experience and the veterinary literature confirm that periodontal disease is not a trivial entity. Once periodontal disease becomes established it triggers disease in other organ systems. Disease in those systems exacerbates periodontal disease — sufferers enter a downward spiral of worsening periodontal and systemic disease.
- Second — feeding on natural foodstuffs serves to cleanse the oral cavity and thus protects a carnivore from periodontal and associated disease. By contrast a starving carnivore suffers calorie deficit and consequences of an unclean mouth.
- Third — in this age of mammals, carnivores sit, as regulators, at the top of the food chain. But regulators also need to be regulated.

When these concepts are placed in the context of Gaia planetary regulation the following equations arise:

- Plants regulate herbivores; in turn, herbivores regulate plants.
- Herbivores regulate carnivores; in turn, carnivores regulate herbivores.
- Carnivores regulate periodontal disease organisms; in turn, periodontal disease organisms regulate carnivores.

Plants <=> Herbivores <=> Carnivores <=> Periodontal disease organisms

The next step to formulation of the hypothesis occurred in a dream. I woke on Christmas morning in 1992 to find a series of propositions running through my mind. In case the ideas evaporated, I tiptoed past the Christmas stockings and committed the words to paper:

Cybernetic hypothesis of periodontal disease in mammalian carnivores

Periodontal disease is the dependable disease which modulates the effects of starvation in wild carnivore population dynamics.

- A 'feedback loop' ensures that daily chewing of raw meaty bones sanitises the oral cavity of the successful carnivore.
- Failure of the 'feedback loop' facilitates multiplication of pathogenic bacteria within plaque and the development of periodontal disease.
- Incremental losses of carnivores and herbivores are thereby facilitated.
- The populations of herbivores, carnivores and bacteria are maintained in dynamic equilibrium.

I must emphasise that this schema is not a statement of established scientific fact but a hypothesis of how balance may be maintained in nature. Some of the technical terms may be unfamiliar to you; however, they do refer to familiar situations, as I shall explain.

Feedback loops

You may be wondering why death by starvation is not the simple regulator of carnivores. While the role of starvation should be acknowledged, taken on its own it would be much too crude. Why is periodontal disease important when there are many other diseases? Once again we should not discount other diseases, but they tend to be too severe in action or too unpredictable in effect. Cybernetic systems and feedback loops tend to be subtle and predictable.

James Lovelock postulated that the Earth is akin to a giant self-regulating organism with multiple cybernetic systems involving feedback loops. He was able to demonstrate that, left to the laws of chemistry, neither the oxygen level nor the temperature of the planet would be conducive to life. Contrary to expectations, conditions have been relatively stable since the emergence of life on the planet. In order to illustrate the meaning of cybernetics — the 'branch of study which is concerned with self-regulating systems of communication and control in living organisms and machines' — Lovelock described a man on the deck of a rolling ship.[6]

A sailor struck dead does not remain upright on the deck of a ship — he falls and then rolls with the movement of the ship. By contrast a living crewman employs a complex action of muscles and bones to keep upright against the effects of the wind and rolling deck. Positioning and repositioning of muscles and bones occur in response to nervous impulses. The eyes focused on the horizon, together with the organs of balance in the ears, provide overall sensitivity regarding position in space. Located in the skin, muscles and joints are sensory nerve endings which communicate subtle changes to the brain. In response to sensory input the brain communicates with and thus controls the muscles which contract and in turn control the stance of the person.

These push/pull cycles of information and action passing through the brain are called feedback loops. At the simple level a nervous impulse is sent to a muscle giving rise to a contraction. Sensors in the muscle detect the contraction and dispatch a negative message to the brain. The brain responds by sending less impulses to the muscle — thereby damping down the contraction. Gentle regulation of action is usually the preferred option and this is enhanced by several negative feedback loops having a modulating impact on the system. For the man on the ship his stance is modulated by negative feedback loops between the brain, muscles, eyes and ears.

Absence of negative feedback or the introduction of positive feedback are further potential enhancements of living systems. Under these circumstances systems accelerate beyond the usual; for instance a mother finding superhuman strength to lift a car off her child. Ordinarily this would be an impossible task due to the negative feedback of pain and psychological signals processed by the brain. Wartime exploits provide further examples of accelerating systems, sometimes out of control. We marvel at tales of courageous conduct and at other times are saddened by atrocities. We describe those caught in harmful, out-of-control feedback loops as being caught in a vicious cycle.

For carnivores natural food provides a negative feedback effect on oral bacteria — they are scrubbed away. Absence of food and therefore absence of the negative feedback loop permit bacteria to proliferate, and periodontal disease develops. Periodontal disease leads to systemic ill health which in turn, by positive feedback, worsens periodontal disease. Carnivores caught in a vicious cycle of worsening starvation and periodontal disease lose their 'appointed part in keeping down [herbivore] numbers' and death becomes inevitable. For the individual this may seem harsh, but for others in the system, whether predators or prey, there are wider cybernetic consequences. Let us use these concepts to see how incremental regulation of a pack of wolves might occur.

Hypothetical example

Wolves living in a finite environment prey on a flock of wild sheep. Without modulating influences population size will likely lurch up and down, being determined solely by food supply. As wolf numbers increase they will eat the sheep and then, when sheep become scarce, the wolves will suffer mass starvation. A few sheep remaining in an environment relatively free of predators will in turn increase in numbers until they exceed the food supply. Starvation will ensue. Violent fluctuations suit neither wolves nor sheep — a modulating influence is required.

By adding periodontal disease to the model we increase the sensitivity of wolves to starvation. In this example there are ten wolves within a pack hierarchy. On day one they catch and eat a sheep. The wolves' hunger is satiated and their mouths are scrubbed clean of bacteria. Pack hierarchy remains intact in readiness for the next hunt. For the sheep in our story, sacrifice of one means that the other flock members will not be troubled by wolves for a couple of days. However, pressure increases as fewer sheep are now available to feed the same number of wolves.

At the next hunt perchance, one wolf is injured, is late to arrive at the kill and consequently remains hungry. For nine wolves things remain much as before. For the injured wolf the outlook changes. He suffers from hunger and is somewhat weakened. Plaque begins to accumulate on his teeth. Over the succeeding days, in the absence of food, things worsen. Periodontal organisms and toxins pass into the various organ systems of the sickening wolf. His stressed immune system exacerbates the developing periodontal disease and feeds back information to other body systems.

At all times the wolves' senses of sight, touch, smell, taste and hearing provide feedback on their position in the pecking order, their position in the environment and their relationship to their prey. Unconscious feelings of physical and immune system well-being create feedback loops within the wolves' internal environment. The nine well-fed wolves become increasingly aware that wolf number ten no longer contributes to the hunt. Rather than share the kill with him they seek to ostracise him. The sick wolf, aware of his bad breath and failing fortunes, moves away rather than endure bullying. As a lone wolf, his days become numbered.

Now let's jump ahead in time to the breeding season. Good rains and bright sunlight produce plenty of herbage. Conditions provide positive feedback to the sheep; they grow fat and many lambs are born. One wolf gives birth to a litter. At first, hunting young lambs is easy and the wolf makes plenty of milk for her cubs. By four weeks of age the cubs' erupting teeth provide an opportunity for plaque organisms. Regular chewing on lamb carcasses limits the establishment of plaque and the cubs remain healthy.

By the age of four months the dynamics begin to change between wolves, sheep and plaque. Many lambs have already been eaten and those which remain are fleeter of foot and harder to catch. Wolf cubs cutting permanent teeth need more food and more gum massage to keep plaque at bay. In the competition for food a differential develops between the strong cubs and the weakest member. Harassed, affected by hunger and worsening periodontal disease the weakling is caught in a vicious cycle and dies. The remaining siblings benefit by the reduction in competition for food and the food (i.e. the sheep) benefit by reduction in wolf numbers.

Love thine enemy

The above example highlights the influence of periodontal disease. In the Diagram (opposite page) a number of organs are shown to depend on and to influence each other. If any one fails, a cascade effect engulfs the other organs within the cybernetic model. Take the heart as a starting point: as it fails it has an adverse effect on the bone marrow, musculoskeletal system, liver and kidneys. These systems themselves have multiple feedback effects:

- A faulty bone marrow produces less red blood cells, thus requiring a greater output from the heart.
- A musculoskeletal system denied sufficient oxygen sends signals to the heart seeking a bigger output.
- The liver suffused with toxins and denied oxygen does not function at full capacity and thus fails to provide sufficient glucose energy to the cardiac muscle.
- Kidneys denied oxygen fail to clear toxins from the blood.
- Circulating toxins affect the heart.

Caught in a vicious cycle, the heart attempts to increase its output, resulting in further cardiac muscle damage.

Poor cardiac output means poor circulation in the gums with resulting build up of toxins and decrease in oxygen supply — a favourable environment for the growth of periodontal bacteria. Other changes in the internal environment of the subject animal contribute to immune changes. Whether hyperimmune, auto-immune, hypo-immune or any combination, each has an effect on periodontal organisms. The bacteria thereby come to 'know' information regarding the internal conditions of the host. We could say the immune system, by virtue of its actions, 'communicates' with the bacteria. The corollary here is that the bacteria 'communicate' with the immune system, which then feeds this information to the internal environment.

This view of the immune system acting as a two-way system of communication between the inner and outer environments is, I believe, an enhancement of the conventional view. In conventional terms the immune system uses 'soldiers' and 'clean-up crews' to maintain internal health of the individual. By according the immune

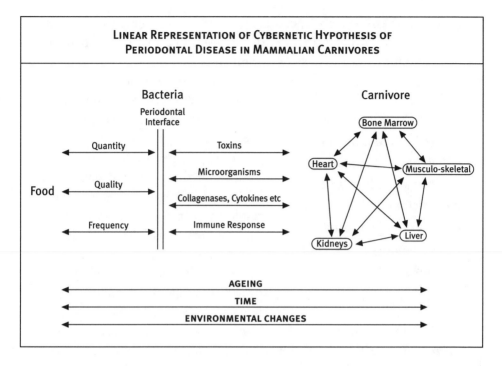

LINEAR REPRESENTATION OF CYBERNETIC HYPOTHESIS OF
PERIODONTAL DISEASE IN MAMMALIAN CARNIVORES

system a communication role, cybernetic control can be exerted between bacteria and individuals, individuals in social groups and social groups within ecosystems.

Communication is triggered at interfaces. A hand-tap to the head and a slap communicate different messages at the interface of hand and scalp. And both giver and receiver get the message. The sight and smell of roses communicate clear messages between lovers through specialised interfaces of eyes and nose. In modern science interactions and perturbations at interfaces are seen as key areas in the complexities of life.[7] For carnivores the key interface with their world is their teeth and gums — at once the source of their greatest strength and also their greatest weakness.

One other aspect of the immune system deserves mention. Under the conventional view the system protects the body. Adherents of this view are perplexed to find that frequently the immune system potentiates disease processes. To the cybernetician this is not a paradox, since depending on circumstances and the intersection of feedback loops, systems can have opposite functions. That the immune system serves both to protect the individual and ultimately to kill that individual is not inconsistent with the needs of either the individual, the community or the wider environment.

> That the immune system serves both to protect the individual and ultimately to kill that individual is not inconsistent with the needs of either the individual, the community or the wider environment.

That is to say that, while life is important, death is no less important to the efficient functioning of natural systems. In our cybernetic model, life and death are two sides of the cycle. Death of a sheep ensured oral good health of our wolf pack with the resultant death of billions of periodontal organisms. The wolf pack of course lived as a result of the death of a sheep. The death of one sheep provided temporary benefit to the remainder of the flock which was able to return to grazing free from the wolves' attention — and incremental death by predation is better than mass death by starvation. When death did befall individual wolves, for the individual it was inevitable and better it was soon over. For the remainder of the pack less competition for food was a benefit. For plaque organisms in the mouths of wolves, sheep are the enemy. But more sheep leads to more wolves that must ultimately die. Plaque bacteria gain their best chance at life during the dying days of wolves.

Programmed cell death

Do not despise death, but be well content with it, since this too is one of those things which nature wills.

MARCUS AURELIUS ANTONINUS (AD 121–180)[8]

The Cybernetic Hypothesis refers to the incremental losses of herbivores and carnivores as a means of controlling their populations. Similar mechanisms appear to be at work elsewhere. Development of a mammalian embryo recapitulates the stages of evolution. At one stage the embryo has gill slits much like a fish, but the cells of the slits die to make way for the mammalian form. Similarly our embryonic fingers are joined together by a web. It is not that the cells of the fingers grow outward; it is in fact a case of the webbing cells being programmed to die at an appointed time.

Prior to 1972 no one suspected that the same programmed cell death is used to shape cell populations in mature animals. In that year a group of cancer researchers published a paper in which they introduced the term *apoptosis*, from the ancient Greek meaning falling of leaves, to describe the social control of cells designed to maintain balance within tissues.[9] At first there was little interest in the subject but now apoptosis is a frequently used word in science and medicine. There is even a Cell Death Society devoted to studying this phenomenon.[10] Speaking about the slow uptake of such ideas, Professor Barbara Osborne of the University of Massachusetts said: 'Sometimes it takes a while for something to sink in as being important. Everybody thought about death as something you didn't want to happen.'[11]

Now researchers have discovered that all cells have a genetically determined 'death pathway' and that under the influence of various chemicals apoptosis is either triggered or suppressed. A common example is that of the lactating breast. In pregnancy hormonal control produces enlarged breasts in readiness for milk production. Once the baby is weaned the milk-secreting cells, having served their purpose, commit suicide in response to hormonal signals. Other cells seem to have intrinsic biological clocks which govern their demise and which are modulated through a cascade of chemical signals. Pollutants, drugs and radiation exert some of their effects by apoptosis — as do the stress hormones, corticosteroids.

With our increasing awareness of the longitudinal and horizontal connections in the web of life we could expect evidence of programmed cell death in other areas. In the February 1995 edition of the journal *Science*, a paper was published describing mechanisms for the maintenance of healthy bacterial populations dependent on programmed death of some of their own kind.[12] Sometimes, however, apoptosis fails to occur as expected. Many cancers are thought to arise by constant proliferation of cells which should under ordinary circumstances die. But even suppression of apoptosis may confer benefits, being just another aspect of cybernetic control.

Now that scientists recognise programmed cell death and the regulatory role of death by predation and disease in populations, the question arises as to where periodontal disease fits in. It appears periodontal disease is the dependable disease of carnivores following on a failure to clean the oral cavity. Chemicals produced by plaque organisms trigger apoptosis of gingival cells.[13] If those same chemicals have a similar action on other cells, including cells of the immune system, this will suggest a possible mechanism of action of the Cybernetic Hypothesis.

Where do bacteria fit?

Nothing is too wonderful to be true, if it be consistent with the laws of nature.

MICHAEL FARADAY[14]

Sheep and wolves — which operate on our time scale and have physical dimensions similar to our own — are easy to conceptualise. Bacteria, though, being for the most part invisible, are easily forgotten. Such treatment of our ancestors is neither respectful nor prudent. Bacteria were here first — 3.5 billion-year-old rocks contain fossilised bacteria — and have always been the most numerous life forms.[15] Long before plants and multi-celled animals appeared the environment of planet Earth was regulated by and for the bacteria.

The Cybernetic Hypothesis, which concerns a subset of the vast range of the phenomena encompassed by Lovelock's Gaia Hypothesis, seeks to link the environment, herbivores, carnivores and plaque bacteria in an interdependent whole. And if we look closely, bacteria are active regulators at every level. Since Charles Darwin it has been known that life evolved

The Cybernetic Hypothesis, which concerns a subset of the vast range of the phenomena encompassed by Lovelock's Gaia Hypothesis, seeks to link the environment, herbivores, carnivores and plaque bacteria in an interdependent whole.

from simple-celled organisms to the wonderfully diverse world of living things in existence today. Darwin commented:

> We cannot fathom the marvellous complexity of an organic being; but on the hypothesis [Darwin's theory of evolution] here advanced this complexity is much increased. Each living creature must be looked at as a microcosm — a little universe, formed of a host of self-propagating organisms, inconceivably minute and as numerous as the stars in heaven.[16]

Lynn Margulis, professor of biology at the University of Massachusetts, provides us with compelling evidence that bacteria living together, and then inside each other, gave rise to humans and the rest of multi-celled life. Rather than an arms race with competing species — as the poet Tennyson put it, 'Nature, red in tooth and claw' — Margulis describes a system of alliances.[17]

A prime example relates to how we came to breathe oxygen. Scientists suggest that when the first microbes emerged more than 3.5 billion years ago the Earth's atmosphere was predominantly carbon dioxide and water vapour. Those first inhabitants lived without oxygen gas (anaerobes) and it was another one billion years before the cyanobacteria appeared on the scene. These primitive forerunners of green plants — with the ability to photosynthesise sugars from carbon dioxide and water — produced oxygen gas as a by-product. Gradually the gas accumulated in the atmosphere until about 1.5 billion years ago, when the composition of the Earth's atmosphere stabilised at around 20 percent oxygen.[18]

Oxygen gas is toxic to anaerobes, which therefore developed ways of eluding the hazard. Some sheltered in mud or under other organisms away from the gas. Others evolved into aerobes which utilised oxygen for the release of energy from carbon compounds. When some oxygen-respiring bacteria took up residence inside anaerobes a blessed alliance was struck. A likely manner in which this occurred arises from the predator/prey interaction.[19] Early predators probably invaded prey cells in ways similar to the modern predatory bacteria. In most such encounters the prey died but in some instances the prey would have resisted to the point that, while weakened, it nonetheless survived. At first such mergers would have been shaky, but with refinement over time the union was perfected.

Both partners in the alliance needed to modify their old free-living ways in exchange for mutual benefits. The invaders gained food and shelter and the host cells the energy production and metabolites generated by the invaders' utilisation of oxygen — host cells were obligated to deliver oxygen to their fussy guests. It is fair to say that our lungs and circulatory systems are a direct response to that need to deliver atmospheric oxygen to the furthermost parts of a complex system of coevolved cells. Of course there were numerous links in the process commencing with coexisting bacteria and culminating in wolves, sheep and people — but it did take more than two billion years.

> **While the evolution of complex species inspires wonder, the fact that many bacteria have remained virtually unchanged since the early beginnings demands equal recognition.**

While the evolution of complex species inspires wonder, the fact that many bacteria have remained virtually unchanged since the early beginnings demands equal recognition. Anaerobes still require an oxygen-free environment, akin to that on the Earth at the time of the origin of life. And the biofilm lifestyle — complex alliances requiring 'check and counter-check' to maintain the balance — probably dates from the development of co-dependency between anaerobe species (aerobes came later).

In the cybernetic model, bacterial communities maintain soil health for growth of herbage to feed sheep, sheep depend on rumen biofilms for the digestion of herbage, and wolves feed on sheep and are thus dependent on biofilms. But wolves as regulators also need regulating. It appears that plaque biofilms help close the ecological loop by hastening the demise of redundant wolves. Within plaque, anaerobes play a key role. They are essential for biofilm homeostasis and give rise to the odour and health effects of periodontal disease. In this age of mammals it appears that conditions on the planet may still be regulated by and for the anaerobes.

Corroborations and refutations

Before the Cybernetic Hypothesis can gain elevation to theory status new evidence will need to be brought to bear. There are three categories of enquiry, with much overlapping among them.

- First, there is the gathering of supporting evidence either from the scientific literature or from field observation — much existing information makes more sense when reinterpreted within a cybernetic framework.
- Second, the attempt to find counter-examples that refute the hypothesis; for instance a community of mammalian carnivores free from periodontal disease and living in balance with their prey. If the hypothesis survives the attempted refutation it is thereby strengthened.
- Third, perhaps the most significant category concerns the predictive and explanatory ability of the hypothesis. In this instance the hypothesis needs to predict and explain phenomena that are considered either unlikely or unexpected according to the current dominant paradigm.

The carnivores' susceptibility to periodontal disease differs from that of herbivores and omnivores. Within the context of the hypothesis this makes good sense. In the extreme a flock of sheep could all be at the brink of starvation when as a result of a rain storm their feeding fortunes recover. No particular advantage would accrue to a flock which suffered severe periodontal disease and reduced its numbers at the onset of a drought.

Paradoxically domestic flocks seem to be widely affected by early onset periodontal disease and resultant incisor tooth loss, regardless of the pasture. If the same occurs in the wild then this could be interpreted as a 'biological clock' mechanism designed to cull older sheep, thus making way for the young.

(Note: The term *periodontal disease* may act as an obstacle to our understanding of how the process intercalates with other influences affecting the biology of species and of the planet generally — other influences that we call *physiological* or *ecological*, and by implication are considered desirable, as opposed to a *disease* that by implication we consider to be harmful. However, in deference to common usage, I continue to refer to periodontal *disease*.)

Human omnivores appear to withstand a level of periodontal disease more readily than carnivores. In a cooperative species even periodontal disease affected individuals can be of benefit to the survivability of the group. But we do know that periodontal disease in modern humans tends to advance with age, which during our primitive evolutionary phase may have been an important regulator of the species.

Periodontal disease is mediated through the immune system which in turn is much affected by stress. As the authors of a paper entitled, 'Nutrition, stress and immune activation' explain in their opening lines:

> The response to stress (physical, social or microbial) provokes an integrated reaction involving the immune system (via cytokines), the central nervous system (via nervous output) and the endocrine system (via hormones) each influencing and influenced by the other physiological responses to environmental change. In this context, the concept of a link between nutrition and immunity is readily appreciated, in that nutritional deficiencies may cause stress or may alter central nervous system output and thereby impact on immune function.[20]

In expanding their argument, the authors propose the concept 'that changes in immune status have a feedback effect on nutrient intake'. If these authors are proved correct then this would lend support to the concept of animals and particularly carnivores entering a downward spiral of periodontal disease, starvation and death as their immune status declines.

The notion of a runaway decline in the health of hungry carnivores is the central theme of the Cybernetic Hypothesis. Multiple influences are thought to impact on the final outcome. It is both interesting to speculate and useful to know which metabolic pathways and feedback loops are responsible. In its August 1998 issue, *Nature* published information on this subject from a group of researchers at the Imperial College School of Medicine, London. In experiments on mice they found that a hormone, leptin, was a likely regulator of the immuno-suppressive effects of acute starvation. Just 28 hours starvation triggered a fall in leptin levels which then precipitated a marked decline in immune function.[21]

Scientists observing the concomitant decline in nutritional status and immune function were surprised.[22] From the conventional viewpoint the immune system is supposed to protect the individual mouse and the conventional evolutionary perspective suggests that the mouse with the strongest immune system survives. But this narrow view seeks to confine the meaning of 'individual'. If we take 'individual' to signify a mouse family or mouse community or the entire species of mice, the emphasis changes. It may well serve the evolutionary interests of the individual wider communities if a single mouse dies. If we then widen our focus to the Gaia world of 'all for one and one for all' we can see that what we may initially perceive as individual weakness may indeed confer strength on the greater whole.[23]

Publishing the cybernetic hypothesis

Coming across a satisfactory explanation for some disparate and seemingly contradictory facts provides a great thrill for any scientist. Following the discovery you want to communicate the information to colleagues. Once published the ideas remain on the record for others to substantiate and accept or to refute and reject. There is a third possibility, and that entails the information being ignored and ultimately forgotten which is much the same as not being published at all. Within a few days of literally dreaming up the Cybernetic Hypothesis I had an article ready for publication. The few established facts used as supporting evidence were kept deliberately brief as a demonstration that the hypothesis was internally consistent and required little in the way of external support — besides, in 1992 I knew nothing of biofilms and apoptosis. In conclusion, I offered a challenge:

> The new-found hypothesis says that wild animals waiting to die suffer periodontal disease. Thanks to the efforts of the pet food industry the majority of pet animals receive calories but not physical cleansing of the oral cavity. These poor unfortunates

are condemned to dwell in the antechamber of death suffering the ghastly consequences of a foul mouth and a variety of immune malfunctions. They are propped up by calorie intake, physical defence against predators and frequent visits to the vet. Alas for them they are denied the rapid and merciful demise of their wild counterparts.

When the furore subsides this hypothesis should emerge strengthened and elevated to theory status. We can expect 'Road to Damascus' style conversions. The germ theory will be subsumed into a new paradigm with corresponding greater explanatory and predictive powers. The pet food industry will be compelled to withdraw its outrageous claims and may be required to compensate its victims. Veterinary teaching could gain a sympathy for its subject and be forever altered. The big question left to boggle the mind of the philosopher/scientist is: What next?[24]

There is an art to gaining publication and luck plays a big part too. Being inexperienced in the matter I decided to start with the *Australian Veterinary Journal* — the journal did invite submissions from ordinary members of the Australian Veterinary Association. I mailed the manuscript on 8 February 1993 and by 5 March I had a response. Both referees declared the paper was unsuitable for publication in the journal. One referee was moved to say:

> The article can also be construed as amounting to an unsubstantiated attack on the pet food industry and I wonder if this might not render the author and/or the *Aust. Vet. J.* liable to adverse criticism at the least if not some form of legal action or litigation.

This left me with the problem of where to direct my next publication attempt. Self-publication was an option, though I didn't seriously consider it. Thoughts of using the Internet did not, for me, exist at that time. And had someone made such a suggestion it would have sounded like science fiction fantasy — about as likely as getting the article published in the *Journal of Veterinary Dentistry*. But time changes things such that reversals are the norm. In March 1994 the *Journal of Veterinary Dentistry*, with minimal changes, accorded the article pride of place. Nowadays, it is also available on the Internet.[25]

What next?

What happens next is anybody's guess. Since carnivores occupy the extreme end of the food chain, some aspects of their biology are unique to them. But other aspects ought to have application further down the chain; for nature uses the same palette of colours at all locations. If the Cybernetic Hypothesis can explain how and why marginalised carnivores die, and if chewing on natural food proves to be the 'miracle prevention', then perhaps something similar applies to humans too?

APPENDICES

Appendix A

Remarks made by
Dr Douglas Bryden at the AVA
annual general meeting, 1993

Mr Acting President, I should say that in speaking I wish to move an amendment to the motion which may not be seen as speaking for the motion or against it. Neither should that be seen as being on the fence. There has been a lot of heat and a lot of emotion in this issue and because of that I think it does warrant consideration by the AVA as a group and as a whole. However I agree with Dr Maddison's comments and I've expressed those comments and sentiments to the two proponents of the motion and in person in recent times and also again in the last few days. I also agree with Dr Prowse [member of the AVA Executive] that it must remain the right of the editor of a publication to decide what material will be included and what will not be included in the publication. Sometimes that will mean that information that should be heard will be suppressed — sometimes in malice, sometimes by mistake — but it's still the prerogative of an editor to make those decisions. Because of the heat and perhaps for other reasons this issue has become a very emotional one.

Earlier this week I had one of the proponents of the motion referred to me as a 'madman'. Now that wasn't by somebody whose opinion I didn't appreciate, it was by a very respected member of the profession. I've not found Dr Lonsdale to be a madman at all. I've found him to be a very dedicated and thinking veterinarian. He is certainly a very intelligent veterinarian. I believe that his ideas are along the right track. I do disagree with some of the ways in which they have been presented and I have mentioned those to him personally.

I would urge all of you who are interested in animal disease and in animal care and who are concerned about this issue to visit Riverstone and to talk to him about what he is doing and what he is achieving. Soak up some of the feeling of the team at Riverstone and look critically at the comments and suggestions that are made and the cases which you will see. I'd urge you, talk to his clients and hear what they say about the therapies which he is instituting. It will be an enlightening experience for you to do that.

I'd like the polarisation which has occurred during this debate to stop. I think it is potentially extraordinarily dangerous to the profession and I think that it is not in the best interests of the community or the patients that we serve. I'd like to promote and enhance the 'getting together' of veterinarians to talk about areas of difference, to talk about the different ideas we have ... in relation to therapy and disease in general. We must remember that not everything is written in the journals. Not everything that is true appears in a refereed journal and not everything that appears in a refereed journal is true...

I know that Dr Lonsdale makes all of us uncomfortable, he makes me uncomfortable, but that should be a signal to us that maybe we should be shifting and looking around us... We need to remember that if we are going to move ahead we must be prepared to be uncomfortable.

I don't believe ... that there is much difference between the ideas of everybody in this room and Dr Lonsdale. I happen to know that his ideas and Stephen Coles' ideas are almost identical. Both of them believe that the type of diet which Dr Lonsdale promotes is necessary...

As an individual veterinarian, as a practitioner — if I can still call myself that after a few years away — I am prepared to stand next to my colleague Dr Lonsdale and say to him: 'Tell me about what you are doing, show me what you are doing. Let me talk to your clients and let me see and make up my own mind about the things you are telling us.'

I would like to move an amendment to the motion —

> That in keeping with the AVA policy of providing forums for the membership, the AVA establish an independent committee to prepare a report on the interaction between diet and disease in companion animals.

Appendix B

$$ \rightarrow\!\!\text{ZOE}\!\!\leftarrow $$

Eating habits of
captive small carnivores

The eating habits of wild carnivores provides a biological model against which to compare the needs of domestic cats and dogs. Neville Buck kindly provided the following information from his observations of captive wild cats and dogs at Howletts and Port Lympne Zoological Parks, Kent, UK. Weights are approximate.

Siberian Lynx (Siberia — 24 kg)

Food	*Result*
Chicken	Pluck feathers, leave gizzard, caecum, wing tips and feet. Everything else eaten.
Rabbit	Everything eaten except tail, stomach, colon and liver. Occasionally the feet are left. It has also been known for the pelt to be turned inside out and left.
Day-old chick	Gizzard, wing tips and toes left.
Guinea pig	Everything eaten except stomach, colon and small amount of fur which has been plucked.
Goat kid	Everything eaten except stomach contents, colon, feet and small amount of pelt.
Piglet	Everything eaten.
Squirrel	Everything eaten except tail.

Grass often eaten. Any food remains are buried under grass. Food items such as goat kid, piglet and guinea pig are often played with before being eaten. Song birds are played with, plucked and left.

Ocelot (South, Central and North America — 14 kg)
Fishing Cat (South-East Asia — 14 kg)

Fish	Everything eaten except sperm sac and roe. Occasionally heads left.
Chicken	Birds under 9 months plucked, leave gizzard and caecum. Eat everything else. Birds over 9 months plucked, leave feet, gizzard and caecum. Eat everything else.
Rabbit	Partially plucked, stomach contents left. Everything else eaten including remainder of hide. The colon is eaten after the contents have been squeezed out by the tongue.
Mouse	Eaten completely.
Rat	Eaten completely. Occasionally plucked, the stomach, colon, liver and tail being left.
Pigeon	Caecum, feet and wing tips left. Everything else eaten.
Quail	Eaten completely after first being plucked. Caecum sometimes left.
Guinea pig	Plucked. Colon left.

They have not been observed eating faeces, either theirs or that of other animals. Grass is regularly eaten. Some animals are known to do this daily. (Evidence in faeces samples and grass vomit.)

Rusty-spotted Cat (India, Sri Lanka — 2 kg)

Mouse	Eaten completely. Very occasionally stomach left.
Rat	Stomach, colon and tail not eaten. Occasionally the liver is also left.
Day-old chick	Wing tips and feet uneaten. Gizzard occasionally left.

They have not been observed eating faeces, either theirs or that of other animals. Grass is regularly eaten. Some animals are known to do this daily. (Evidence in faeces samples and grass vomit.)

Desert Cat (Pakistan, India — 4 kg)

Fish	Everything eaten except sperm sac and roe. Occasionally heads left.
Day-old chick	Gizzard, wing tips and feet are occasionally uneaten.
Mouse	Eaten completely.
Rat	Stomach, colon and tail not eaten. Occasionally the liver is also left.
Pigeon	All internal organs, feet and wing tips left. Plucked before eaten.
Quail	Eaten completely after first being plucked. Caecum sometimes left.
Guinea pig	Plucked. Colon left. Occasionally the pelt is turned inside out and left.

They have not been observed eating faeces, either theirs or that of other animals. Grass is occasionally eaten.

Caracal (Africa, Middle East, India — 15 kg)

Day-old chick	Gizzard, wing tips and feet are occasionally uneaten.
Rabbit	Partially plucked, stomach and colon and their contents left. Stomach usually burst. Occasionally the pelt is turned inside out.
Chicken	Plucked, gizzard and colon left.
Mouse	Eaten completely.
Rat	Stomach, colon, liver and tail not eaten.
Pigeon	All internal organs, feet and wing tips left. Plucked before eaten. Occasionally the rib cage also left.
Quail	Eaten completely after first being plucked. Caecum sometimes left.
Guinea pig	Plucked. Colon left. Occasionally the pelt is turned inside out and left.

They have not been observed eating faeces, either theirs or that of other animals. Grass is occasionally eaten.

Timber Wolf (Canada, USA — 33 kg)

Calf, horse, deer, goat	Carcass opened at groin, liver and heart eaten, lungs often left. The rumen is usually dragged across the enclosure; when this ruptures the contents are left where they lie. The colon, once dragged from the carcass, is usually left. The contents of the rumen are frequently rolled on by all members of the pack. The hide is turned inside out and left. Fur is not eaten. Horns are left although antlers are chewed and partially eaten. Hooves are eaten but only if from the carcass of a young animal. Bones from a young animal are mostly eaten, the exception being the larger bones. Bones from a larger animal are generally chewed on the ends. Particularly strong-smelling male goats are avoided by most animals.
Rabbit	Sometimes eaten completely, at other times the pelt is left.
Fish	Eaten completely. Often rolled on.
Chicken	Preferred when feathers removed. Carcass turned inside out to get at flesh.

They have not been observed eating grass or faeces, either theirs or that of another animal.

African Wild Dog (Africa — 25 kg)

Calf, horse, deer, goat	Carcass opened at groin, all internal organs eaten. Rumen and colon mostly eaten along with a small amount of their contents. Colon and contents of the rumen are usually rolled on. Small amount of fur is eaten along with the hide. Horns are chewed, antlers are chewed and partially eaten. Hooves are eaten but only if the carcass is from a young animal. Bones from a young animal are mostly eaten, the exception being the larger bones. Bones from larger animals are generally chewed on the ends. Particularly strong-smelling male goats are avoided by most animals.

Rabbit	Sometimes eaten completely, at other times the pelt is left.
Fish	Eaten completely. Often rolled on.
Chicken	Preferred when feathers removed. Carcass turned inside out to get at flesh.

Grass often eaten.

Bush Dog (South America — 6 kg)

Chicken	Eaten completely. Gizzard and colon occasionally left.
Rabbit	Eaten completely.
Quail	Eaten completely.
Rats	Eaten completely.
Fish	Eaten completely.
Pigeon	Eaten completely. Wing tips, gizzard and colon occasionally left.
Fruit	Bananas, pears and grapes offered. Small amounts eaten.
Antlers	Antlers in velvet (during the annual growth phase) mostly eaten, hardened antlers partially eaten.

Grass often eaten.

Appendix C

Diet guide for domestic dogs and cats

Dingoes and feral cats keep themselves healthy by eating whole carcasses of prey animals. Ideally we should feed our pets in the same manner. Until a dependable source of whole carcasses becomes available, pet owners need a satisfactory alternative. The following recommendations, based on raw meaty bones, have been adopted by thousands of pet owners with excellent results.

The diet is easy to follow and cheap, and pets enjoy it. It's good for ferrets too.

- Fresh water constantly available.
- Raw meaty bones (or carcasses if available) should form the bulk of the diet.
- Table scraps both cooked and raw (grate or liquidise vegetables, *discard cooked bones*).

Puppies and kittens

From about three weeks of age puppies and kittens start to take an interest in what their mother is eating. By six weeks of age they can eat chicken carcasses, rabbits and fish.

During the brief interval between three and six weeks of age it is advisable to mince chicken carcasses or similar for the young animals. The meat and bone should be minced together. This is akin to the part-digested food regurgitated by some wild carnivore mothers. Large litters will need more supplementary feeding than small litters.

Between four and six months of age puppies and kittens cut their permanent teeth and grow rapidly. At this time they need a plentiful supply of carcasses or raw meaty bones of suitable size.

Puppies and kittens tend not to overeat natural food. Food can be continuously available.

Natural foods suitable for pet carnivores

Raw meaty bones

Chicken and turkey carcasses, after the meat has been removed for human consumption, are suitable for dogs and cats.

Poultry by-products include: heads, feet, necks and wings.

Whole fish and fish heads.

Goat, sheep, calf, deer and kangaroo carcasses can be sawn into large pieces of meat and bone.

Other by-products include: pigs' trotters, pigs' heads, sheep heads, brisket, tail bones, rib bones.

Whole carcasses

Rats, mice, rabbits, fish, chickens, quail, hens.

Offal

Liver, lungs, trachea, hearts, omasums (stomach of ruminants), tripe.

Quality — Quantity — Frequency

Healthy animals living and breeding in the wild depend on the correct *quality* of food in the right *quantity* at a correct *frequency*. They thereby gain an appropriate nutrient intake plus the correct amount of teeth cleaning — animals, unlike humans, 'brush' and 'floss' as they eat.

Quality

Low-fat game animals and fish and birds provide the best source of food for pet carnivores. If using meat from farm animals (cattle, sheep and pigs) avoid excessive fat, or bones that are too large to be eaten.

Dogs are more likely to break their teeth when eating large knuckle bones and bones sawn lengthwise than if eating meat and bone together.

Raw food for cats should always be fresh. Dogs can consume 'ripe' food and will sometimes bury bones for later consumption.

Quantity

Establishing the quantity to feed pets is more an art than a science. Parents, when feeding a human family, manage this task without the aid of food consumption charts. You can achieve the same good results for your pet by paying attention to activity levels, appetite and body condition.

High activity and big appetite indicate a need for increased food, and vice versa.

Body condition depends on a number of factors. The overall body shape — is it athletic or rotund — and the lustre of the hair coat provide clues. Use your finger tips to assess the elasticity of the skin. Does it have an elastic feel and move readily over the muscles? Do the muscles feel well toned? And how much coverage of the ribs do you detect? This is the best place to check whether your pet is too thin or too fat. By comparing your own rib cage with that of your pet you can obtain a good idea of body condition — both your own and that of your pet.

An approximate food consumption guide, based on raw meaty bones, for the average pet cat or dog is 15 to 20 percent of body weight in one week or 2 to 3 percent per day. On that basis a 25 kilo dog requires up to five kilos of carcasses or raw meaty bones weekly. Cats weighing five kilos require about one kilo of chicken necks or similar each week. Table scraps should be fed as an extra component of the diet. Please note that these figures are only a guide and relate to adult pets in a domestic environment.

Pregnant or lactating females and growing puppies and kittens may need much more food than adult animals of similar body weight.

Wherever possible, feed the meat and bone ration in one large piece requiring much ripping, tearing and gnawing. This makes for contented pets with clean teeth.

Frequency

Wild carnivores feed at irregular intervals. In a domestic setting, regularity works best and accordingly I suggest that you feed adult dogs and cats once daily. If you live in a hot climate I would recommend that you feed pets in the evening to avoid attracting flies.

I suggest that on one or two days each week your pets be fasted — just like animals in the wild.

On occasions you may run out of natural food. Don't be tempted to buy artificial food, fast your pets and stock up with natural food the next day.

Puppies, kittens or sick and underweight animals should not be fasted (unless on veterinary advice).

Table scraps

Wild carnivores eat small amounts of omnivore food, part-digested in liquid form, when they eat the intestines of their prey. Our table scraps, and some fruit and vegetable peelings, are omnivore food which has not been ingested. Providing scraps do not form too great a proportion of the diet they appear to do no harm and may do some good. I advise an upper limit of one-third scraps for dogs and rather less for cats. Liquidising scraps, both cooked and raw, in the kitchen mixer may help to increase their digestibility.

Things to avoid

- Excessive meat off the bone — not balanced.
- Excessive vegetables — not balanced.
- Small pieces of bone — can be swallowed whole and get stuck.
- Cooked bones — get stuck.
- Mineral and vitamin additives — create imbalance.
- Processed food — leads to dental and other diseases.
- Excessive starchy food — associated with bloat.
- Onions and chocolate — toxic to pets.
- Fruit stones (pits) and corn cobs — get stuck.
- Milk — associated with diarrhoea. Animals drink it whether thirsty or not and consequently get fat. Milk sludge sticks to teeth and gums.

Take care

- Old dogs and cats addicted to a processed diet may experience initial difficulty when changed on to a natural diet.
- Pets with misshapen jaws and dental disease may experience difficulties with a natural diet.
- Create variety. Any nutrients fed to excess can be harmful.
- Liver is an excellent foodstuff but should not be fed more than once weekly.
- Other offal, e.g. ox stomachs, should not exceed 50 percent of the diet.
- Whole fish are an excellent source of food for carnivores, but avoid feeding one species of fish constantly. Some species, e.g. carp, contain an enzyme which destroys thiamine (vitamin B_1).
- There are no prizes for the fattest dog on the block, nor for the fastest. Feed pets for a lifetime of health. Prevention is better than cure.

Miscellaneous tips

Domestic dogs and cats are carnivores. Feeding them the appropriate carnivore diet represents the single most important contribution to their welfare.

Establish early contact with a dependable supplier of foodstuffs for pet carnivores.

Buy food in bulk in order to avoid shortages.

Package the daily rations separately for ease of feeding.

Refrigerated storage space, preferably a freezer, is essential.

Raw meaty bones can be fed frozen just like ice cream. Some pets eat the frozen article, others wait for it to thaw.

Small carcasses, for example rats, mice and small birds, can be fed frozen and complete with entrails. Larger carcasses should have the entrails removed before freezing.

Take care that pets do not fight over their food.

Protect children by ensuring that they do not disturb feeding pets.

Feeding bowls are unnecessary — the food will be dragged across the floor — so feed pets outside by preference, or on an easily cleaned floor.

Ferrets are small carnivores which can be fed in the same way as cats.

For an expanded description of dietary requirements, including the potential hazards, please consult the other pages in this book or the Web site:

www.rawmeatybones.com

IMPORTANT: Note that individual animals and circumstances may vary. You may need to discuss your pet's needs with your veterinarian.

Appendix D

⟶ ꝺ◉ꜱ ⟵

Edited transcript of
ABC 2BL program broadcast at
11.50 am on 5 February 1993

Julie Steiner (Interviewer):

It mightn't only be a play or a good night out that can put you in high spirits. Often the same can be said about the love we have for our domestic pets. After a horrible day when you've been shouted at, yelled at and you end up feeling totally unloved, the therapeutic value of being met at the front gate by the family pet can be immeasurable and, of course, the temptation is to return that display of love with a treat. It may be an extra sliver of fish or a creamy bowl of milk for the family cat, but the problem is that you may be killing your cat with kindness. Well, that's a warning from Petcare, an organisation set up to promote the value of pets and the best ways to look after them. Cats are evidently much like children: they seem to enjoy a lot of the food and drink that simply isn't good for them. Too much fish, wrong diets and, surprisingly, giving the cat a bowl of milk is about the worst thing you can do for them. So what is the perfect diet. Denise Humphries is a consultant for Petcare and she joins me on the line this morning. Hello, Denise.

Denise Humphries:

We all tend to think that cats need milk because they enjoy it so much but many cats, a very high percentage of cats, have a lactose intolerance which means that milk actually makes life pretty uncomfortable for them and sometimes the owner too. It can cause quite severe diarrhoea if your cat has a lactose intolerance.

If we have a cat who particularly likes milk — and we like to spoil our cats and give them milk as a treat — then there are low-lactose pet milks available. Cow's milk doesn't have all the necessary nutrients that the cat needs but the pet milks that are available are both low-lactose and have the added nutrients, so if we want to spoil them we're able to do it that way by looking for the pet milks that will suit them.

Interviewer:

Denise, what about fish? Again it's part of the stories of childhood that we should give our cats fish because that's the thing they love best. Is that in fact true?

Denise Humphries:

No, I think all cats or most cats find fish very palatable, but I guess if we thought about it, it wouldn't be a great part of their diet in their natural state. We like to spoil our animals, we like to feed them things that we think they like. And the problem is that many of the canned cat foods that are available don't have the essential fatty acids in them that a cat needs, nor the necessary energy requirements. So it's very important that if we have a cat who likes fish and we'd like to spoil him once again and give him some fish, then it's important to read the label carefully and see that fatty acids and nutrients have been added to the can. We must read the label to see that it says that it is a completely balanced or a nutritionally complete food. If it doesn't say that then the diet shouldn't be based on it.

Interviewer:

What would you, then, suggest? If people were starting from scratch, what should they think about in terms of feeding their cats?

Denise Humphries:

It's important with kittens that they're actually fed a kitten food, not an adult food, because kitten foods are growth foods with extra nutrients that the kitten will need. So it would be a good idea to start by feeding kitten foods — by reading the labels to make sure that it says either it's nutritionally complete or it is a balanced diet — and introducing a cat to a variety.

We believe that the meat-based products should form the basis of the diet and the fish varieties are not to be the chosen diet.

Interviewer:

Mmmm. What do you suggest for keeping cats' teeth in good order too?

Denise Humphries:

Cats don't have a great deal of problem with their teeth if the owners are careful. As with elderly people, animals are living a lot longer these days than they did before; probably because of the better nutrition that's available instead of all the homemade diets. Most of us now are able to go and buy a commercially prepared diet which has everything in it that the animal needs. And our animals are living longer and as a result of that we're tending to see older animals with dental problems sometimes. It's up to the owners to check the teeth and in the older animals if they see any problems occurring go off to the vet just as we would go off to the dentist.

Interviewer:

Mmmm. Is there such a thing as dental floss for cats?

Denise Humphries:

Well, now you can buy pets' toothbrushes.

Interviewer:

I haven't seen pets' toothbrushes but I have seen owners attack cats and dogs with a good rub of the toothbrush.

Denise Humphries:

Well, certainly dogs do develop some tartar on their teeth. Some dogs seem to have a predisposition to do this and toothcare is just part of the normal grooming routine. And, as I said, now there are toothbrushes and there's even doggy toothpaste available which is a little more palatable than the human one.

Interviewer:

OK. Well, Denise, thanks very much for that. Good advice, I think, for cat or, dare I say moggy, lovers. Thanks very much for your time.

Denise Humphries:

Pleasure.

Interviewer:

That was Denise Humphries, who is a consultant to Petcare.

APPENDIX E

Whistleblower
information and contacts

When contemplating blowing the whistle you may want help and guidance. Self-help and liaising with other whistleblowers are the best strategy because, as Brian Martin, author of *The Whistleblower's Handbook*, advises, 'some of the most worthwhile [whistleblower] organisations are seriously overloaded and cannot respond effectively to every request'.

Recommended publications

The Whistleblower's Handbook, **Brian Martin**

Jon Carpenter Publishing, 1999, ISBN 1 897766 52 1 and Envirobook 1999 ISBN 0 85881 167 7

Web: www.uow.edu.au/arts/sts/bmartin/dissent/

ORDER FROM:

UK and Europe: Jon Carpenter Publishing, Alder House, Market Street, Charlbury, Oxfordshire OX7 3PH
Phone/fax: 01608 811969
E-mail: joncarpenterpublishing@compuserve.com

Australia: Envirobook, 38 Rose Street, Annandale, NSW 2038
Telephone: 02 9518 6154

New Zealand: Addenda, PO Box 78224, Grey Lynn, Auckland.
Telephone: 09 834 5511

USA and Canada: order from bookstores. The distributor is: Paul and Company, PO Box 442, Concord, MA 01742
Telephone: 978 369 3049

The Whistleblower's Survival Guide: Courage Without Martyrdom

Washington, DC: Fund for Constitutional Government, 1997

Order from:

Government Accountability Project, 810 First Street, NE Suite 630, Washington, DC 20002 Telephone: 202 408 0034 or summary available at

Web: www.whistleblower.org/gap/

Contacts

Australia

Whistleblowers Australia
PO Box U 129
Wollongong NSW 2500
Australia
Tel: 02 9810 9468

South Africa

Freedom of Expression Institute
(FXI)
PO Box 30668
Braamfontein 2017
South Africa
Phone/fax: 011 403 8309

United Kingdom

Freedom to Care
PO Box 125
West Molesey
Surrey KT8 1YE
UK
Phone/fax: 020 8224 1022
E-mail: freecare@aol.com
Web: www.freedomtocare.org/

USA

The Government Accountability
Project
1612 K St., NW, Suite 400
Washington DC 20006
USA
Tel: 202 408 0034
Fax: 202 408 9855
E-mail: gap1@erols.com
Web: www.whistleblower.org/gap/

West coast office
1402 Third Avenue, Suite 1215
Seattle WA 98118
USA
Phone/fax: 206 292 2850
E-mail: gap@whistleblower.org

Veterinary associations and regulatory authorities

Each country, or State within a country, has its own regulatory structure. If you wish to make enquiries or lodge a complaint you may need to make a series of telephone calls in order to locate the correct agency. The government information line is often the best place to start. Alternatively you may wish to contact the relevant veterinary association for information. Sometimes the local police station or court house may be able to assist.

When contacting political representatives consider writing to members of government and opposition parties.

Australia

Australian Veterinary Association
PO Box 371
Artarmon NSW 1570
Australia
Tel: 02 9411 2733
Fax: 02 9411 5089
Web: www.ava.com.au

Veterinarians are regulated by State Veterinary Boards.
There are State and Federal consumer protection laws.

Canada

Canadian Veterinary Medical Association
339 Booth Street
Ottawa
Ontario K1R 7K1
Canada
Tel: 613 236 1162
Fax: 613 236 9681

Enquiries and complaints regarding false and misleading advertising:
Industry Canada
Consumer Products Directorate
Place du Portage
50 Victoria Street, 16th Floor
Hull
Quebec K1A 0C9
Canada

New Zealand

New Zealand Veterinary Association
PO Box 11-212
Manners Street
Wellington
New Zealand
Tel: 471 0484
Fax: 471 0494
E-mail: nzva@vets.org.nz

South Africa

South African Veterinary Association
PO Box 25033
Monument Park
Pretoria 0105
South Africa
Tel: 27 12 346 1150/1
Fax: 27 12 346 2929

United Kingdom

British Veterinary Association
7 Mansfield Street
London W1M OAT
United Kingdom
Tel: 020 7636 6541
Fax: 020 7436 2970
E-mail: bvahq@bva.co.uk

British Small Animal Veterinary Association
Woodrow House, 1 Telford Way
Waterwells Business Park
Quedgeley
Gloucester GL2 4AB
United Kingdom
Tel: 01452 726700
Fax: 01452 726701
E-mail: adminoff@bsava.com
Web: www.bsava.com

The United Kingdom veterinary profession is regulated by the Royal College of Veterinary Surgeons. The RCVS Guide to Professional Conduct can be viewed at Web: www.rcvs.org.uk/Guide/index.htm

Royal College of Veterinary Surgeons
Belgravia House
62-64 Horseferry Road
London SW1P 2AF
United Kingdom
Tel: 020 7222 2001
Fax: 020 7222 2002
Web: www.rcvs.org.uk

Enquiries and complaints regarding false and misleading advertising, and adverse effects of artificial pet foods should be addressed to your local Member of Parliament.

USA

American Veterinary Medical Association
1931 North Meacham Road Suite 100
Schaumburg IL 60173
USA
Tel: 847 925 8070
Fax: 847 925 1329

Veterinarians are regulated by State Boards.

Enquiries and complaints regarding false and misleading advertising:

Federal Trade Commission
Advertising Practices
6th Street and Pennsylvania Ave NW
Washington, DC 20580
USA

Enquiries and complaints regarding harmful effects of artificial pet foods:

Director
Center for Veterinary Medicine
Food and Drug Administration
Rockville MD 20857
USA

Artificial pet food company details

Contact details for manufacturers appear on the labels of cans and packets. You may prefer to deal with the subsidiary of a company located in your country or alternatively with the head office. Helplines can provide details.

Head offices of five large pet food companies

Colgate-Palmolive

Colgate-Palmolive Company
300 Park Avenue
New York, NY 10022
USA

Heinz

Heinz
600 Grant Street
Pittsburg, PA 15219
USA

Mars

Mars, Inc.
6885 Elm Street
McLean, VA 22101
USA

Nestlé

Nestlé S.A.
Avenue Nestlé 55
CH - 1800
Vevey
Switzerland

Ralston Purina

Ralston Purina
Checkerboard Square
St. Louis, MO 63164
USA

GLOSSARY

acidosis A pathological condition resulting from accumulation of acid or depletion of the alkaline reserve (bicarbonate content) of the blood and body tissues.

ad libitum feeding Food constantly available for the free choice of the animal.

ambit Precincts; bounds; compass, extent.

arachidonic acid Essential fatty acid necessary as a precursor for some hormones and structural fats. Cats are susceptible to deficiency, due to an inability to convert linoleic acid.

bacteremia Bacteria, usually in small numbers and temporarily, in the blood. From the blood the bacteria can gain access to joints, lungs, brain and other organs and set up infection.

biochemical A chemical found in living things or an adjective used to describe physico-chemical processes in living things.

biofilm A well organised community of microorganisms adherent to each other and/or to surfaces and interfaces.

caecum The first part of the large intestine forming a dilated pouch. Birds have a double caecum.

carnivora Order of flesh-eating animals, particularly mammals.

caveat emptor Latin term for 'let the buyer beware'.

Corgi Small to medium short-legged dog popular with the British Royal family.

cybernetics Branch of study concerned with self-regulating systems of communication and control in living organisms and machines.

cytotoxic Toxic to cells of the body.

defaecation Passage of faeces from the rectum via the anus.

dentine Main part of tooth composed of hard dense tissue.

discospondylitis Infection of vertebrae and intervertebral discs.

encephalopathy Degenerative disease of the brain.

encyst Enclose in a cyst or bladder.

endodontic Relating to the pulp cavity of the tooth.

endorphin An opiate-like chemical produced within the body and having effects similar to morphine.

endotoxaemia Endotoxins, from the outer membranes of bacteria, circulating in the blood.

epidemiology The study of diseases in communities with reference to the factors which determine the frequency and distribution.

et al. Abbreviation of the Latin *et alii*; means 'and others' (that is, other people).

fascia Fibrous, white and shiny tissue which lies under the skin and wraps muscles and various body organs.

fibroblast Fibre-producing cell of connective tissue.

flatus Gas in bowels (or stomach), usually expelled through the anus.

gastritis Inflammation of the stomach lining.

gastroenterology Study of the gastrointestinal tract and its diseases.

gingiva The Latin word for gum.

glomerulonephritis Inflammation of the capillary loops in the kidney. It may be secondary to infection or immune mechanisms.

haematology Science and study of blood and blood-forming tissues in health and disease.

halitosis Foul breath odour.

herbage Collective term for herbs and the succulent parts of herbs.

histidine An amino acid, essential for optimum growth of the young.

histopathology A word combining histology (the science and study of minute structure and function of tissues) and pathology (the science and study of disease).

HIV Human immunodeficiency virus.

homoeostasis/homeostasis A process of constant readjustment whereby biological systems maintain a state of constancy although their environment changes.

homogeneous Uniform, of the same quality, composition or structure.

humectant A moistening agent.

hydatid A cyst-like structure, often used in reference to the cyst of the tapeworm *Echinococcus granulosus*.

hydrolyze Chemical cleavage of a compound by addition of water.

hyperkalaemia Abnormally high concentration of potassium in the blood.

immunopathology The study and science of immune reactions associated with disease. Some immune reactions are beneficial, others harmful and some without effect.

ketone Chemical products of metabolism. Excess production leads to excretion of ketones in the urine.

knackery A factory which processes butchers' waste, diseased, debilitated, dying and dead stock (4D stock). The resultant tallow, meat and bone meal is used for animal feedstuffs and fertilisers.

Luddite A member of a nineteenth century band of rioters against the introduction of machines. In modern usage one who opposes the introduction of new machines and techniques.

macrophage Large cells of the immune system noted for their ability to ingest microbes and dead tissues.

metabolism The physical and chemical processes by which the living body is maintained. Large molecules are broken down to provide energy and raw materials by the process known as catabolism. Anabolism is the recombining of chemicals for growth and repair.

metabolite Chemical product of metabolism.

methionine An essential amino acid in the diet of mammals.

microflora Microscopic organisms which reside more or less permanently in a given area, for instance on skin or in oral cavity. Includes bacteria, viruses, protozoa and fungi.

moggie Affectionate slang term for a cat.

musculoskeletal Pertaining to muscle and skeleton.

mutagenic Inducing genetic mutation, either by physical or chemical means.

mutt Slang term, either affectionate or derogatory, for a dog.

myocarditis Inflammation of the muscular wall of the heart.

necropsy Post-mortem examination of a body (autopsy).

neutrophil White blood cell with lobulated nucleus.

odontoblast A connective tissue cell responsible for laying down dentine.

odontoclast A connective tissue cell responsible for absorbing dentine.

oocyst The resistant stage in the life cycle of coccidia.

osteoarthritis Degenerative joint disease involving joint cartilage and bone.

osteoblast Cell involved in bone production.

osteoclast Cell involved in bone resorption.

outback The remote and usually uninhabited inland districts of Australia.

pandemic (Disease) prevalent over wide geographical area.

pathophysiology The physiology of disordered function.

peptide Two or more amino acids chemically linked.

per se Of itself, intrinsically.

pharynx The throat immediately behind the tongue.

physiology 1. The science and study of the functions of the living organism and its parts. 2. The physical and chemical factors and processes in an organism or its parts.

phytate Synonymous with phytic acid. A phosphorus-rich compound abundant in plants.

phytin Calcium and magnesium salt of phytic acid.

polyarthritis Inflammation of several joints.

polyvasculitis Inflammation of several blood vessels.

potentiate Enhance an agent or process, producing a greater overall effect.

premolar Tooth in front of molars but behind canines.

protozoa Single celled organisms with nucleus. Often complex life cycle. May be pathogenic (harmful) or non-pathogenic to animals.

pruritus Another name for itching. Allergic inflammation and parasitic infestations of the skin frequently give rise to pruritus.

purine A chemical compound found in DNA and RNA.

purulent Containing or forming pus.

retinopathy Non-inflammatory disease of the retina.

rumen The first and largest compartment of the forestomach of ruminant animals (those which chew the cud).

sheep station A large Australian/New Zealand sheep farm.

spicule Short, sharp-pointed body.

streptococcal Pertaining to or caused by a streptococcus (a spherical bacterium occurring in pairs or chains).

thyroiditis Inflammation of the thyroid gland.

tonne Measure of weight or mass; one tonne = 1000 kg.

tosh Slang term for rubbish or twaddle.

vasculature The blood vessels of the body or part of the body.

vesicle A small bladder or sac, frequently seen as a small blister in skin diseases.

whistleblower Person who, on discovering evidence of perceived harm (e.g. fraud, waste, corruption, health hazard) affecting the community or workplace or similar, seeks, by appealing to those in authority and/or others, to end or reduce the perceived harm.

NOTES

Chapter 1

Disturbing the peace

1. Thurston, M E (1996) History in the Making, in *The Lost History of the Canine Race,* Andrews and McMeel, Kansas City, MI p 268

2. *Waltham Focus,* (1997) 7:3 32. See also Web: www.waltham.com

3. Thurston, M E (1996), pp 235–237

4. Lonsdale, T (1991) Oral disease in cats and dogs, *Control and Therapy* No 3128, Post Graduate Committee in Veterinary Science, University of Sydney

5. Muir, B (1991) Canned pet food not the healthiest, *Australian Veterinary Association News,* December 1991, p 28

6. Coles, S (1992) Dentistry — let's get it straight, *Australian Veterinary Association News,* April 1992, p 23

7. Billinghurst, I (1986) Feeding dogs — client handout, *Control and Therapy* No 2275, Post Graduate Committee in Veterinary Science, University of Sydney

8. Paxton, D (1995) Censorship and sealing wax, *Australian Veterinary Association News,* May 1995, p 14

9. *Australian Veterinary Association News,* November 1994, p 19

Chapter 2

Mouth rot and dog breath

1. Penman, S and Emily, P (1991) Scaling, Polishing and Dental Home Care, *Waltham International Focus,* 1:3 2–8

2. Harvey, C E and Emily, P (1993) Periodontal disease, in *Small Animal Dentistry,* Mosby, St Louis, p 92

3. Colyer, F (1947) Dental disease in animals, *British Dental Journal,* 82 31–35

4. Page, R C and Schroeder, H E (1982) Periodontitis in other mammalian animals, in *Periodontitis in Man and Other Animals,* Karger, Basel, p 213

5. Coghlan, A (1996) Slime City, *New Scientist,* 2045 p 34

6. Coghlan, A (1996), p 35

7. Blood, D C and Studdert, V P (1999) *Saunders Comprehensive Veterinary Dictionary,* 2nd Edition, W B Saunders, London

8. Costerton, J W et al (1995) Microbial biofilms, *Annual Reviews of Microbiology,* 49 p 739

9. Gunter Grass (1970) Local anesthetic, New York: Harcourt Brace Jovanovich, Inc. cited in Mandel, I D and Gaffar, A (1986) Calculus revisited: a review, *Journal of Clinical Periodontology,* 13: 249–257

10. Pilkey, D (1994) *Dog Breath, The Horrible Trouble with Hally Tosis,* Scholastic Inc, New York.

Chapter 3

Ugly facts

1. Harvey, C E and Emily, P (1993) Function, Formation, and Anatomy of Oral Structures in Carnivores, in *Small Animal Dentistry,* Mosby, St Louis, p 6 (Eruption schedules vary with breed and size of animal.)

2. Crossley, D A, Web page December 1998, http://ourworld.compuserve.com/homepages/vetdent_uk/toothcar.htm

3. *Australian Veterinary Association News* (1994) Diet and disease link — final report, February, pp 1 and 6

4. *Australian Veterinary Association News* (1994), pp 1 and 6

5. *Australian Veterinary Association News* (1994), pp 1 and 6

6. O'Connor, J J (1950) Affections of the teeth in *Dollar's Veterinary Surgery,* 4th Edition, Baillière, Tindall and Cox, London, p 601

7. Beard, G B (1991) Gingivitis and Periodontitis, *Dental Seminar,* Post Graduate Committee in Veterinary Science, University of Sydney, No 169, p 15

8. Penman, S and Emily, P (1991) Scaling, Polishing and Dental Home Care, *Waltham International Focus,* 1:3 2–8

9. Hamlin, R L (1991) A theory for the genesis of certain chronic degenerative diseases of the aged dog, *Veterinary Scope International Edition,* The Upjohn Company, Kalamazoo, pp 6–10

10. DeBowes, L J (1994) Systemic effects of periodontal disease, *Proceedings of the 12th American College of Veterinary Internal Medicine Forum,* San Francisco, pp 441–445

11. 1998 Pet Dental Health Month, Web: www.petdental.com/

12. DeBowes, L J et al (1996) Association of Periodontal Disease and Histologic Lesions in Multiple Organs from 45 Dogs, *Journal of Veterinary Dentistry,* 13 (2): 57–60 Web: www.petdental.com/html/4c3_aging.htm

13. Hefferren, J J (1996) Relations of Oral and Systemic Health and Disease, Proceedings of a Conference on Companion Animal Oral Health, University of Kansas, Lawrence, March 1–3, 1996, Sponsored by an Educational Grant from Hill's Pet Nutrition, Inc. Web: www.petdental.com/html/4c1_disease.htm

14. Jotwani, R and Cutler, C W (1998) Adult periodontitis — specific bacterial infection or chronic inflammation?, *Journal of Medical Microbiology,* 47 187–188

15. Piggot, M, Medical Notes, *The Sunday Times,* 13 July 1997

16. DeStefano, F et al (1993) Dental disease and risk of coronary heart disease and mortality, *British Medical Journal,* 306:6879 688–691

17. DeBowes, L J (1994)

18. Healthy Gums: Key to More than a Bright Smile? Researchers in Field of Periodontal Medicine Link Oral and Reproductive Health, *Harvard Focus,* June 25 1999 Web: www.med.harvard.edu/publications/Focus/June25_1999/alum.html

19. Hefferren, J J (1996)

20. Lonsdale, T (2000) The Association of Periodontal and Systemic Health, *Control and Therapy* No 4192, Post Graduate Committee in Veterinary Science, University of Sydney

21. Hefferren, J J (1996)

22. Rifkin, B R, Vernillo, A T and Golub, L M (1993) Blocking Periodontal Disease Progression by Inhibiting Tissue-destructive Enzymes: a potential therapeutic role for tetracyclines and their chemically-modified analogs, *Journal of Periodontology,* 64 (8 Suppl): 819–827

23. DeBowes, L J et al (1996)

24. *Commonwealth Serum Laboratories Product Manual* (1995) Anthrax Vaccine, p A1

25. Floss or die: Bad gums linked to heart disease, premature births, *Augusta Chronicle,* 18 June 1997, Web: http://augustachronicle.com/stories/061997/fea_floss.html

26. West-Hyde, L and Floyd, M (1994) Dentistry, in *Textbook of Veterinary Internal Medicine,* 4th Edition (Eds Ettinger S J and Feldman E C) W B Saunders, Philadelphia, p 1104

27. Zuber, R M (1993) Systemic Amyloidosis in Oriental and Siamese Cats, *Australian Veterinary Practitioner,* 23:66

28. Zuber, R M (1999) Systemic amyloidosis in cats, *The Veterinarian,* November 1999 pp 14–15

29. Lonsdale, T (2000) Periodontal disease and systemic amyloidosis, *The Veterinarian,* February 2000 p 18

30. Duval, D and Giger, U (1996) Vaccine-Associated Immune-Mediated Hemolytic Anemia in the Dog, *Journal of Veterinary Internal Medicine,* 10:290–295

31. Kuwahara, J (1986) Canine and feline aural hemotoma: Clinical, experimental, and clinicopathologic observations, *American Journal of Veterinary Research,* 47:10 2300–2308

32. Pedersen, N (1997) Immunologic diseases of the Cat, in *Feline Medicine,* Proceedings of the Post Graduate Foundation in Veterinary Science, University of Sydney, Sydney, 289 p 203

33. Jotwani, R and Cutler, C W (1998) Adult periodontitis—specific bacterial infection or chronic inflammation?, *Journal of Medical Microbiology,* 47:3 187–188

34. Medline address for definition of Reactive Oxygen Species: http://www.biomednet.com/db/medline/mesh/MESH.Reactive+Oxygen+Species Scope note: Reactive intermediate oxygen species including both radicals and non-radicals. These substances are constantly formed in the human body and have been shown to kill bacteria and inactivate proteins, and have been implicated in a number of diseases. Scientific data exist that link the reactive oxygen species produced by inflammatory phagocytes to cancer development.

35. Stohs, S J (1995) The role of free radicals in toxicity and disease, *Journal Of Basic And Clinical Physiology And Pharmacology,* 6:3-4 205–228

Chapter 4

Raw vs cooked food

1. Clark, W R (1995) Hypersensitivity and Allergy, in *At War Within: The double edged sword of immunity,* Oxford University Press, New York, p 88

2. Billinghurst, I (1993) *Give Your Dog a Bone,* Billinghurst, POBox WO 64, Bathurst 2795 Australia Tel: +61 2 6334 2009 Fax: +61 2 6334 2140 E-mail: barfdiet@ix.net.au

3. National Academy of Sciences (1985) Nutrient Requirements and Signs of Deficiency, in *Nutrient Requirements of Dogs,* National Academy Press, Washington, p 14

4. National Academy of Sciences (1985) p 16

5. Hazewinkel, H A et al (1987) Influences of different calcium intakes on calciotropic hormones and skeletal development on young growing dogs, *Frontiers of Hormone Research,* 17:221

6. National Academy of Sciences (1985) p 20

7. Muller, G H, Kirk, R W and Scott, D W (1992) Environmental diseases, in *Small Animal Dermatology,* 3rd Edition, Saunders, Philadelphia, p 663

8. NutriPet P/L (1993) *NutriPet News,* Campbellfield, Victoria, Australia

Chapter 5

What's in the can?

1. National Academy of Sciences (1985) *Nutrient Requirements of Dogs,* and (1986) *Nutrient Requirements of Cats,* National Academy Press, Washington

2. Kronfeld, D S (1983) Feeding and nutrition of dogs and cats, in *Nutrition,* Proceedings of the Post Graduate Committee in Veterinary Science, University of Sydney, Sydney, 63 p 31

3. Kronfeld, D S (1983) p 143

4. Kronfeld, D S (1983) pp 238–242

5. Kronfeld, D S (1983) p 165

6. (1989) in Former tables, *Composition of Foods — Australia,* Australian Government Publication

7. Kelly, N C (1996) Food types and evaluation, in *Manual of Companion Animal Nutrition & Feeding,* 1st Edition, Eds. Kelly, N and Wills, J, British Small Animal Veterinary Association, Gloucester, pp 24–25

8. Wheeler, S J (1996) Feline neuropathy associated with contaminated food, *The Veterinary Record,* 139:13 323

9. O'Connor, J J, Stowe, C M and Robinson, R R (1985) Fate of sodium pentobarbital in rendered products, *American Journal of Veterinary Research,* 46:8 1721–17214

10. (1996) *Nutrition in Practice,* Edition 3/1996 Uncle Ben's of Australia, Albury Wodonga

11. Kronfeld, D S (1983) p 365

12. Kelly, N C (1996) p 13

13. Pedigree PAL Professional Formula, Conditioning Diet for adult dogs, Package notes on 4 kg pack, Uncle Ben's of Australia, Raglan, NSW

14. Allen, T A (1998) High blood pressure, Published at Hill's Pet Nutrition, Inc. Web: www.hillspet.com/public/nutrition/bloodpressure.html

15. Blood, D C and Henderson, J A (1968) Diseases Caused by Chemical Agents — 1 in *Veterinary Medicine,* 3rd Edition, Baillière, Tindall and Cassell, London, pp 782–785

16. Allen, T A (1998)

17. Animal Protection Institute (1997), *What's Really in Pet Food,* Web: www.api4animals.org/Petfood.htm

18. National Academy of Sciences (1986) Other Food Constituents, in *Nutrient Requirements of Cats,* National Academy Press, Washington, p 34

19. World Cancer Research Fund/American Institute for Cancer Research (1997) Food additives, in *Food, Nutrition and the Prevention of Cancer: a global perspective*, American Institute for Cancer Research, Washington, p 485

20. World Cancer Research Fund/American Institute for Cancer Research (1997) p 486

21. Reyes, F G, Valim, M F and Vercesi, A E (1996) Effect of organic synthetic food colours on mitochondrial respiration, *Food Additives and Contaminants*, 13:1 5-11

22. Katamine, S et al (1986) Iodine content of various meals currently consumed by urban Japanese, *Journal of Nutritional Science and Vitaminology* (Tokyo), 32:5 487–495

23. Wills, J M and Morris, J G (1996) Feeding Puppies and Kittens, in *Manual of Companion Animal Nutrition & Feeding*, 1st Edition, Eds Kelly, N and Wills, J, British Small Animal Veterinary Association, Gloucester, p 60

24. FDA Veterinarian July/August 1996 Vol XI, No IV
Web: www.fda.gov/cvm/fda/infores/fdavet/1996/796fdavet.html#RTFToC16

25. McIntosh, G H et al (1986) Acute intoxication of marmosets and rats fed high concentrations of the dietary antioxidant 'ethoxyquin 66', *Australian Veterinary Journal*, 63:11 385-6

26. Rubel, D M and Freeman, S (1998) Allergic contact dermatitis to ethoxyquin in a farmer handling chicken feeds, *Australasian Journal of Dermatology*, 39, 89–91

27. Dzanis, DA (1991) Safety of ethoxyquin in dog foods, *Journal of Nutrition*, November, 121:11 Suppl S163–164

28. FDA Veterinarian September/October 1997 Vol XIII, No V
Web: www.fda.gov/cvm/fda/infores/fdavet/1997/997fdavet.html#ETHOXY

29. World Cancer Research Fund/American Institute for Cancer Research (1997) p 486

30. Kronfeld, D S (1983) p 245

31. *Journal of Veterinary Dentistry* (1997) 14:3

32. Anderson, R S (1996) Feeding Older Pets, in *Manual of Companion Animal Nutrition & Feeding*, 1st Edition, Eds Kelly, N and Wills, J, British Small Animal Veterinary Association, Gloucester p 98

Chapter 6

Unpleasant diseases; painful death

1. Penman, S and Emily, P (1991) Scaling, Polishing and Dental Home Care, *Waltham International Focus,* 1:3 2–8

2. Dr Mark Beale, Macquarie Street, Sydney (1992) — letter to author

3. Australian Broadcasting Association, Radio National Transcripts, The Health Report, Nutriceuticals, 5th February 1996 Web: www.abc.net.au/rn/talks/8.30/helthrpt/hstories/hr050201.htm

4. National Academy of Sciences (1985) *Nutrient Requirements of Dogs,* National Academy Press, Washington, p 32

5. Kronfeld, D S (1983) Hypersensitivity: Food and Nerves, in *Nutrition,* Proceedings of the Post Graduate Committee in Veterinary Science, University of Sydney, Sydney, 63 p 339

6. Kronfeld, D S (1983) p 230

7. Mugford, R A (1987) The influence of nutrition on canine behaviour, *Journal of Small Animal Practice,* 28, 1046–1055

8. Markwell, P J and Edney, T B (1996) The Obese Animal, in *Manual of Companion Animal Nutrition & Feeding,* 1st Edition, Eds. Kelly, N and Wills, J, British Small Animal Veterinary Association, Gloucester, p 109

9. Kronfeld, D S (1983) p 308

10. Markwell, P J and Edney, T B (1986)

11. Andrews, S (1997) Acute diarrhoea, *Waltham Focus,* 7:3 32

12. Hall, E (1996) Gastrointestinal Problems, in *Manual of Companion Animal Nutrition & Feeding,* 1st Edition, Eds Kelly, N and Wills, J, British Small Animal Veterinary Association, Gloucester, pp 144–152

13. Hall, E (1996) p 146

14. Burrows, C F and Ignaszewski, L A (1990) Canine gastric dilatation-volvulus, *Journal of Small Animal Practice,* 31, 495–501

15. Kronfeld, D S (1983) p 259

16. Bellenger, C R and Beck, J A (1994) Intussusception in 12 cats, *Journal of Small Animal Practice,* 35, 295–298

17. Lonsdale, T (1994) Revitalising Veterinary Science, Letter submitted to *Journal of Small Animal Practice,* Web: www.rawmeatybones.com/Revital.html

18. Dr Bob May, Chipping Norton, NSW — personal communication

19. Hamlin, R L (1991) A theory for the genesis of certain chronic degenerative diseases of the aged dog, *Veterinary Scope International Edition,* The Upjohn Company, Kalamazoo, pp 6–10

20. Hungerford, T G (1992) Periodontal Disease, Gingivitis, Foul Mouth In Dogs and Diet, *Control and Therapy* No 3315, Post Graduate Committee in Veterinary Science, University of Sydney, Sydney

21. Lonsdale, T (1992) Feline Eosinophilic Granuloma Complex, *Control and Therapy* No 3271, Post Graduate Committee in Veterinary Science, University of Sydney, Sydney

22. Taylor, J E and Schmeitzel, L P (1990) Plasma cell pododermatitis with chronic footpad hemorrhage in two cats, *Journal of the American Veterinary Medical Association,* 197:3 375–377

23. Lonsdale, T (1996) Plasma cell pododermatitis resolution after dental and dietary therapy in two cats, Web: www.rawmeatybones.com/Podo.html

24. World Cancer Research Fund/American Institute for Cancer Research (1997) Liver, in *Food, Nutrition and the Prevention of Cancer: a global perspective,* American Institute for Cancer Research, Washington, p 205

25. World Cancer Research Fund/American Institute for Cancer Research (1997) pp 15–16

26. World Cancer Research Fund/American Institute for Cancer Research (1997) p 72

27. World Cancer Research Fund/American Institute for Cancer Research (1997) p 72

28. Johnston, N W (1991) Feline Dental Disease – The Neck Lesion, *Veterinary Scope International Edition,* The Upjohn Company, Kalamazoo, pp 15–17

29. Doherty, G (1999) Ulcerative Stomatitis in Cats, *Control and Therapy* No 4144, Post Graduate Committee in Veterinary Science, University of Sydney, Sydney
Malik, R (2000) Use of Bonjela® Gel to Treat Calicivirus Faucitis in Cats, *Control and Therapy* No 4225, Post Graduate Committee in Veterinary Science, University of Sydney, Sydney

30. Senior, D F (1995) Feline Lower Urinary Tract Disease, in Proceedings of The Australian Small Animal Veterinary Association 22nd Annual Conference, pp 60-65

31. Senior, D F (1995)

32. Buffington, C A (1996) Diet and Lower Urinary Tract Disease, British Small Animal Veterinary Association Congress Papers Synopses, p 42

33. Lambert, A (1998) Good News For Cats, 9 April letter from Veterinary Business Director, Pedigree Petfoods to British veterinarians

34. Gruffydd-Jones, T J (1995) Hyperthyroidism, in *Feline Practice,* Proceedings of the Post Graduate Foundation in Veterinary Science, University of Sydney, Sydney, 243 pp 223–231

35. Gruffydd-Jones, T J (1995)

Chapter 7

Foul-mouth AIDS

1. Nance, J (1992) The Fido Fad: Out with tinned roo, in with alfalfa and raw carrot, 'New age' pets get on health kick, *Sunday Telegraph,* Sydney, 28 June, p 23

2. Lonsdale, T (1992) Raw Meaty Bones Promote Health, *Control and Therapy* No 3323, Post Graduate Committee in Veterinary Science, University of Sydney, Sydney

3. Blood, D C and Studdert, V P (1999) *Saunders Comprehensive Veterinary Dictionary,* 2nd Edition, W B Saunders, London, p 1107

4. English, R V et al (1994) Development of Clinical Disease in Cats Experimentally Infected with Feline Immunodeficiency Virus, *The Journal of Infectious Diseases,* 170:543–552

5. Jacobs, R M, Lumsden, J H and Vernau, W (1992) Canine and feline reference values, in *Current Veterinary Therapy XI, Small Animal Practice,* Eds, Kirk, R W and Bonagura, J D, W.B. Saunders, Philadelphia, pp 1250–1251

6. Lonsdale, T (1993) Putting FLUTD in context, *Journal of Small Animal Practice,* 34, 592 Web: www.rawmeatybones.com/FLUTD.html

7. Lonsdale, T (1995) Periodontal disease and leucopenia, *Journal of Small Animal Practice,* 36, 542–546

8. Cribb, J (1994) Processed food killing pets, say vets, *The Australian,* 10 March, p 3

9. Cribb, J (1996) AIDS-like disease threatens family pets, *The Weekend Australian,* 16–17 March, p 8

10. Professor Hughes, Dean, School of Veterinary Science wrote, in a letter to author, 8 July 1996: 'I can advise that Professor Robinson was consulted by the Australian Companion Animal Council and that the opinion provided by him was in a private capacity.'

11. Clarke, D E and Cameron, A (1998) Relationship between diet, dental calculus and periodontal disease in domestic and feral cats in Australia, *Australian Veterinary Journal,* 10 690–693

12. Maddison, J (1997) Today on Saturday, TCN9 Television Sydney 8 am 23 August 1997

13. Pedersen, N (1997) Immunologic diseases of the Cat, in *Feline Medicine,* Proceedings of the Post Graduate Foundation in Veterinary Science, University of Sydney, Sydney, 289 p 203

Chapter 8

The right diet

1. Whitehouse, S J O (1977) The diet of the dingo in Western Australia, *Australian Wildlife Research*, 4:2 145–50

2. Newsome, A E et al (1983) The feeding ecology of the dingo, *Australian Wildlife Research*, 10:3 477–486

3. Dr Peter Darvall, Chinchilla, Queensland — personal communication

4. Ben Savage, York, Western Australia — personal communication

5. Coman, B J and Brunner, H (1972) Food habits of the feral house cat in Victoria, *Journal of Wildlife Management*, 36:3 848–853

6. Ewer, R F (1973) Food and food finding, in *The Carnivores*, Cornell University Press, Ithaca, New York, p 153

7. Kronfeld, D S (1983) LIVER: A Natural Supplement, in *Nutrition*, Proceedings of the Post Graduate Committee in Veterinary Science, University of Sydney, Sydney 63 p195

8. Hungerford, T G (1992) Periodontal disease, gingivitis, foul mouth in dogs and diet, *Control and Therapy* No 3315, Post Graduate Committee in Veterinary Science, University of Sydney

9. Billinghurst, I (1993) Dogs eat bones. in *Give Your Dog a Bone*, Billinghurst, PO Box WO 64, Bathurst 2795 Australia Tel: +61 2 6334 2009 Fax: +61 2 6334 2140 E-mail: barfdiet@ix.net.au p 113

10. Kendall, P, Too much supplementation may be harmful, in *FEEDING The Dog & Cat*, Uncle Ben's of Australia, Albury Wodonga

11. Billinghurst (1993) p 190

12. Fuller, T K and Keith, L B (1980) Wolf population dynamics and prey relationships in northeastern Alberta, *Journal of Wildlife Management*, 44:3 583–602

13. *FEEDING The Dog & Cat Nutrition. Clinical Nutrition. Product Information*, Uncle Ben's of Australia, Albury Wodonga, June 1990

14. Recommended Daily Feeding Portions, Eukanuba The Original Premium, The IAMS Company Australia

15. Liberg, O (1984) Food habits and prey impact by feral and house-based domestic cats in a rural area in southern Sweden, *Journal of Mammology*, 65:3 424–432

16. Fuller and Keith (1980)

17 Mech, L D (1970) Food habits, in *The Wolf: the ecology and behaviour of an endangered species*, Natural History Press, Doubleday, New York, p 181

18. Fuller and Keith (1980)

19. Mech (1970) p 182

20. Mech (1970) p 182

21. Edney, A T B (1991) Nutrition and Disease, in *Canine Medicine and Therapeutics,* 3rd Edition, Eds E A Chandler, D J Thompson, J B Sutton and C J Price, Blackwell, Oxford, p 760

22. Hungerford (1992)

23. Nine Network Australia (1996/7) Money. Pet food savings, 26 June 1996 and 16 July 1997, Fact sheet information, Money, PO Box 107 Willoughby NSW 2068

24. Dr Grant Guilford — personal communication

25. Kronfeld (1983), p 149

26. Buck, N (1996) Small carnivores, in *Help,* 18 Friends of Howletts and Port Lympne, Kent, p 21

27. Wilson, G J (1999) Slab Fractures of Carnassial Teeth in Dogs, *Australian Veterinary Practitioner,* 29:2 84–85

28. Turner, A J (1997) Knackeries and the salvage of cadavers for pet meat in Victoria. An appraisal of the knackery industry, Department of Natural Resources and Environment, Attwood, Victoria

29. Consumers Union of US, Inc (1998) Chicken: What you don't know can hurt you, Consumer Reports Online, March 1998 Web: www.consumerreports.org/ @@uPXKToQM1LSupw4A/Categories/FoodHealth/Reports/9803chk0.htm

30. Jacobs, D E and Fox, M T (1991) Endoparasites, in *Canine Medicine and Therapeutics,* 3rd Edition, Eds E A Chandler, D J Thompson, J B Sutton and C J Price, Blackwell, Oxford, p 704

31. Stevenson, W J and Hughes, K L (1988) Parasitic diseases, in *Synopsis of Zoonoses in Australia,* 2nd edition, Australian Government Publishing Service, Canberra, p 220

32. Stevenson and Hughes (1988), p 200

33. University of Nebraska (1996) Common Infectious Diseases That Cause Abortions in Cattle, University of Nebraska Webguide publication: http://www.ianr.unl.edu/pubs/AnimalDisease/g1148.htm

34. Bernstein, L A (1998) An Overview of Neospora Caninum and Raw Food Diets. Client information handout, Natural Holistic Pet Care, N Miami Beach, Florida Web: www.naturalholistic.com

35. Soulsby, E J L (1982) Taenia saginata, in Helminths, *Arthropods and Protozoa of Domesticated Animals,* 7th Edition, Baillière Tindall, London, pp 107-111

36. Soulsby (1982), p 112

37. Soulsby (1982), p 119-122

38. Stevenson and Hughes (1983), p. 173

39. Australian Broadcasting Corporation Television (1993) The Investigators, Sydney

Chapter 9

The bite on veterinary dentistry

1. Dalton, P (1996) President's Reflections, *News Bulletin,* Australian Dental Association, 239, 3

2. Gillings, K J R (1993) Preventistry, The goal of all dentistry should be prevention. *News Bulletin,* Australian Dental Association, 199, 15-21

3. Australian Dental Association *News Bulletin,* Dental Health Week campaign gets the message across and scores over $1 million in exposure value, 227, 5-7

4. Higgins, P (1987) Preventative dentistry, in *Teeth open wide,* Proceedings of the Post Graduate Committee in Veterinary Science, University of Sydney, Sydney 100, 181-184

5. Dental health Information, Your smile: Gums are just as important as teeth. Dental Health Foundation – Australia, The University of Sydney, S82

6. Bartold, P M (1994) Periodontal test systems, *News Bulletin,* Australian Dental Association, 214, 35, 38, 40-42

7. Royal College of Veterinary Surgeons (2000) *Guide to Professional Conduct 2000,* p 3 Web site: www.rcvs.org.uk/Guide/index.htm

8. Abbott, P V (1996) The changing face of dentistry. Endodontics, Insert in: *News Bulletin,* Australian Dental Association, April 1996 232

9. Horrobin, D F (1990) The Philosophical Basis of Peer Review and the Suppression of Innovation, *Journal of the American Medical Association,* 263:10 1438–1441

10. Correspondence on file. Name withheld to preserve anonymity.

11. Alt Vet Med, Premium (Natural) Pet Foods: 'Following is a list of manufacturers of premium (natural) pet foods. These manufacturers use premium ingredients and do not use artificial preservatives and additives. You should contact the manufacturers directly for information on their products and names of local distributors in your area.' March 2000 Web: www.altvetmed.com/premfood.html

12. Muir, B (1991) Canned pet food not the healthiest, *Australian Veterinary Association News,* December 1991 p 28

13. Wynn, S (1996) Dental Care. At Alt Vet Med March 2000 Web: www.altvetmed.com/dental.html

14. Colmery, B (1992) Veterinary Dental Therapeutics in Companion Animals. Presentation Remarks — Guide for a Series of Ten Symposia to Veterinarians and Students in Australia Through the Sponsorship of The Upjohn Company, 20–31 July 1992, p 9

15. Harvey, C E (1993) Managing Pet Oral Health — Diet and Home Care, in *Veterinary Dentistry,* Proceedings of the Post Graduate Committee in Veterinary Science, University of Sydney, Sydney, 212, 214–215

Chapter 10

Misdirected science

1. Gleick, J (1987) *Chaos: Making a new science,* Cardinal, London, p 241

2. French, S (1993) The World According to GAIA, *Country Living* (UK), May 1993, p 38–40

3. Lumley, J (1993) Raw Meaty Bones: Dogs and Cats, *Control and Therapy* No 3406, Post Graduate Committee in Veterinary Science, University of Sydney, Sydney

4. Pietroni, P (1990) Tyranny of Excellence, in *The Greening of Medicine,* Gollancz, London, p 43

5. Kuhn, T S (1970) *The Structure of Scientific Revolutions,* 2nd Edition, Enlarged, The University of Chicago Press, Chicago (quote from Science on back cover)

6. Kuhn, T S (1996) Preface, in *The Structure of Scientific Revolutions,* 3rd Edition, The University of Chicago Press, Chicago, p x

7. Root-Bernstein, R (1993) The role of HIV in AIDS, in *Rethinking AIDS: The tragic cost of premature consensus,* The Free Press, New York, p 106

8. Blood, D C, and Studdert, V P (1999) *Saunders Comprehensive Veterinary Dictionary,* 2nd Edition, W B Saunders, London

9. Pietroni (1990), p 12

10. Williams, B (1978) The Project, in *Descartes: The Project of Pure Enquiry,* Penguin Books, London, p 32

11. World Cancer Research Fund/American Institute for Cancer Research (1997) Scientific evidence and judgment, in *Food, Nutrition and the Prevention of Cancer: A global perspective,* American Institute for Cancer Research, Washington, p 83

12. Gleick, J (1992) Far Rockaway, in *Genius: Richard Feynman and Modern Physics,* Abacus, London, p 40

13. Personal recollections of a radio interview in San Francisco late 1960s

14. Blood, D C, and Studdert, V P (1999) *Saunders Comprehensive Veterinary Dictionary,* 2nd Edition, W B Saunders, London

15. Atwell, R B (1992) A Practical Approach to Respiratory Medicine, in *Small Animal Internal Medicine,* Proceedings of the Post Graduate Committee in Veterinary Science, University of Sydney, Sydney, 187, p 334

16. Association of American Feed Control Officials, Inc (1993) Official Publication, p 282 (Copies from: Charles P Frank, AAFCO Treasurer, Georgia Department of Agriculture, Plant Food, Feed and Grain Division, Capitol Square, Atlanta, GA 30334 (404) 656-3637

17. Association of American Feed Control Officials Inc, pp 286–287

18. Wysong, R L (1993) *Pet Health Alert,* Wysong Corporation, Midland, Mi 48640–8896 Quoting: Collings, G F et al, *Veterinary Forum,* October 1992, p 34

19. Klenk, V (1989) Introduction to Logic, in: *Understanding Symbolic Logic,* 2nd Edition, Prentice-Hall, New Jersey, pp 1–12

20. Maggitti, P, Feeding your cat, in *A Cat of Your Own,* Salamanda Books, ISBN 1 875566 26 0, p 117

21. National Academy of Sciences (1985) Formulated Diets for Dogs, in *Nutrient Requirements of Dogs,* National Academy Press, Washington, p 42 and (1986) Formulated Diets for Cats, in *Nutrient Requirements of Cats,* National Academy Press, Washington, p 30

22. Guest, G B (1992) Correspondence on file, 18 September 1992

23. McCance, I (1995) Assessment of Statistical Procedures Used in Papers in the *Australian Veterinary Journal, Australian Veterinary Journal* 72: 322–330

24. Ludbrook, J (1995) Words on Numbers, *Australian Veterinary Journal,* 72: 321

25. Fahey, T, Griffiths, S and Peters, T J (1995) Evidence Based Purchasing: Understanding results of clinical trials and systematic reviews. *British Medical Journal,* 311:1056–1059

26. Altman, D G, and Bland, J M (1996) Absence of Evidence is Not Evidence of Absence, *Australian Veterinary Journal,* 74: 311

27. Rose, M (1998) Questions and Answers, in *Ethics, Money and Politics: Modern Dilemmas for Zoology,* Transactions of the Royal Zoological Society of New South Wales, Mosman, NSW, p 31

28. National Health and Medical Research Council (1997) *Australian code of practice for the care and use of animals for scientific purposes,* Australian Government Publishing Service, Canberra, p 32

29. Petcare Information and Advisory Service, Secret Power of Pets, Reprinted from the *New Scientist,* October 1993 Edition, ISBN–0–646–19002–4, Petcare Information and Advisory Service, Melbourne

30. Ewing, T (1997) Pet Food Kings Fret as Mutts Lose Shine, *The Age,* 28 July 1997, p 6

31. Anderson. W P (1996) The Benefits of Pet Ownership, *Medical Journal of Australia,* 164 441–442

32. Heady, B, and Anderson, W (1995) *Health Cost Savings: The impact of pets on Australian health budgets,* ISBN 0 949492 16 7, Petcare Information and Advisory Service, Melbourne

33. Newby, J (1997) *The Pact for Survival: Humans and their animal companions,* ABC Books, Sydney, back cover

34. Hare, J (1997) Pet Theories, in *Living Well,* Winter 1997, Medical Benefits Fund of Australia Ltd, Sydney, pp 20–23

35. Jorm, A F, et al, (1997) Impact of Pet Ownership on Elderly Australians' Use of Medical Services: An analysis using Medicare data, *Medical Journal of Australia,* 166 376–377

36. Cumming, F (1997) Pet Theory on Heart Disease Savaged, *The Sun-Herald,* 8 June p 41

37. Pets and the Health of Senior Citizens, *Vic Vet,* Newsletter of the Victorian Division of the Australian Veterinary Association, Autumn 1999, p 13

38. *Vic Vet,* Autumn 1999, p 13

Chapter 11

Collaboration at every level

1. Day, R A (1995) The Review Process (How to Deal with Editors) in *How to Write and Publish a Scientific Paper,* 4th Edition, Cambridge University Press, Cambridge, pp 102–103

2. Barber, B (1961) Resistance by Scientists to Scientific Discovery, *Science,* 134 596–602

3. Horrobin, D F (1990) The Philosophical Basis of Peer Review and the Suppression of Innovation, *Journal of the American Medical Association,* 263:10 1438–1441

4. Costerton, J W et al (1995) Microbial Biofilms, *Annual Review of Microbiology,* 49: 711–745

5. *Australian Veterinary Association News,* (1994) Diet and disease link — final report, February, pp 1 and 6

6. Smith, R (1998) Beyond Conflict of Interest, *British Medical Journal,* 317:291–292

7. Altman, E (1997) Scientific and Research Misconduct in *Research Misconduct: Issues, Implications, and Strategies,* Eds E Altman and P Hernon, Ablex, Greenwich, CT p 5

8. Wolf, K H (1999) Professional Misconducts: Research under whistleblower's scrutiny, *The Whistle,* Newsletter of Whistleblowers Australia Inc, March pp 6–8

9. Rockwell, T (2000) Scientific Integrity and Mainstream Science, *The Scientist,* 14 [5]:39 Web: www.the-scientist.com/yr2000/mar/opin_000306.html

10. Peter, L (1977) *Quotations for Our Time,* Souvenir Press, London, p 182

11. Martin, B (1997) Suppression: It's everywhere, in *Suppression Stories,* Fund for Intellectual Dissent, Wollongong University, Wollongong, p 26

12. Conway, A (1988) The Research Game: A view from the field, *Complementary Medical Research,* 3:1 29–35

13. Web: www.rawmeatybones.com/VetResearch.html

14. *Report of the Committee of Enquiry into Veterinary Research* (1997) The Welcome Trust, London, ISBN 1 869835 98 0, pp 48–49

15. *Report of the Committee of Enquiry into Veterinary Research* (1997) p 29

16. Walsh, M (1993) The Bottom Line, In the snake pit everyone covers their own asp, *The Sydney Morning Herald,* 11 June p 21 Quoting the book *Knowledge for Action,* Jossey-Bass, San Francisco

17. Carroll, L (1965) Chapter 6 Humpty Dumpty in *The Annotated Alice, Alice's Adventures in Wonderland and Through the Looking-Glass,* Introduction and notes by Martin Gardner, Penguin Books, London, p 269

18. Beder, S (1995) SLAPPs — Strategic Lawsuits Against Public Participation: Coming to a controversy near you, *Current Affairs Bulletin,* 72: 3 22–29 Web: www.uow.edu.au/arts/sts/bmartin/dissent/documents/Beder_SLAPPS.html

19. Beder (1995)

20. Lynch, P (2000 52nd Parliament — Veterinary Surgeons Investigating Committee — 10/8/2000, *Hansard,* Sydney p 65 Web: www.parliament.nsw.gov.au/

Chapter 12

There's a cuckoo in the nest: a deceptive bird

1. Cummins, J (1999) Human Fertility ABC Radio National, Ockham's Razor 18 July 1999 Web: www.abc.net.au/rn/science/ockham/stories/s37385.htm

2. Thurston, M E (1996) The Way to a Dog's Heart, in *The Lost History of the Canine Race,* Andrews and McMeel, Kansas City, MI pp 234–236

3. Thurston, M E (1996), p 241

4. May 1993 Television commercial. See also: The right diet for cats, *Australian Veterinary Association News,* February 1993, p 19

5. Shoebridge, N (1991) Pack tries new tricks but PAL remains top dog, *Business Review Weekly,* 5 April 1991, 68–70

6. Thurston, M E (1996), pp 239–243

7. Let's get the facts straight!, Advertisement in *Australian Veterinary Journal,* 76:11 November 1998

8. Thurston, M E (1996), p 240

9. Brenner, J G (1999) To the Milky Way and Beyond, in *The Emperors of Chocolate: Inside the secret world of Hershey and Mars,* Random House, New York, p 67

10. Cleary, P (1996) Billions in tax being lost to multinationals, *The Sydney Morning Herald*, 28 October 1996

11. Peter, L (1977) *Quotations for Our Time*, Souvenir Press, London, p 310

12. Lexicon Branding, Inc, Web site: www.lexicon-branding.com/story/

13. Sargant, W (1959) *Battle for the mind*, Pan Books, London

14. Brenner, J G (1999), p 188

15. Shoebridge, N (1991)

16. Shoebridge, N (1991)

17. Littlemore, S (1997) Media Watch, Australian Broadcasting Corporation, 3 March 1997

18. Department of Surgical Research (1998) Dogs'n'kids, The New Children's Hospital, Westmead, 4 December 1998.

19. *Australian Veterinary Association Annual Conference Handbook* (1998), p 58

20. Williams, R (1992) letter to T Lonsdale, 5 November 1992

21. Australian Broadcasting Corporation, Radio National Web site: http://www.abc.net.au/rn/science/ss/ss.htm

22. Rotherham, S (1998) Variety is the spice of life, *The Veterinarian*, May 1998 p 8

23. Newby, J (1994) Pet Care, *The Australian Women's Weekly*, September 1994, p 273

24. Williams, R (1996) Cruel to muzzle age-old love, *The Australian*, 6 February 1996, p 18

25. Lloyd-James, A (1999) letter to T Lonsdale and B Muir, 30 September 1999

26. Ewing, T, (1997) Pet food kings fret as mutts lose shine, *The Age*, Late edition, 28 July 1997, p 6

27. Littlemore, S (1997)

28. ABC Radio National Science Unit (1997) Media Release, The Science Show 'Animal Friends' Series, 21 February 1997

29. Ackland, R (1998) Media Watch, Australian Broadcasting Corporation, 13 July & 12 October 1998

30. Fitch, H M and Fagan, D A (1982) Focal Palatine Erosion Associated With Dental Malocclusion in Captive Cheetahs, *Zoo Biology*, 1:295–310

31. Pratkanis, A R and Aronson, E (1992), p 3

32. Parker-Pope, T (1997) For You, My Pet, *The Wall Street Journal*, 3 November 1997

33. Parker-Pope, T (1997)

34. Newby, J (1994) p 232

35. Hopkins, D (1991) Teacher Information Sheet 4(c), *PetPEP Manual* (Trial), Australian Veterinary Association, Sydney

36. Hopkins, D (1991) Adapted by Curriculum Corporation (1995), *PetPEP Manual,* Australian Veterinary Association, Sydney

37. Editor's note (2000) *Australian Veterinary Journal,* 78:9 598

38. Burke, T, Deputy Director-General (Teaching and Learning) (1995) correspondence to Dennis Eager, Chief Executive Officer, Australian Veterinary Association, 13 September 1995 and 9 November 1995

39. Sillince, J (1995) Open Letter to Tom Lonsdale, *Australian Veterinary Association News,* December 1995, p 14

40. Gilmore, H (1995) PEP food talks end in dogfight, *The Sun-Herald,* 19 November 1995, p 43

Chapter 13

Righting the wrongs: charting a new course

1. Peter, L (1977) *Quotations for Our Time,* Souvenir Press, London ,p 260

2. Carson, R (1962) The Obligation to Endure, in *Silent Spring,* Penguin Books, London, p 28

3. Carson, R (1962), p 29

4. Kingston, M (1998) Public opinion shows the way, *The Sydney Morning Herald,* 26 May 1998, p 17

5. Kuhn, T S (1996) Preface, in *The Structure of Scientific Revolutions,* 3rd Edition, The University of Chicago Press, Chicago, p 151

6. (1999) *The Whistle,* Newsletter of Whistleblowers Australia Inc, frontpage

7. Lennane, K J (1993) "Whistleblowing": a health issue, *British Medical Journal,* 307: 667–670

8. Martin, B (1999) Building support, in *The Whistleblower's Handbook,* Jon Carpenter Publishing, Charlbury, Oxfordshire, p 75

9. Association of American Feed Control Officials, Inc. (1993) Official Publication, Copies from: Charles P Frank, AAFCO Treasurer, Georgia Department of Agriculture, Plant Food, Feed and Grain Division, Capitol Square, Atlanta, GA 30334 (404) 656–3637 p 62

10. Royal College of Veterinary Surgeons (2000) *Guide to Professional Conduct 2000,* p 3 Web site: www.rcvs.org.uk/Guide/index.htm

11. (1997) Today on Saturday, TCN9 Television Sydney, 23 August 1997

12. Smithcors, J F (1958) Fourteenth century, in *Evolution of the Veterinary Art,* Bailliere, Tindall and Cox, London, p 139

13. Gee, R W and Auty, J H (1999) Surgeons or sow gelders, *Vic Vet,* Newsletter of the Victorian Division of the Australian Veterinary Association, Autumn 1999, 3–7

14. Watson, A D J (1994) Diet and periodontal disease in dogs and cats, *Australian Veterinary Journal,* 313–318

15. (1999) American toothbrush lawsuit, Australian Dental Association *News Bulletin,* 267, 27

16. (1999) Petfood Industry Online, Dental Diet Receives Seal, Web site: www.wattnet.com/NewsRoom/ViewNews.cfm?PG=4&ST =155475&nwsNum=6638

17. Honorary Associate Professor P D Barnard personal communication to T Lonsdale

18. Borthwick, R (1986) The Distribution, Prevalence and Some Factors Associated with Periodontal Disease in Dogs and Cats, University of Edinburgh Report to The Animal Studies Centre, Waltham-on-the-Wolds

19. Groom, B (1994) Nestlé's formula for disaster, *Marketing,* May 1994 66–67

20. Pietroni, P (1990) The Feminine Principle, in *The Greening of Medicine,* Gollancz, London, p 122

21. Court of Appeal of England and Wales Decisions, HELEN MARIE STEEL and DAVID MORRIS v. MCDONALD'S CORPORATION and MCDONALD'S RESTAURANTS LTD [1999] EWCA 1397 (31st March, 1999) Web: www.bailii.org/ew/cases/EWCA/1999/1397.html

22. Langton, J (1998) Now clean livers have a beef with burger industry, *The Sydney Morning Herald,* 26 May 1998, p 13

23. Cleary, T (1996) Distinctions Between Aggressors and Defenders, in *The Lost Art of War,* Harper Collins, San Francisco, p 101

24. *Australian Veterinary Association News,* (1994) Diet and disease link — final report, February, pp 1 and 6

25. (1999) *Immunity and Disease,* Proceedings of the Post Graduate Foundation in Veterinary Science, University of Sydney, Sydney, 323

Chapter 14

A cybernetic hypothesis of periodontal disease

1. O'Connor, M (2000) The Beginning in: *The Olive Tree: collected poems,* Hale & Iremonger, Alexandria, NSW, p 16

2. Mee, A (1950) in *The Children's Encyclopedia,* The Educational Book Company Ltd, Vol 1, Ch 4, p 417

3. Lovelock, J E (1987) Introductory in *Gaia: a new look at life on earth,* Oxford University Press, Oxford, p 11

4. Tickell, O (1996) Healing the rift, in *Independent on Sunday,* 4 August 1996, p 40

5. Lovelock (1987), p 22

6. Lovelock (1987), p 48

7. Lewin, R (1993) Edge of Chaos Discovered, in *Complexity: life at the edge of chaos,* J M Dent, London, pp 44–62

8. Marcus Aurelius Antoninus (AD 121–180) *The Meditations* Web: http://classics.mit.edu/Antoninus/meditations.9.nine.html

9. Kerr, J F, Wyllie, A H and Currie, A R (1972) Apoptosis: A basic biological phenomenon with wide-ranging implications in tissue kinetics, *British Journal of Cancer,* 26:4 239–257
For a detailed etymology see Mauro Degli Esposti, Apoptosis and the Classics, Web: http://celldeath-apoptosis.org/HistOfApoptosis.html

10. The Cell Death Society, Web: http://celldeath-apoptosis.org/

11. Lewis, R (1995) Apoptosis Activity: Cell death establishes itself as a lively research field, *The Scientist,* Vol 9 #3 p. 15 February 6 1995, p 15
Web: www.the-scientist.library.upenn.edu/yr1995/feb/apo_1_950206.html

12. Yarmolinsky, M B (1995) Programmed Cell Death in Bacterial Populations, *Science,* 267, 836–837

13. Sorkin, B C, and Niederman, R (1998) Short chain carboxylic acids decrease human gingival keratinocyte proliferation and increase apoptosis and necrosis, *Journal of Clinical Periodontology,* 25:4 311–315

14. Milton, R (1994) Too Wonderful to be True, in *Forbidden Science,* Fourth Estate, London, p 3

15. Schopf, J W (1993) Microfossils of the Early Archean Apex Chert: New evidence of the antiquity of life, *Science,* 260, 640–646, (Paper cited on Science Show, ABC Radio National, 8 May 1993)

16. Margulis, L, and Sagan, D (1987) Introduction: The Microcosm, in *Microcosmos: Four billion years of evolution from our microbial ancestors,* Allen & Unwin, London, p 34

17. Capra, F (1996) The Unfolding of Life, in *The Web of Life: A new synthesis of mind and matter,* Harper Collins, London, p 226

18. Capra (1996), p 228–236

19. Margulis, L (1993) Mitochondria, in *Symbiosis in Cell Evolution: Microbial communities in the Archean and Proterozoic Eons,* 2nd Edition, W H Freeman, New York, pp 305–326

20. Husband, A J and Bryden, W L (1996) Nutrition, Stress and Immune Activation, *Proceedings of Nutrition Society of Australia,* September 1996, Sydney, Australia

21. Lord, G M et al (1998) Leptin modulates the T-cell immune response and reverses starvation-induced immunosuppression, *Nature,* 394 897–901

22. Day, M (1998) Sick of Hunger. A simple hormone may buy time for starving people, *New Scientist,* 2149 4

23. Lewin, R (1996) All for One, One for All, *New Scientist,* 2060 28–33

24. Lonsdale, T (1994) Cybernetic Hypothesis of Periodontal Disease in Mammalian Carnivores, *Journal of Veterinary Dentistry,* 11:1 5–8

25. Lonsdale, T (1994) Web: www.rawmeatybones.com/Cybernetic.html

ACKNOWLEDGEMENTS

In a sense, it's taken fifty years to research and write this book and as a consequence I am indebted to many people and many influences. Looking back over the period, some events stand out and some are hazy in the memory. Some events, at the time, seemed pointless excursions into dead-ends but now, in retrospect, appear as journeys toward enlightenment.

Some people have shown great patience when attempting to impress small points upon me — school masters for instance. Others, especially family members, have been ever patient and helpful. Perhaps those showing the greatest trust were my animal patients and their owners who helped in charting a new course.

Latterly I have been advised by professionals — editors, lawyers, publishers — whose contributions I much appreciate. Several drafts of the manuscript were commented upon by friends. I am most grateful for their time and expertise and the improvements they have suggested.

Four people I would like to mention by name for having stood shoulder-to-shoulder with me, often when the going was tough. Veterinary colleagues Breck Muir and Alan Bennet, founder members of the Raw Meaty Bone Lobby, have provided selfless help and advice. Two veterinary teachers, Oliver Graham-Jones and Arthur Hayward, who provided help and inspiration during my days at the Royal Veterinary College in the late 1960s and early 1970s, are now well into their retirement — but, still as patient as ever, offer assistance.

Where weaknesses occur in this book, they are my responsibility. Any strengths can, almost invariably, be traced to others — they know who they are and to them I express my gratitude.

Copyright Acknowledgements

—————⟫●⟪—————

Grateful acknowledgement is made to the following publishers for granting permission to reproduce extracts of previously published material:

Ashley Conway's 'The Research Game: A view from the field', *Complementary Medical Research*, (1988) 3:1, 29–36
Web: www.tandf.co.uk

Definitions of 'Koch's postulates', 'cause' and various terms in the Glossary have been reprinted from or derived from *Saunders Comprehensive Veterinary Dictionary*, 2nd Edition, D C Blood OBE & V P Studdert pp 1–1243 (1999) W B Saunders, London

Front cover — AAP Information Services, Julian Cribb, *The Weekend Australian* (16–17 March 1996), *The Sydney Morning Herald, The Herald and Weekly Times* and *The Age*.

INDEX

ONLINE ORDERS

Secure online ordering at:
www.rawmeatybones.com

OFFLINE ORDERS
AND TRADE ENQUIRIES

PLEASE CONTACT:

Rivetco P/L
PO Box 6096
Windsor Delivery Centre
NSW 2756
Australia

Telephone: +61 2 4574 0537
Facsimile: +61 2 4574 0538
E-mail: rivetco@rawmeatybones.com
Web: www.rawmeatybones.com